"A one-woman fina
At heart, Orman is a per...
people to take control of their money life. She's playing a vital role
in the financial education of many people." —*USA Today*

"Suze Orman can't let a stranger walk by . . . without asking, 'Do
you have credit card debt?' She needs to know so she can help.
So she can change a life. And not later or a little bit. But now,
profoundly. . . . Her optimism comes from a belief that all of us
have the power within us to improve how we save and spend our
money and thus the power to forge lives that are better, fuller and
richer in every way." —*Time,* "The 2009 Time 100"

"She possesses an encyclopedic command of financial planning."
—*Money*

"Ms. Orman is a success because she knows how to reach many
people, and shows some sympathetic understanding of their con-
crete problems." —*The Wall Street Journal*

"There's an enormous number of Americans who don't know any-
body earning more than $250,000 a year; Suze Orman can speak
to these Americans—and especially the women among them—
like no one else in or out of government. When she does so, she
gives good advice. That advice might not always be followed to
the letter, but thanks to Orman, there are now millions of Americans who have a very good idea what they *should* be doing, financially." —*Portfolio.com*

"Orman can be a fierce critic with exacting standards. But what
clearly animates her is creating new possibilities in the lives of her
viewers. Orman's emotion and energy peak when she's knee-deep
in the challenge of helping people get out of their own way. . . .
Orman doesn't trade empathy for expectations, or expectations
for empathy. She reveals both in almost every interaction she has
with her audience." —*Harvard Business Review*

SPI
EGE
L&G
RAU

THE
MONEY
CLASS

THE MONEY CLASS

HOW TO STAND
IN YOUR TRUTH AND
CREATE THE FUTURE
YOU DESERVE

SUZE ORMAN

SPIEGEL & GRAU TRADE PAPERBACKS
NEW YORK
2012

2012 Spiegel & Grau Trade Paperback Edition

Copyright © 2011 by Suze Orman, a Trustee of the Suze Orman Revocable Trust
Introduction copyright © 2012 by Suze Orman, a Trustee of the Suze Orman Revocable Trust

Published in the United States by Spiegel & Grau, an imprint of The Random House Publishing Group, a division of Random House, Inc., New York.

SPIEGEL & GRAU and Design is a registered trademark of Random House, Inc.

Originally published in hardcover in the United States by Spiegel & Grau, an imprint of The Random House Publishing Group, a division of Random House, Inc., in 2011.

Library of Congress Cataloging-in-Publication Data

Orman, Suze.
  The money class: how to stand in your truth and create the future you deserve / Suze Orman.
    p. cm.
  ISBN 978-0-8129-8213-8
  eBook ISBN 978-0-679-60470-9
  1. Finance, Personal—United States.   2. Wealth—United States.   I. Title.
  HG179.O75764 2011
  332.024'01—dc22   2011001394

Printed in the United States of America

www.spiegelandgrau.com

9 8 7 6 5 4 3 2 1

Book design by Susan Turner

To all the great teachers who've taught me everything I know

CONTENTS

How to Enter The Classroom

Welcome to *The Money Class*. The information in this book provides the foundation for your work: The facts describe the new financial reality we have to apprehend, both collectively and individually. The new perspective offered paves the way for the inner work—the emotional and psychological shifts—to be considered. The financial guidance and information contained in this book are supported by a number of important tools and resources that are housed in The Classroom on my website. It's also where I'll post any information updates you need to know.

To gain access, go to the home page of my website, **www .suzeorman.com.**

Click on **The Classroom** icon.
You will be asked to enter a passcode.
The code is: **999 999 999**

In The Classroom you will find everything you need to put the lessons learned in this book into action. Throughout the book, this icon will alert you to the additional information you can find online.

In The Classroom you will also find a special offer for readers of *The Money Class* that you can learn more about on page 156 of this book.

INTRODUCTION

DREAM DEFERRED?

When *The Money Class* was first published in early 2011 there was a quiet exhalation starting to sweep the nation. There was a glimmer of hope that we had finally come out the other side of the devastating financial crisis. To be sure, there was nothing to celebrate, given the magnitude of the damage done to so many facets of our financial lives. But there was a sense that we had reached a bottom from which rebuilding could commence, and that meant job and economic growth would pick up. We were starting to feel better, not the least reason being that our battered 401(k)s were healing nicely as the stock market nearly doubled from the depths of its March 2009 lows. The recovery was on.

Or so we thought.

As time went on it became increasingly evident that 2011 was to be a year of great expectations unmet. The strong economic growth that spurs job creation has yet to materialize. The only appreciable increase we've seen is the growing concern that we are on the verge of another recession. Housing remains in shambles in many parts of the country. The foreclosure crisis has not abated, and an astounding one in four homeowners with a mortgage are underwater. Most distressing, the unemployment rate remains stuck at a horrific level, and the official word out of Washington is that we won't see any significant improvement before 2014.

Against that backdrop the pressure grew for our elected officials to step in and step up with measures to prevent a painful economic backslide. Yet we got just the opposite. Not only did Washington fail to buoy the economy, it made the crisis worse! The wholly unnecessary debt-ceiling debate in Congress in the summer of 2011 was an attack on the well-being of every American household, further confirmation that special interests have come to dominate the political agenda. This hijacking of the national conversation spiraled so far out of control that it triggered a downgrade of our nation's credit rating and the ensuing weeks of record volatility in the stock market. Here's what some in Congress worked overtime to obscure: The debt ceiling has absolutely nothing to do with future spending choices. The debt ceiling is a mechanism that allows the government to continue to pay off debts it has already accrued. It's how we stand up and make good on what we've already spent. Yet Washington decided to hold the debt ceiling as a political hostage in discussions about future spending. And the ransom we all paid was to see Standard & Poor's lower our pristine AAA credit rating a notch. Not because it questioned the ability of our government to make good on its debt payments, but out of concern over our political dysfunction.

I have to tell you, the gridlock in Congress is one of the most terrifying threats to your financial security. The inability—or should I say, the unwillingness—of Washington to step up and address our most pressing economic needs is stupefying. Retreating to your political corners and digging your heels in is unconscionable in a world where we still have 9% unemployment nearly two years after we've been told the recession officially ended. This is not a time for party and politics above all. Doing nothing is a dereliction of duty in a world where there are 14 million Americans unemployed, another 9 million underemployed, and job growth so slow it barely is enough to keep up with the natural growth in the working-age population.

And to be clear, it's not as if Congress doesn't know the damage it is doing. Federal Reserve chairman Ben Bernanke spent much of 2011 telling Congress he's pretty much exhausted his toolbox and he needs Capitol Hill to do its part by enacting programs that can help prevent a backslide into recession.

But as I write this in the autumn of 2011, Congress has not taken action. In fact, doing nothing has become the goal. Capitol Hill's playbook for crisis management: Play politics, don't govern. So much for People First.

I am not suggesting that Congress has the power to solve everything. But choosing to make matters worse—in the midst of a deepening crisis!—by subjecting us to the debt-ceiling debacle and refusing to address the unemployment situation is an abomination.

Let me be very clear: There is plenty Congress can do—and this we can all agree on, no matter your party affiliation or agenda. Here's but one example: If ever there was an economic no-brainer for these times, focusing on infrastructure spending is it. Our transportation systems are in serious need of upgrading in order for us to remain globally competitive. And we have a ready workforce to step in: all the laid-off construction workers. Moreover, we can finance this at record low interest rates. Yes, that means spending more. That's the only way to move us out of this economic morass; fiscal austerity is to be saved for discussions about our long-term goals. Not now. That said, we must spend smartly. And infrastructure spending surely qualifies. According to the Congressional Budget Office, every dollar invested on infrastructure produces an average increase in GDP of $1.60. Yet, as of this writing, we are still waiting to see if Congress will in fact embrace investing in infrastructure, and on a scale large enough to make a positive impact on employment and economic growth.

It's also time to get serious about dealing with the housing mess. There is no question that moral hazard—"rewarding" some people with the tax dollars of others—is a very big concern. But I think the reward also flows to the greater community if assistance can bring stability to those markets.

Do we help everyone? No. Some who bought never had the

financial stability to be homeowners. But what about the family that could once handle the mortgage but is struggling now because of a layoff? More than 30% of unemployed Americans have been out of work for more than a year. There is no emergency fund that can easily absorb that jolt. Offering bridge loans, or temporary assistance to those families so they can stay current on their payments until they are reemployed, makes a lot of sense. The alternative is more short sales and foreclosures.

To dismiss help of any kind, for anyone, at this juncture resigns all of us to many more years of economic hardship. And I do mean all. When a significant portion of households are struggling to make the mortgage or are worried that they will never get out from being underwater, that means a significant portion of American households are in no position to spend money. When you hear mention of the fact that our economy is suffering from a lack of demand, do you know what that means? It means no one wants to spend or has money to spend. We need to arrive at a targeted approach to providing relief to qualified homeowners if we are serious about keeping our economy moving forward.

As the Occupy Wall Street movement that emerged this fall so rightfully implored, the inequity in this country should be a national disgrace, not something vehemently defended and aided by so many in Washington. We have record corporate profits while nearly 24 million Americans are unemployed or underemployed. We have corporations sitting on more than $2 trillion in cash, a sizable chunk of which is stashed overseas, waiting until our government gives them a "holiday" to bring those profits back home with the promise of a low tax bill. For the record, we did this back in 2004, on the assumption that all that repatriated money would spur investment and job growth. It didn't. But here we are amid a jobs crisis, and we are pretending that a big tax gift for corporate America and its shareholders will in some way trickle down to benefit the broader economy.

All of this is occurring while average workers wages adjusted for inflation have grown just 4% since 1990, and median household income today is no higher than it was more than a decade ago. And in a time when the top 1% of Americans own more than

40% of our financial wealth and have seen their tax rates go ever lower, we can't have a serious conversation about tax reform.

You are right to wonder who's looking out for your interests. I wish I had a reassuring answer. Instead, I am still shaking my head in disbelief over the incredible act of Washington hubris that ran Elizabeth Warren out of town. Warren had championed the Consumer Financial Protection Bureau into existence as part of sweeping financial reform that managed to pass Congress as the embers of the 2008–2009 crisis were still glowing. But by 2011, protectors of the financial service industry—some in Congress, plus legions of lobbyists—had regained their leverage and made sure she would not be confirmed as director of the CFPB. Why? Well, she had the gall to insist that consumers should understand what financial products they were being sold. She was going to require that fees and expenses be clearly explained in easily accessible formats, not buried in pages and pages of fine-print legalese.

Long before Occupy Wall Street had coalesced into a movement, Elizabeth Warren was out front representing "the other 99%." That made her a huge threat to the profit flow for the financial services industry. So they turned loose their lobbyists to make sure Warren would not get the job. And guess what? The lobbyists won. And they are not done. They are determined to weaken or obliterate what remains of the financial reform. In the meantime, some banks are already starting to hand the bill for financial reform over to consumers, charging new fees to make up for having to lower other fees per new federal regulations. Not to cover expenses, but to keep their profits sky high.

Given this intractable economic state we're in, my expectation is that we will not be fully healed and in a stronger growth mode until at least 2015. That's not a new position for me. As I shared in my *2009 Action Plan* book, I believed the magnitude of the problems at the heart of the financial crisis could not be resolved quickly, and I predicted the economy would not be back in solid growth mode until 2014 or 2015. As I explained back then, I anticipated that we would have periods of encouraging growth and progress interrupted by periods of retrenchment. Two steps forward, one step back. Indeed, it is far too easy for me to envision that 2012 will include yet another step backward as it is becoming harder to see how the United States—and other foreign economies—will be able to avoid becoming engulfed in more financial turmoil.

DREAM ON

As certain as I was a year ago that the timing was perfect for me to share my lessons on building and rebuilding a new American dream, the events of the past year make this new paperback edition even more timely. As much as you and I can hope that the gridlock lifts and Washington begins to govern for our collective well-being, that's not something we can count on. And even if Washington decides to take action, its role will be focused on short-term crisis management. We have every right to expect that our government will stand and deliver with stimulus and safety nets during a crisis. But in the long term we must recognize that the hard work of building lasting financial security is very much a personal matter.

What you save in your 401(k)s and IRAs will determine your comfort level in retirement. How honest you are with your kids about what you can afford—and not afford—for their college education will determine your family's future financial stability. Whether you create a lifestyle that allows you to have money left over each month to put toward long-term goals is the key to your success. You, not your government, are the catalyst for that. Righting your financial life at this juncture is very much a public-private partnership.

That's why I was so passionate about the need for *The Money Class*. This updated version has all the lessons you need to be the agent of change that moves your life forward. My focus is not how to help you get by this year or next. The lessons in this book are about building lifelong security. All that you need to bring to the table is the resolve to build a better life for you, your family, and future generations. Thankfully, that's one commodity that is absolutely yours for the taking.

I have long said that every money challenge can be solved by the person you see in the mirror. That's never been as true as it is now. You can't control much of what goes on around you, but you do have complete control over how you choose to respond. I'm here to show you the way forward.

Suze Orman
November 2011

THE
MONEY
CLASS

CLASS

THE NEW AMERICAN DREAM

The American Dream. As a concept, it is so ingrained in our collective imagination that it doesn't even need to be defined, right? Think about it: Did you ever need to have it explained to you? My guess is you did not and that even from a young age, you, like me, knew it represented a promise—of opportunity, of possibility—that came with being American.

But on closer inspection, it is not just an American impulse that the American Dream describes, it is a human one, and it unites us. No matter your socioeconomic, ethnic, or religious background, we all aspire to the same things: We seek to provide for our family and keep them safe, no matter what shape that family takes, no matter if we are talking about our parents or our children, a blended family or a family "by choice," not blood. We want future generations to have even more opportunity than we ourselves have, a dream that is intrinsically linked with education and the advancement that follows from it. We want to live in a home that is secure in every sense—as a haven for our loved ones and as a wise place to have spent our money. We want the guarantee that our hard work will pay off, that it will support us financially, that it will allow us to achieve our goals, and that when it is time to stop working, we will reap the benefits of those years of dedicated service and live out the rest of our lives comfortably in retirement.

As universal as these desires are, we refer to them as the American Dream because for centuries this country has, for the most part, been able to make good on this promise of America as the land of opportunity. This belief has played a defining role in shaping our national psyche. It is at the heart of our Declaration of Independence—that we each possess "certain unalienable Rights, that among these are Life, Liberty, and the Pursuit of Happiness."

How truly terrifying, then, to take stock of the American Dream today and to question the truth of it—to wonder if it still exists in reality or if it has become an illusion, a myth. Take a look around: As of October 2011, nearly 14 million Americans were out of work; another 8.9 million were working only part-time because they cannot find full-time employment. That is nearly 23 million people who are struggling to make ends meet. Many of those lucky enough to still be employed in their 60s are looking to hang on to their jobs as long as possible because they simply cannot afford to retire—which also means there are fewer job openings for young people entering the workforce.

In many areas of the country, the dream of homeownership has backfired. Real estate values have deflated to such an extent that a record number of people owe more than their homes are worth. That's not an American Dream—it's a nightmare.

Because of the dire economic conditions of recent years, many parents are unable to afford the high cost of college tuition for their children. And there is a record number of student loans in default, making people question whether they ever should have taken them on to begin with.

The sum total of all these facts and figures? The home, the job security, the education, the retirement—the very standard of living that all of us took for granted for so long is completely under siege.

Whether we speak about it or not, we are grappling with the frightening possibility, the fear, that we no longer live in a land where effort applied to opportunity produces a better life. The doors leading to more and greater things, once wide open, now seem to be closing. It is hard to move up in an economy where there has been no job or wage growth over the past decade. Once a manufacturing powerhouse—"Made in the U.S.A." was our calling card—we have ceded that engine of growth, and the jobs that go with it, to other countries as our own economy now relies on our ability to consume, not produce.

The impact of these economic shifts has been felt deeply within our homes. While the median household income for adults born in the 1960s is indeed higher than the income of their parents' generation, much of that is a function of smaller household size and the fact that there are now likely two wage earners per household. It takes more of us working more to maintain our forward progress. Even so, the pace of our growth has slowed considerably. According to a study commissioned by the Pew Charitable Trusts, family income doubled in the postwar years, between 1947 and 1973, but in the three decades since then the increase has been a mere 20%. That statistic provides important context to why household debt relative to income more than doubled over the same period: For many, borrowing was a way to keep up with our parents and grandparents. To put it in more emotional terms, it is why so many of us wonder how our parents and grandparents seemed able to enjoy a higher standard of living even though their means were so much less than ours.

The meritocracy that underpins our economy and culture—work hard, move up the ladder—has also been weakening, as the distribution of income has become increasingly uneven. In the 1950s and 1960s, our national economic growth trickled down across a broad spectrum of income levels. Since the 1970s it has been more fractured, with much of the economic gains benefiting upper-income households. This concentration of wealth leaves the middle class, the heart and soul of this country, struggling just to hang on.

The epic financial crisis—and there really is no other way to describe it—that began in 2008 may have delivered a decisive blow to the stubborn optimism that we held on to in spite of the on-the-ground reality of how our financial lives have been marked by increasing struggle. For many, the crisis was a rude awakening; for others, it was a grim confirmation of the creeping anxiety we've been feeling about how we are going to make it all work. Either way, it is hard to find a family that was untouched by this financial disaster. It was a galvanizing moment for us as a nation—it has forced us to reckon with our beliefs in our country and our individual ideals.

Is it time, then, to pronounce the American Dream dead?

In many ways it pains me to say this, but in my opinion the American Dream as we knew it *is* dead.

But listen to me: That is not such a bad thing. The old American Dream has been in need of revision for quite some time; we have just been very good at avoiding that truth. It's time to take that dream back into our hands and reshape it. It's time to create a New American Dream that is based in honesty, authenticity, good intentions, and genuine need.

What is important to understand is that the American Dream is not something to put your faith in, to pray for, to embrace blindly, and hope that everything turns out okay—despite its long, dependable run. Rather, it is a concept, a loose set of goals that beg for individualization. The American Dream was never one-size-fits-all. The New American Dream asks you to fashion a dream that suits you—not one based on false premises and the expectations of others. It asks you to take measure of your own needs and understand what it will take to provide for yourself and those around you—your family, your community, and those less fortunate.

The truth is, we are on the threshold of an important moment. We can come together, right here, right now, and each one of us can envision our own New American Dream—a dream that is rooted in reality, not superficiality; in truth and integrity, not illusion and faslehood.

MAKING CHANGE

I am a great believer in the power of perspective. Often when we find ourselves in a difficult situation we come to believe we have no options. We convince ourselves there is no way out. Despair and frustration take root and convince us that things are more desperate than they may actually be. When I've found myself in those situations in my own life, I have learned that a change in perspective can change everything. What seemed insurmountable can be overcome. Not without difficulty, but through ingenuity and dedication. We can make a difference when we think differently. If you have any doubt about the truth of that statement, think of any significant achievement throughout American history, from our founding as a nation built on those inalienable rights and freedoms, to the civil rights movement.

What we need first and foremost then, to erase the feelings of hopelessness and to ease our fears, is a change in perspective. Let us recognize what the American Dream no longer is, in order to give birth to a New American Dream.

We must abandon any vestige of the old dream that suggested it was delivered on a silver platter as a matter of national birthright, and that our economy would forever be the rising tide that lifts all boats. The dream I am asking you to create—this New American Dream—is a very individualistic pursuit. It calls upon you to take stock of the challenges we face as a nation with an economy that is still struggling to recover from the effects of a crippling recession. And then it calls upon you to take stock of your own life, your own needs, your own security. We must transform ourselves from dreaming society's dreams and putting our faith in a false and misleading sense of entitlement, to being a society where each of us strives for dreams that are personal and realistic and that are in the best interests—in the truest and most honest sense—of us and our family. I am calling upon each of us to rethink the very way we dream.

WHAT I LEARN FROM YOU

I am confident you are up to the challenge. I know you are absolutely capable of everything I am going to ask you to do. I also can feel that lurking just beneath your fear and frustration is an even more powerful resolve not to resign yourself to a life of less. You are resilient. It is a hidden upside to times of great turmoil. When we are shaken to our core, when the status quo no longer works for us on any level, we are motivated to change. Transformation becomes not just possible, but imperative. How do I know this? I have been listening to you—so many of you—over the years. I have heard your hopes and fears; I have made it my job to expose the falsehoods and deceptions we perpetrate on ourselves and others and encourage honesty and truth. And I hear how ready you are for change.

To that end, may I share some more statistics with you that I know you will find as heartening as I do? In a 2010 survey conducted by Charles Schwab & Company, 29% of respondents chose the phrase "Decade of Hope" to describe the coming years. Another 27% said "Decade of Great Change" and 20% chose "Decade of Personal Responsibility." Three-quarters of respondents understand what it is going to take to create a new, sustainable, and achievable dream: hope, change, and personal responsibility.

Those are the very elements I ask you to bring to *The Money Class*. At the core of the change I am asking for is a willingness to stand in the truth. To take a clear-eyed accounting of exactly where you are today, what your circumstances are, and then plot a course that addresses your truth. The pendulum has swung out to an extreme and we now must ease it back to a more stable and sustainable sense of equilibrium. To do that, I am going to challenge each of you, after years of overextending yourselves, to put into effect a correction. I am going to challenge you not merely to live within your means, but to live *below* your means. This is not meant to be a punitive strategy; it is a course in self-awareness, a return to values that our grandparents and their parents embraced. It is at the very core of the American Dream of old. Yes, there is still a beating heart in that dream. It is our duty now to rescue what was so right about it: the virtues of hard work and sacrifice; of self-knowledge and steadfastness in achieving one's goals; of aiming for something greater and longer-lasting than the fleeting rewards of instant gratification and indulgence.

THE MONEY CLASS CURRICULUM

I named this book *The Money Class* because what I can provide is knowledge—of what actions to take, what behaviors to correct, how to fortify yourself in the face of economic challenges, how to fashion a responsible dream and achieve it—and knowledge is the key. I can take you from here—a place of fear and despair—to there—a place of security and hope. You will need to learn and in some instances relearn what has changed in our world and in your life, and how you must adapt to those changes.

I understand fully: At this moment in time, you are in fear of the unknown. You don't know exactly what to do or where to turn because you aren't sure what works anymore. You don't know who or what institutions to trust. The truth is, you must learn to trust yourself. To follow a path that is right for you, to make choices that are realistic for you and your family. And becoming that person requires an education, a course of study.

The nine classes that make up this book begin right here, with a lesson in learning how to dream. In the next class, "Stand in Your Truth," I will teach you what it takes to become honest and stay honest. That lesson is the catalyst for everything that follows. The subsequent chapters on family, home, career, and retirement can only be put into action if you bring along a commitment to stand in the truth. Each class will begin with an explanation of the important elements that have changed and require us to rethink our assumptions and reimagine what's possible. Next I will lay out the essential strategies to help you reach your newfound goals. With my guidance and your commitment, we can be a formidable team.

It is time to move beyond materialism in order to set our sights on authentic happiness. *Authenticity* is a word I find myself returning to again and again these days. I would ask you to put your finger on what is authentic in your own life—and what endures. Surely that is our relationships—with those we love, with our community, with the earth. We strive for connection, we gladly sacrifice and find strength in working toward a greater purpose, a sense that there is a reward in being true to yourself and honoring the limitless power that comes from living a life of integrity. More than anything else, isn't that the legacy each of us would like to leave behind? Wouldn't we take pride in knowing that future generations will look to us for inspiration, just as we look for inspiration to the greats who came before us? Then let us embrace the ideals that forged the American Dream, then and now: honesty, integrity, dedication, commitment, courage, and hope. And let us turn toward the future.

The Money Class is now in session.

CLASS

2

STAND IN YOUR TRUTH

How do we usher in this new era of personal responsibility? By taking an honest inventory of exactly where you are today and what you want most for your future. Sounds like it shouldn't be so hard, right? But trust me—getting honest is the hard part. Based on my experience of working with people and their finances for three decades, I can tell you that culturally we have become a nation that hides from that truth.

I see it week in and week out when working on my television show on CNBC. The most popular segment of the show is "Can I Afford It?" in which viewers ask my opinion about a financial purchase they are considering. It is a very simple concept: Viewers want me to tell them whether they can truly afford to buy something.

Before I render my Approved or Denied verdict I insist on finding out everything I can about a viewer's financial situation. And I do mean everything. My staff and I pore over detailed financial information each guest must submit to be considered for the segment. Invariably we go back and forth a few times with the guest before the show is taped, until I am absolutely clear about whether they will be Approved or Denied.

Those of you who watch the show know that more often than not I have to tell guests they are Denied. I know that many of you think the people who are featured on the "Can I Afford It?" segments are just playing a game. I can't tell you how often people come up to me on the street and say, "Oh Suze, I saw the show last weekend and there is no way those people were for real—it was crazy what they thought they could afford!"

I am here to tell you they are most definitely real. What you don't see is that after they have been Denied and the taping is complete, the guests start trying to negotiate with me and my staff. They come back to us and change their story just a little bit in the hope that I will change my mind. The guests most desperate to change the verdict are caught up in what they wish were true; their desires about what they want in the here and now push them to bend the truth, to hide from the truth, just so I will tell them they are Approved.

I wonder if deep down on some level you are struggling with the same urge. That kind of wishful thinking is not unique to the guests who ask me "Can I Afford It?"; it's something many of us indulge in because it allows us to avoid tough decisions and owning up to a difficult reality that we may not be ready to face.

There is no blame, no finger-pointing that accompanies my observation. As we embark on *The Money Class* I want to be crystal clear about my motivation for writing this book: empathy. I understand how painful it can be to face reality. Especially given the realities we are all facing, detailed in the opening class. It often seems to be in conflict with a healthy optimistic impulse.

So trust me when I say that I know it is not easy. But it is necessary. No, make that *vital*. As I explained in the first class, I am convinced that we can all move toward a better future, but in order to do so we must create a new template for achieving our dreams. An important starting point to these classes is the recognition that the events of the past fifteen years or so that culminated in the financial crisis were caused by a collective disconnect from reality.

The most fundamental lesson of *The Money Class* is this: In order to create lasting security you must learn to stand in your truth. You must recognize, embrace, and be honest about what is real for you today and allow that understanding to inform the choices you make. Only then will you be able to build the future of your dreams.

In this class we will learn:

- Finding Your Truth: A Personal Financial Accounting
- Living Truthfully: How to Stand Tall in Your Reality
- The Foundation of All Truthful Living: The Power of Cash

LESSON 1. FINDING YOUR TRUTH: A PERSONAL FINANCIAL ACCOUNTING

Moving toward new realistic dreams starts with an honest appraisal of exactly where you are today. I am not going to try to cajole you into this first lesson with some fancy window dressing. I am going to stand in this truth: There's no way around the fact that every lesson that follows in *The Money Class* can only be helpful if you first take the time to create a personal balance sheet that shows you exactly what you currently spend and owe (your liabilities) and what you have managed to save for your future (your assets).

I realize that sounds like drudgery. But you have it so wrong. Stick with me here, commit to this exercise, and I promise you the experience will be revelatory.

If you already use a software program that helps you track your spending and saving, great. But I suspect that many of you really don't have such a strong grip on where your money is going, month after month. If that is the case, I would like you to go to my website, www.suzeorman.com, and click on the link for The Classroom. The Classroom is where all the tools and resources referenced in *The Money Class* are housed. There you will find my Expense Tracker tool. I have made it as easy as possible for you to determine your monthly income and outgo. But please know that your ability to stand in the truth comes down to how honest you are about inputting the data requested. Please do not guess or estimate. I am asking you to take the time to go through all your statements and documents so you can input dollar amounts into each line item that are a realistic reflection of your actual spending. Be prepared—it could take hours, but that kind of ruthless honesty is necessary to beginning this lesson on a firm and true foundation.

The next piece of information we need is your credit score. You can get that at myFICO.com. If you have a FICO credit score that is below 700, you have some work to do.

Improving Your FICO Score

Your FICO score is important for many reasons, which you know if you've been following my advice for years, but it's even more so today. Before the financial crisis a strong FICO score simply enabled you to qualify for the best deals. Now you must have a strong FICO score to qualify for a loan, period. Typically that means a FICO credit score of at least 700–720, and often lenders reserve their best terms for borrowers with FICO credit scores of 740 or higher. A great source of information on FICO scores can be found at ScoreInfo.org, a consumer site created by FICO.

Once you complete those worksheets and get a FICO score, please print them out. Hold those papers firm and give yourself credit. You have just taken a giant step toward getting honest. I realize many of you will not like what the numbers tell you. Do not panic. Do not beat yourself up. And do not give up. Making those numbers "work" for you is in fact the basis of the rest of this book.

Understand that we are not going to fix anything here in this class. Our focus right now is on facing the facts, so you can identify the areas of your financial life that are causing you stress. I realize you probably have a sense of that without going through these exercises. But it may be just a sense, or an inkling, or a hazy dread. When you take the time to put it all down on paper it brings everything into a sharp clarity. You are no longer guessing, or able to "bend" the truth. With the facts right in front of you, you have the building blocks of a solid foundation that will enable you to stand in your truth.

LESSON 2. LIVING TRUTHFULLY: HOW TO STAND TALL IN YOUR REALITY

Now that you have a clear-eyed accounting of your financial reality, our next challenge is to give you the means to take action based on what those worksheets tell you. I need to repeat myself: Do not be ashamed or upset. Know that in spirit I am sitting right beside you and I am excited for you: You have taken a giant step toward getting honest! That is no small achievement.

In the classes that follow I present a series of lessons that will guide you through making the adjustments and taking the proper actions to help you realize your dreams. Those chapters contain all the nuts-and-bolts information you will need. To be honest, the how-to part of those chapters is relatively easy; it is just a matter of understanding some basic financial rules, regulations, and truths and making smart choices based on that knowledge.

What I want to focus on in this lesson is how you find it in yourself to make those choices. The success of *The Money Class* is not just what I can teach you, but ultimately, what you are able to put into action for yourself, for your family, and for the benefit of future generations.

Here are the cornerstones of the better financial life you can build with the lessons that follow:

FOCUS ON WHAT IS REAL TODAY . . .

The only way you can move forward is to loosen your grip on the past. I know for many of you it is quite difficult to not look in the rearview mirror. You are still hoping your home's value gets back to where it was in 2006, or you are stuck thinking about how much more your retirement accounts were worth a few years ago, or how much easier it was to generate income when interest rates were higher than they are today. Those of you looking for work are unwilling to settle for a job that pays less than your last one.

Please know that I say this with full knowledge of how deeply wrenching it is: We must let go of the past. The decisions you make today must be based on what is realistic today—not what may have been true in the past, but what you know for a fact is an honest accounting of what is happening for you right here, right now.

. . . AND WHAT YOU WILL NEED TOMORROW

What derails so many of our good intentions is that we find it hard to make decisions today that will serve us well in the future. So we spend today rather than save for tomorrow. Or we say yes to something—a vacation with friends, a cousin who is looking for investors in a new business—even though spending that money now will impede our ability to reach long-term goals. The process of standing in the truth must work for you not just in terms of what is right today, but also with a clear appreciation of the measures required to attain a secure future. Money you spend today is money that will not be able to grow and help you reach your most important future goals, be it a child's college education, paying off your mortgage before retirement, or being able to live comfortably in retirement.

PUT MONEY IN ITS PLACE

Over the years you may have heard me say that money has no power of its own. It might have given you a moment's pause when you first heard it, but maybe the truth behind it didn't stick with you. So let's dwell on it a moment here, because it's truly an important concept.

When you are staring at the numbers on your worksheets, I want you to recognize that you have been the catalyst that made the decisions to spend, save, and invest those dollars. Money has no power on its own. It is the car; you are the gas, ignition key, and driver. Without you nothing happens. That should actually make you optimistic. You have the power to make the right and honest decisions about how you handle your money. And finding your power will set off a wonderful chain reaction: When you take the necessary measures to regain security—or build it for the very first time—you bring happiness into your life. You are better able to be present and connect with your family; you are less preoccupied by financial anxiety.

I am asking you to recognize and embrace this concept with your head and your heart: Your money has no power of its own; you are what gives it power. That you are here with me in *The Money Class* tells me you are ready to own that power, fix what isn't working, and build lasting security.

LIVE BELOW YOUR MEANS BUT WITHIN YOUR NEEDS

The reality is that in order to reach your goals, and maintain those goals once they are achieved, you must live below your means. If you do not have money left over each month you will have nothing to put toward fulfilling your dreams. So "below your means" means making a commitment not to spend every last dollar you take home. "Within your needs" requires that you make a clear-eyed assessment of what exactly you are putting in that category. Yes, it is the act of separating needs from wants, something that I've discussed in previous books; but now, in fact, I am asking you to take a more penetrating look.

You need a house, but do you need a house that eats up 35% or more of your monthly income? Could your family be just as content in a less expensive house where the rent or mortgage is just 20% of your monthly income?

I find it so interesting that over the past thirty years the average square footage of a new home grew 42%, even though the number of people living in that house actually decreased. That's a lot more house to pay for, to heat and cool, to furnish and repair. We all need a place to live, but perhaps a smaller, less expensive place would help us achieve our new dreams. You are meeting your needs with the less expensive house but given the lower cost it will allow you to live below your means, and that can free up significant money to put toward other goals.

You need a car to get to work and shuttle the kids around. But can you honestly tell me you bought a car that met your needs but was as inexpensive as possible? The new dream car is one that is less expensive and that you drive for as long as possible.

I understand the desire to have the things that you want. You feel you work hard, so you deserve those things. But the truth of the matter is that they are just things and those things will never make you happy. Peace of mind will make you happy. Being able to sleep at night will make you happy. Not worrying about being able to retire one day will make you happy.

I want you to appreciate where I am coming from: My call to live below your means is the path to having more. Living below your means—but within your needs; this is not about punishing deprivation—will allow you to create more to put toward your goals. I need you to recognize, right here, right now, that your dreams for tomorrow reside in the choices you make today.

THE PLEASURE OF SAVING IS EQUAL TO THE PLEASURE OF SPENDING

I want to share a dream of mine: Someday, hopefully not too far in the future, I will have people call in to my television show or stop me on the street and excitedly share with me their latest savings triumph. I mean, let's just say no one has ever asked me if they can afford to save another $500 a month, if you catch my drift. But a girl has gotta dream . . .

I am not suggesting you never allow yourself to spend money today. But what is painfully absent from so many of your lives is an appreciation that what you manage to save today is in fact what gives your family security, hope, and opportunity. When you see it from that vantage point, you begin to understand what I mean by the pleasure of saving. It is what makes your dreams possible.

To be sure, some of you do understand the pleasure that comes from saving. But those families seem to be the exception, not the norm. So my dream is that each and every one of you can embrace the power, security, and control that comes from saving:

- When I see a family that has an eight-month emergency fund, contributes to their workplace retirement funds, and also makes annual contributions into their own IRAs, I know they understand the pleasure of saving and that their family is not beset with financial stress.
- When I see a family that drives a six-year-old car they own outright that runs perfectly fine, and even though they can afford to buy a new one they do not, I know they are standing in the truth.
- When I meet families, as I have so often these past few years, that tell me with well-earned pride that they have cut back on their household spending and have reduced their credit card debt by 30%, I know they get it. When you stop me in the street to tell me you have managed to cut your food expenses dramatically by cooking dinner at home and reserving fancy restaurant meals for special occasions, I see that you've got a handle on your priorities.
- When you tell me you stopped yourself cold in the mall and put down an impulse purchase because you recognized it really wasn't something you needed, I am happy for you, for you have experienced the pleasure that comes from saving.

One of the goals of this book is to make savings part of our national conversation. It's my dream that someday soon we will share and measure ourselves by our saving exploits, rather than judging ourselves and others by what we spend. I've heard newscasters and pundits refer to this shift as the "New Frugality," but I have to tell you, the negativity of that phrase turns me off. Finding equal pleasure in savings as you do in spending strikes me as something far more hopeful and exciting. It carries with it the promise of freedom, of liberation, for when you make it a priority to save, to fund your current expenses and future goals, you are in fact buying yourself freedom from crushing debt, from having to cross your fingers that the markets—real estate and stock—will generate the money you want and need. With savings comes control. And I think we can all agree that on many levels what went so wrong in the recent past and came to a head during the financial crisis is that we lost all control over our future. We borrowed it from the banks, or based it on unrealistic expectations.

YOU DEFINE YOURSELF BY WHO YOU ARE, NOT WHAT YOU HAVE

With all the spending of the past few decades came a not-too-surprising by-product. Money became our identity; we became defined by what we owned, or what we dreamed of owning. The New American Dream is rooted in a definition of self that has everything to do with character and intention and nothing to do with material things. When you are motivated by your own beliefs, aims, and principles, you possess the clarity and single-mindedness to achieve that which is truly valuable: security and peace of mind.

YOU CAN SAY, "I'M GLAD I DID," RATHER THAN "I WISH I HADN'T"

Making tomorrow's dreams a reality requires being able to make the right choices today. As you consider the options before you, I ask that you take a few moments to consider how that particular decision might play out over the next year, the next decade, the next generation, and imagine how you might grade your decision with hindsight. You will know you are standing in your truth today if during this exercise you can imagine your future self saying, "I'm glad I did make that decision," rather than "I wish I hadn't." For a decision to be powerful it must not only provide you immediate gratification or relief, it must in fact be a choice that brings long-lasting satisfaction.

YOU ARE AN ELEPHANT

Don't be offended—I mean that as a compliment!

I have a favorite saying that I recall whenever I need help to stand in my truth: *The elephant keeps walking while the dog keeps barking.*

The elephant stays on course, moving toward its goal, regardless of all the barking and noise that swirls around him. I do what is true and right for me. I listen to advice. I seek advice. But ultimately I know when I am standing in the truth because my mind and my gut are in agreement. The goal is to achieve an internal calmness that comes when your intellect and your instincts are operating in harmony.

Why is this saying so important for you? If you are going to stand in your truth then you will have to be strong and tenacious. You will have to be committed to your goal and determined to stay the course. You may feel pressured at every turn to spend money; there are many enticements all around us trying very hard to get you to part with your hard-earned cash—the sounds of excitement coming out of restaurants and clubs, the heady scents that waft out the doors of department stores, persuasive ads, the pages of glossy magazines telling you about the "must haves" of the season. Let me tell you, it's not easy to ignore all that barking. A lot of time and money and invention is spent on coming up with ways to seduce you to spend. But if you are steady and true and you are able to just keep walking when your friends say let's go skiing this weekend, let's go out to eat, come on, live a little—if you can just keep walking then you will end up where you want to be, regardless of the obstacles thrown in your path. An elephant walks where it wants—surely and steadily it arrives at its destination, and that is the truth that I want you to stand in.

In the New American Dream we must all aspire to be elephants. We must decide what is true and right for ourselves and our family and then stay devoted to actions and behavior that are in service to our greatest goals. We must not let the barking dogs distract us.

LESSON 3. THE FOUNDATION OF ALL TRUTHFUL LIVING: THE POWER OF CASH

In the following chapters I dive into detailed advice on how to maneuver through the big financial decisions in your life. But before you venture into those lessons you must first make sure you and your family have a solid foundation to build upon. And that brings me to the last element of what it takes to stand in your truth: embracing the power of cash.

While you will always need to borrow to purchase a home, and many families will need to borrow for college as well, one of the fundamental principles of the New American Dream is to pay for as much as possible with cash. Spend what you have today, not what you hope to have tomorrow.

Paying with cash—be it good old dollar bills or a debit card—cuts down on the temptation to charge more on a credit card than you can truly afford. And studies show that when we use cold, hard cash to pay for things, we tend to spend less; it's a more tangible experience to part with actual money than to hand over a credit card with a too-generous limit that won't require us to pay in full.

DEBIT CARD RULES

Using a debit card tied to your bank or credit union checking account is the next best thing to paying with cash and it's undeniably convenient. And talk about standing in your truth! The whole MO of credit cards is to encourage you to live beyond your means—to spend based on your credit limit, not your bank account. On the other hand, debit cards actually encourage you to spend only what you can truly afford. For that reason alone, I think it makes a lot of sense to use a debit card over a credit card. However, you must truly understand how debit cards work to be assured that the card you choose to use offers you the best possible deal.

Two Types of Debit Cards

There are two different types of debit cards: There is the debit card that is tied to your bank or credit union checking account, or there is the increasingly popular option of a prepaid debit card that you can load money onto and then pay bills or make purchases up to that amount. As your balance gets lower you have the option of "reloading" your card by putting more money on it.

Here's how to be a smart debit-card user:

Decline overdraft protection. Thanks to a federal regulation that went into effect in 2010, you should have been asked whether you wanted this service; if you said yes or if you can't remember what you chose, please check right away. I never want you to be enrolled in the overdraft program. An overdraft is a sign of dishonesty. You are spending money you don't have. And it makes me nuts when you end up being stuck with expensive overdraft fees. When you are standing in your truth and living below your means, you don't need overdraft protection.

Monitor your account every other day. If someone has managed to hack into your account and withdraw money using your debit card info, your liability is limited to $50 if you notify your bank or credit union within two business days. Otherwise you could be held liable for up to $500 in fraudulent charges. If your debit card offers email or text alerts for all transactions, that's a smart way to monitor your account.

Understand the fees. Yet another new regulation that went into effect in mid-2011 reduces how much some debit card issuers can charge *retailers* for debit card transactions. To make up for that lost fee income, you better believe the card issuers are actively looking for ways to charge *you* more when you use your debit card.

For those of you with debit cards tied to your checking account, there may be a new or higher monthly charge, or you may be hit with a fee for every transaction.

Fees can be an even bigger issue for prepaid card users. In addition to potential ATM and per-swipe charges, some prepaid debit cards charge a fee of $9.95 a month. Alternatively, the arrangement might be a lower monthly fee, but you may be charged more for other services. For example, many cards charge you 50 cents for every bill you pay online. If you're not careful you can end up with total monthly charges that approach $50! That is highway robbery!

Please take the time to read the fine print before you sign on to any card plan to verify you will not be hit with outsized fees.

FICO Scores and Debit Cards

As I explained on page 14, a FICO credit score can play a huge role in your family's financial life. It affects your loan terms, your car insurance premiums, and your ability to rent an apartment, among other things. Moreover, the data inside your personal credit report can also be accessed by prospective employers.

When you use a credit card your payment habits on that card are shared with the three major credit bureaus that compile your credit reports (Equifax, Experian, and TransUnion). When you use a credit card you are building up data inside of your credit report, and that in turn is what your all-important FICO score is based on.

The problem with debit cards is that your payment history isn't tracked by the three major credit bureaus (this is true as I write this in late 2011), which makes it hard, if not impossible, for FICO to calculate credit scores for you. Even though some prepaid cards advertise that they report your payment history to a credit bureau, what they don't tell you is that it's not one of the three major credit bureaus, so that makes the report pretty useless. The vast majority of lenders and businesses that check credit scores look at one or more of your three FICO credit scores that are based on the data in your Equifax, Experian, and Trans-Union credit reports. If your debit card doesn't report to one of those three major credit bureaus, it's not helping you build a strong credit history that will translate into a strong FICO credit score.

The Approved Card: My Consumer-Friendly Pre-Paid Debit Card

As much as I love how debit cards can help Americans live within their means, I am not in love with how expensive some of these cards are once you tally up all the fees. And it's so frustrating that no debit card issuer shares your payment history with one of the three major credit bureaus.

That's why I have created a truly consumer-friendly debit card: **The Approved Card**. In addition to a low monthly fee of just $3 per month, the Approved Card will be the first prepaid debit card in history to share your payment history with one of the three major credit bureaus. TransUnion intends to study the transaction patterns of Approved Card users over an 18-month period to determine if it is a solid predictor of creditworthiness. If TransUnion finds that debit card habits are a viable indicator of a user's financial habits, the data will then be used to compute a FICO credit score for Approved Card users.

It is my hope that this will be the start of a truly important shift in credit scores: People who rely on debit, rather than credit, should be celebrated, not penalized. You can learn more about my Approved Card at www.suzeorman.com and www .theapprovedcard.com.

LIFE HAPPENS

I've said it before and I'll say it again: You need an eight-month emergency savings fund. Why so long? Well, it's not just because 4 in 10 people who are unemployed today have been out of work for more than six months. Being laid off indeed creates a dire emergency, but there are less dramatic and more frequent emergencies that happen throughout the course of any given year. Your car may need new brakes. Your water heater goes on the fritz. Your kid tears a ligament playing soccer and suddenly you have $1,000 in copays for the doctor bills.

I have to admit, I regret casting these events as emergencies. They really aren't; they are just life. So if it helps you embrace the necessity of this account to be well funded, we can call it a "life happens" fund.

Every New American Dream must rest on the foundation of a robust savings account that can absorb life's emergencies, big and small.

CREDIT UNIONS: A GREAT PLACE TO SAVE

Credit unions are nonprofits and that makes them a whole lot nicer to do business with because they aren't motivated to squeeze every dollar out of you with penalties and exorbitant fees. They are also less likely to shut down your credit card for no reason, and the fees they do charge are typically lower than bank-issued credit cards. Best of all, especially for those of you who are still not out of credit card debt, the maximum interest rate on all federally charted credit union credit cards is capped by law at 18%, whereas some bank cards are charging 28% or more these days.

Credit unions are also a smart place for your checking and savings accounts. You often can qualify for absolutely free checking at many credit unions, and the interest rates paid on your bank deposits are typically better than at many banks that are in the business of making money for themselves, not you.

You must be a member of a credit union, and some credit unions limit membership to people with a specific affiliation; it can be through an employer, or a community group. But many credit unions are in fact more than happy to invite "outsiders" to become members, often for a small fee of $5–$20 or so. You can search for federally insured credit unions that you may be eligible for at the website of the National Credit Union Administration. Go to www.asmarterchoice.org or CreditCardConnection.org.

There is just one trick to joining a credit union: Please make sure it is a member of the National Credit Union Association (NCUA). That means your deposits are federally insured in the same way bank accounts are backed by the FDIC. The base level of protection in an NCUA-member credit union is $250,000. That is, if anything were to happen to that credit union, the federal government would step in and pay you back every penny up to $250,000. You can learn more at www.ncua.gov.

Go to The Classroom at www.suzeorman.com: Depending on how you set up your accounts you can in fact have more than $250,000 protected by federal insurance at either a bank or credit union. At my website I have a detailed explanation of how you can use different accounts to increase your total coverage at one individual credit union.

SAFETY FIRST WITH YOUR SAVINGS

In late 2011, most basic checking accounts are not paying more than 1% interest. We may see those rates persist at least into mid-2013 as the Federal Reserve is determined to keep short-term rates low to help spur economic growth.

As low as the yields are on super-safe bank and credit union deposit accounts, they are indeed the best place for your emergency fund. You must keep this savings account safe and sound. You need to know that money is available to you whenever you need it—and you need to know exactly how much is there.

Don't use a money market mutual fund for your emergency savings. It's not just that money market mutual funds are not federally insured. The problem is that they charge an annual fee. It can be quite small, maybe one-tenth or two-tenths of a percentage point, but right now that small sum is actually huge given how low general interest rates are. You want to earn as much interest income as possible.

I also want you to stay away from putting this money into a certificate of deposit account that matures in more than 12 months. These accounts, especially ones that have longer terms (five years or more), are not where you want to be when interest rates start to rise.

SAVING FOR BIG-TICKET ITEMS

The New American Dream also requires that you have ample savings beyond your "life happens" fund in order to borrow less for major purchases. Be it the cost of a new car, a 20% down payment on a home, or the full cost of a kitchen renovation, I want you to do your very best to have that money saved up—completely—before you embark on this expenditure. That is how our grandparents did it and it is the way of the future.

I have news for you: This isn't just about my wanting you to borrow less. As I write this in late 2011, you probably will not qualify to borrow money from banks and credit unions unless you have a sizable amount of your own savings to bring to the deal.

You need a down payment to make a deal. It is that simple. (Yes, I am well aware homebuyers can make just a 3.5% down payment and qualify for an FHA-insured loan. But as I explain in the Home Class, I do not think a 3.5% down payment is in any way standing in your financial truth.)

Here are a few tips on how to save for a capital expense.

Open a separate savings account for each goal. Your emergency fund should be its own separate account. And every additional savings goal should have its own dedicated savings account.

Set up an automatic monthly transfer from your checking account into your savings account(s). All banks and credit unions offer this service for free and I would encourage you to take advantage of it. It's hard to have the discipline on your own to make sure you are setting aside money every month. By committing to an automatic transfer each month that the bank handles for you, you are making sure the money will in fact make it into your savings account every month. You can set up this service online, or by dropping into a local branch.

At my website, in the Suze Tools section you will find a free online Compound Interest Forecaster that will show you how your savings will grow over time. Play around with that calculator to get a sense of what you want to save each month to be able to make a sizable down payment for a future goal. Just promise me you will stand in your truth: If that goal is within the next 5–10 years, your money must stay in a super-safe savings account. So set your interest rate at just 1% or 2%. When rates rise, as I expect they will in the coming years, you can come back to the Forecaster and see how that will speed up your savings. But right now, we are standing in the truth that safe savings are growing at just a 1% to 2% rate. Agreed?

THE TRUTH WILL INDEED SET YOU FREE

As I said earlier in this chapter, in many ways "Stand in Your Truth" is the most important class I have to teach, for it is only when we turn inward and locate what is right and true for us that we can begin to move forward toward creating our new dreams.

From learning to live below your means, to insulating your family from the unexpected major expenses that are a part of all our lives, your new dreams will begin to take shape only once you've begun to stand in your truth.

The challenge is to make this new way of living—this pursuit of genuine happiness—a long-term commitment. I ask you to do it from a place of sincerity and hope for the future, not just because you are afraid of what is happening to you at the moment. It is inevitable that the economy will improve at some point. That is something we are all hoping for. But as grateful as we will all be when those better times come, I hope you hold fast to the lessons in this class. Your future and that of your children and grandchildren, whether they've been born yet or not—all of us collectively will benefit from a commitment made to living a life of integrity, from moment to moment, of resisting the ephemeral temptations of immediate gratification, and staying steady with the dreams of your shining future squarely in your sights.

Trust me, it will not be long before the banks and financial services industry as a whole will be back offering you enticing ways to get you to stray from your path. Credit card limits will be loosened, home loans and home equity lines of credit will become easier to obtain. Get-rich-quick schemes will never die. My hope for you—for all of us—is that you will be able to stand tall in your truth and stay committed to the path that will lead you to peace, financial security, and happiness.

LESSON RECAP

- Give a fresh review to all your spending and expenses; learning to live below your means creates the opportunity to fund your long-term dreams.
- Make a conscious decision to derive pleasure—yes, pleasure!—from the act of saving. When you value saving as much as spending you are standing in your truth.
- An eight-month Life Happens fund is a nonnegotiable necessity if you are to stand in your truth.

CLASS

3

FAMILY

THE TRUTH OF THE MATTER

Family has always been at the heart of the American Dream. We work, we strive for the sake of our family. We want our children to have endless opportunity, to be free to achieve and create and flourish. We want our parents to enjoy good health, to reap the benefits of a lifetime of hard work and sacrifice on our behalf, to live out their golden years free of financial worry. *Sacrifice*—that word was so ingrained in a generation of immigrants who came to America to make a better life, not necessarily one they themselves would realize, but for future generations. That is still true to this very day. No matter the current state of the American Dream, the promise still shines and American shores still beckon: If you work hard, you can improve your life and the lives of your loved ones.

I cherish that promise, as an American and a woman whose grandparents, full of hope, emigrated from Eastern Europe at the turn of the last century. And certainly if you read my books or watch me on TV, you know how important family is in my own life. I'm blessed to have my mother with me, to have a spouse, to be surrounded by siblings and nieces and nephews at holidays, and to be able to enjoy and share the gifts life offers us and the fruits of what we have been able to create with those we love best.

So is this aspect of the American Dream intact? Well, I'd have to say in theory, in our hearts, it is still alive and well. In practice, however, too often we fall prey to good intentions. We sacrifice the wrong things for the right reasons. We put our financial security at risk to make someone we love happy. We put wants before needs because we mistakenly think it's a way to show our love. For the past two decades so many of us have spent more than we had any right to spend, all in the name of providing for our families. We used credit cards to buy things we couldn't really afford. We bought bigger, more expensive homes, with bigger, more expensive mortgages, and then we used the equity in those homes to finance everything we couldn't manage to save for: a vacation, a college education, retirement. The American Dream of more and bigger and better got distorted. And in the process, we lost the truth that one of the greatest gifts we can teach our children and put into practice for ourselves is self-sufficiency.

Sadly, even families that have behaved with more financial responsibility have been buffeted by punishing economic headwinds. A layoff or a stalled career that hasn't produced a promotion or substantial raise in recent years can mean that your standard of living has not markedly improved for quite some time; it may even feel like it's getting harder and harder just to make ends meet. And even as you work to regain your financial bearings, you may also find that your grown children and elderly parents need financial assistance now too. Add to that poor returns on your retirement portfolio and a decrease in your home value and you have plenty of cause for worry all around.

No matter what the current state of the American Dream in your family, we have arrived at a point in time that is defined by this one incontestable truth: How your family spends and saves money, and how money flows through the generations of your family, needs to be revisited. For many of you the challenge is to rein in your family's spending so you can achieve the long-term financial goals you have set for yourself. For others, the task is more complex and far-ranging; it may require a reassessment of your very way of life—an honest reappraisal of your immediate needs and a realistic reworking of your priorities in the decades ahead.

No matter what your starting point, the first step, the first thing I'm going to call on you to do, is the same: Start talking.

The New American Dream is rooted in honesty—and honesty must be a family affair. With honesty as your foundation you can then lay down the framework of how as a family you intend to create and achieve sustainable dreams. The lessons in this class run the gamut, from how parents can instill the right money values in young children to how adult children can help their aging parents live a comfortable and secure life. You never really graduate from the Family Class, as you shall see. It is an ongoing lesson—a practice and a privilege for those of us blessed to share our lives with the ones we love.

A silver lining to emerge from the recent economic crisis is the fact that we are finally getting it. More Americans are paying down their debt; we are, sometimes painfully, facing up to the consequences of rash financial behavior; we are starting to learn what it means to stand in the truth. I am hopeful that on a large scale and individually we are recognizing the virtues and integrity of the generations who came before us, who understood what it meant to save, to sacrifice, to set a goal and work diligently and selflessly to achieve it. I speak to so many of you—at my lectures, in the course of producing my TV show, via email and social networks—and I am encouraged to see that there seems to be a new maturity, a new sobriety taking hold. That is a sea change, the beginning of a paradigm shift, that has occurred in the span of just a few years. With that promise in our hearts, let's head into the Family Class.

I have organized the Family Class into the following lessons:

- How to Build Honest Family Relations
- How to Raise Young Children to Stand in the Truth
- How to Create a Financially Honest College Strategy
- How to Help Adult Children Facing Financial Challenges

- The Conversation Every Adult Child Should Have with His or Her Parents
- Advice for Grandparents: How to Build a Lasting Legacy

LESSON 1. HOW TO BUILD HONEST FAMILY RELATIONS

One of the great mysteries to me is how we have convinced ourselves that it is okay to lie to our loved ones.

When your credit card balance is full of purchases you made because your kids asked for something, you are in fact lying to yourself and your kids about what your family can honestly afford.

When you loan your sister money to cover her chronic shortfalls and that money depletes your emergency fund, you are lying to yourself and your sister that you can afford to help her—or that you are in fact helping her by enabling her irresponsible behavior.

When you tell your kids to focus on getting into the best college and not worry about the cost, even though you will have to spend your retirement savings to cover the bills, you are not being honest with them about the sacrifices you are prepared to make. What you are doing, in effect, is mortgaging their future. Who, after all, will you have to lean on in retirement if you haven't planned well, but your children?

When your parents need financial help and your siblings assume you will take care of anything because you make the most money, and you participate in this disproportionate share of responsibility, you are encouraging a financial codependence that will surely lead to conflict and animosity. That is a shared dishonesty.

Your rationale for behavior of this sort seems so irrefutably pure and right: love. You give, and give, and give out of love. No questions asked. Because that is what family is all about.

I want you to know how sensitive I am to the good intentions behind all these choices. But there is no way to build sustainable dreams on a foundation of financial dishonesty.

OPEN THE LINES OF COMMUNICATION

Having taught you to stand in your truth in the second class, I am now going to ask that you go public with your truth. Bring everyone in your family on board, because we are always stronger and more successful in reaching our goals when we have the support and encouragement of our loved ones. But you must also open the lines of communication and share your financial truths because they will in many cases have a direct impact on your family. How you explain to a ten-year-old child why you will not be sending him to sleepaway camp this year is obviously different than how you express to your adult siblings your desire to change the gift-giving traditions in your family. But both conversations are a must. If you fail to communicate you leave it to those around you to fill in the backstory. That can be especially dangerous with children, who will think it is somehow their fault, or that they are being punished. A lack of communication also creates distance between you and your loved ones. That's never a good outcome, but it seems especially ill timed when you are embarking on a new stage of your life and could benefit greatly from bringing your family into the process.

TAKE PRIDE IN YOUR HONESTY

I know that many of you think having truthful conversations with your family about your financial situation is embarrassing or painful. You feel so defeated by having to admit what is going on. Please listen to me: You have it all wrong. When you stand in the truth, and you are able to communicate that truth, you should feel proud and triumphant. For when you take the step forward to live your life with honesty you are at your most powerful and your most admirable. It takes strength and resolve to stand in your truth. Your family will love you all the more for your ability to embrace the changes you need to move toward your new realistic dreams.

Now, that said, if there are young children involved, a transi-

tion to a more modest lifestyle will no doubt be met with some re-
sistance. That's to be expected. And you must respect that they
need time to absorb and adapt to the shift. But your words, your
body language, and your spirit throughout will set the tone for
them. Stand in your truth with pride and confidence and you will
be parenting in a way that will benefit your children not just next
week and next month, but for decades to come. You are imparting
the invaluable lesson of living life honestly.

GIVE IT SOME THOUGHT

One of the reasons you find it so hard to act with financial honesty
when it comes to your family is that you tend to act in the moment,
rather than step back and contemplate before you make a decision.
You say yes without ever stopping to think if you can in fact afford
to say yes.

That needs to change. For you to build and reach your new
dreams you must carefully weigh each and every money decision.
This is not simply about what you can afford. Obviously if you do
not have money to spare you cannot give it away. But even when
you do have the money to share, I am asking you to take the time
to think through whether you are helping that person stand in his
or her truth.

When you cosign a loan for a child who can't get a car loan because she has a lousy credit score, are you helping her stand in her
truth? When you give a brother $15,000 to get out of credit card
debt, is that helping him stand in his truth? I realize your intentions are good, but you need to distinguish between helping and
enabling. People who are standing in the truth and need financial
assistance deserve your help, if you can in fact afford to give financial help. People who are looking for your money to solve
(probably temporarily) a problem of their own creation are not
standing in their truth. My advice? Guide them, with love and encouragement, toward personal accountability and financial honesty. Don't allow your money to do the talking for you; it will send
the absolute wrong message.

LESSON 2. HOW TO RAISE YOUNG CHILDREN TO STAND IN THE TRUTH

One of the saddest aspects of our national borrowing binge of the past few decades is the damage it has done to an entire generation of children. Parents who used credit cards and home equity lines to finance a lifestyle way beyond the family's means have left their children with no experience, understanding, or appreciation for what it means to live a financially honest life.

I am not interested in assigning blame or provoking feelings of guilt. I raise this important issue in the hope that from this day forward all parents will devote themselves to instilling a strong set of values in their children and teaching them essential money management skills. Survey after survey reports that, in the wake of the financial crisis, parents worry that their children's future will be limited. That is what we are addressing head-on in this class, so you will not live in a state of anxiety about your children, but you will in fact act to secure their future, right here, right now.

YOUR PRICELESS LEGACY

Children in their teens who are aware of what is going on in our economy—and within their own family's finances—are less likely to repeat the same mistakes. They can feel the stress and worry and they are way too smart to want the same for themselves. But what makes me truly optimistic about the future of today's children is the fact that so many of you, their parents, have financial regrets. In "Stand in Your Truth" we talked about changing your inner dialogue from "I wish I hadn't" to "I am glad that I did." Well, there is no more important proving ground for that intention than to raise children who from an early age respect the value of money and know how to make smart money choices. Much of this comes down to creating an environment where those lessons are woven into the daily rhythms of your family's life. Raise a child in a home where money is valued, and that child is likely to be an adult who values money. It is really that simple.

Life Insurance: The Ultimate Gesture of Love

So many of you tell me you would do absolutely anything to protect your children, yet when I ask about your life insurance policy you look at me sheepishly and admit you don't have one. That is an unacceptable act of hypocrisy. If you love your children and if those children are financially dependent on you to provide them food, shelter, and education, then you must have life insurance. There are no ifs, ands, or buts here. If your death or the death of your spouse or partner would leave your family unable to continue to pay its bills and maintain the lifestyle you help provide today, it is your obligation to have life insurance. And I do mean obligated. Life insurance is a must when you have dependent children.

Purchasing that protection is neither hard nor expensive. In the vast majority of situations all your family needs is a term life insurance policy. Just as an example, a 40-year-old male in good health could purchase a $1,000,0000 policy—meaning his survivors would receive $1 million tax free upon his death—for a monthly premium of $80 or so.

In 2011 a new hybrid version of term life insurance—called term/universal—was being offered by a handful of insurers. Do not get thrown by the word "universal." This is a different animal—it's not the kind of universal life I do not like. In fact, in my opinion the new term/universal policies are certainly worth investigating. The selling point for term/universal life insurance is that instead of being insured for just a set period (the term), you have the option to continue coverage after the initial term is over. If you are absolutely certain you need term for only a set period, a straight term policy could still offer the best pricing for you. But if you think you might be interested in possibly extending your coverage past the initial term, then I recommend looking at a term/universal policy. For the initial term the price should be similar to that of a straight term policy—that's what you want to compare. The difference with the term/universal is that at the point you purchase the initial policy you will also be told what your new premium would be if—and only if—you decide to extend the policy past the initial term. The premium you are quoted will never change; it is guaranteed to be honored 10, 20, or 30 years down the line when your initial term expires. Most important, that new premium will be level for the rest of your life, meaning it will never rise.

Go to www.suzeorman.com: In The Classroom you will find a detailed explanation of how term life insurance works, what features you want in a policy, and resources for working with top-notch insurance agents, as well as additional information on term/universal.

SET THE RIGHT TONE

Your family will take its cues from you. If your words and actions telegraph that you are scared, or sad, then that is exactly what you are going to transmit to those who depend on you.

Do not apologize. There will obviously be instances when standing in your truth requires saying no to spending you previously said yes to. Be compassionate. Be patient. But please do not ever apologize. There should not be any regret. That is not respectful of yourself, and it also sends a message to your children that you feel bad about these changes.

Focus on what will be gained, not lost. Make sure your family understands why you want to make changes. When you present your truth in the context of wanting to move toward realistic new dreams, you set the tone that this is not about loss or defeat. This is a triumphant step forward into a new life where you can build lasting financial security for yourself and your family. Every spending cut is an appropriate measure that moves you closer to your family's greater goals.

Be patient but strong. I am not going to pretend this is going to be in any way easy if your kids have grown accustomed to having everything they want, when they want it. They are going to be upset. There will likely be tears. I realize that can be excruciatingly hard to impose—on all parties—but please focus on your long-term goals. You are not punishing them. You are not punishing yourself. Just the opposite. I think you will be surprised at how quickly your kids will adapt to your new ways, but you need to summon the strength to stand firm during the transition. Resist caving. Keep reminding yourself that by standing in your truth today you are creating a better future for your children, and you are also instilling in them an attitude toward money that will help them reach their dreams when they are adults.

IMPARTING GOOD VALUES WHEN IT COMES TO MONEY

Talk about what you love. The first and most important money lesson you need to teach your children is to put money in its place. Ask your children—even children as young as four or five—what they love most. Do not guide them, just listen to what they value. Is it people or is it things? Did they talk about loving you, and their grandparents, a sibling, a pet? A favorite food? Or was their list about possessions? It is perfectly natural for every human being—child and adult—to desire and enjoy material possessions. But you need to make sure you are raising your children to have a broad view of what is important in life. Many of you know my motto: *People first, then money, then things.* If your child has moved things to the front of the line, that's a clear sign you have some work to do. I would start by making sure you communicate, through words and actions, what you love most. If you are clear that you care most about your family, about the well-being of others, rather than what you own, you are telegraphing an important lesson.

If you don't particularly like what you hear, I have to point out that you are the issue here. Kids don't do as you say, they do as you do. They are watching and mimicking your behavior. If you are constantly shopping, or ordering things online, or focusing on your latest mall conquest, what else can you expect than for your young child to assume that is the absolute best way to behave? After all, you are the all-knowing and all-wonderful parent they worship and take all their cues from. Including your cues about how to value material possessions.

MONEY LESSONS FOR YOUNG CHILDREN, AGES 3 TO 6

Establish the work-pay-purchase connection. As far as I am concerned there is no age too young to start learning that money must be earned to buy the things your family needs.

Explain why you work. It makes me absolutely nuts when I see parents kiss their young children goodbye in the morning and say, "I hate that I have to leave you to go to work, but I need to make money." All that does is teach your child that work and money is a bad thing. What your children need to hear from you is that you are incredibly grateful that you get to go to work and get paid money and that that money enables you to take care of them. Also let them know that you personally get satisfaction from your work.

Explain how you earn money and what it does. Unless you make a concerted effort to explain how money is earned, your children will think it is simply something anyone can get by punching a few keys at the ATM. Or worse, they will have no concept of real money—actual dollar bills—because you are always using a credit card. You must explain that your work earns you money, that money goes into the bank, and that you can only take out as much money as you have earned at your job.

Explain that the groceries in the refrigerator and the toys in the playroom were bought with the money you earned. The electricity that keeps the computer humming has to be paid for too. Once your child is old enough to understand the concept of dollar bills, I want you to have them join you on your errands from time to time, and have them pay the cashier with real dollar bills. Physically connecting to money—real dollar bills—helps us focus on what we are spending. That is a lesson you should be teaching your kids from an early age.

Teach giving. Two times a year sit down in your child's room or the playroom and together sort through all the clothes, toys, books, and crafts that they no longer use. Whether you give these away to a friend, a charity, or a thrift store, I want your child to be the one to make the physical transfer. It is such an important lesson to learn the power of giving. A friend recently made her five-year-old's birthday party into a pajama party, asking children to come in ther PJs and to bring a new set of pajamas instead of a gift. The pajamas were donated to the Pajama Program (www .pajamaprogram.org), a charity that gives new pajamas and books to children in need, in the United States and around the world. I thought this was a great idea that created a real opportunity to teach small children about our obligation to help those less fortu- nate.

Have a clear toy/gift policy. This is one area where I see so many parents completely drop the ball. Instead of reserving gifts for special occasions such as birthdays, they have become your go- to solution to help you get through your way-too-hectic day with- out an upsetting meltdown (yours or theirs). So you promise a gift for good behavior, or you hold out the carrot of a stop at the toy store if your child behaves well while you are running other er- rands. Toys—big and small—have become pacifiers at home. When your child starts to get a little cranky and your first line of talking it through doesn't work, you pull out a "little something" from your hidden stash in the closet to shift their energy and attention.

I am asking you to think about the message you are sending your child: If they act up, you will give them a toy. Then you won- der why when you are at the toy store your child has a meltdown because you have just said he can have one (less expensive) toy, not the big toy he has his eyes on. Your kid is doing exactly what I would expect him to. He has learned from you that if he gets cranky he will get what he wants. You are the problem here, not your little one.

I understand how overloaded your life is; trust me, I know how exhausted you are after a full day. But please try to find your way through to a better approach to how you use toys and gifts. They are for celebrations. Not behavior modification.

And if you do find yourself in the midst of an in-store melt- down, I am asking you to please find the courage not to cave in. Your first impulse, understandably, is to make the spectacle stop. But if you don't deal with this properly, it is just going to keep hap- pening. My hope is that you can take a deep breath, usher your child to a quiet corner—or out of the store—until they are calm

enough to listen to you explain—clearly and gently; no scolding—
why it is you are saying no. Will a lightbulb miraculously go off inside that little head and everything will be instantly okay? Not
likely. At least not on the first try . . . or the second . . . but try you
must. You have to start somewhere. I am asking you to stand in
the truth of how your actions affect how your child sees the world.

I would also suggest that one way to reduce the likelihood of
those unfortunate meltdowns is to set expectations before you
head into a store. Talk about what you are going to be shopping
for. Set parameters—in an age-appropriate way. Then, if your
child's eye wanders off to something inappropriate, you have that
conversation to turn to as a reference point for both of you to "discuss" the situation.

MONEY LESSONS FOR CHILDREN, AGES 6 TO 10

Introduce work-pay into your family. I am vehemently anti-
allowance. In my opinion, it is such a disservice to your children to
mindlessly hand over money week after week, just because they
are your kids. And the notion that their allowance should increase
just because they get older breeds a ridiculous sense of entitlement.
You have an opportunity to instill a work ethic in your children,
even at this young age. Tell them that you will pay your children
for doing household chores. I recommend you substitute the term
work-pay for *allowance*. They work, you pay. The more work you
do, the more you get. And the *better* you work, the more you get.
That's how you earn a raise in real life; why not introduce that
concept now?

I have a few important ground rules:

- **First, establish nonpaying chores.** These are the basic cour-
  tesies you all do for the benefit of the family.
- **Never pay for good behavior or good grades.** You do not reward a child for meeting your expectations.
- **Draw up a list of work-pay chores.** Show the potential earnings for each job. Allow your children to choose their jobs—

but make it clear that they have to work their way up from the smaller to the greater chores; they can't just cut right to the higher-paying ones. And the job must be done well, not just done. Teach them that they must start with the lesser tasks and work their way up the ladder. I promise you, your kids will learn to work more quickly and efficiently to get to the higher-paying jobs—and they will look forward to working in order to earn more.

- **Make payment a weekly ritual.** Bring some formality to the process by setting a date and time for when you will review the work from the past week and make the payment. Maybe it's Saturday morning when you are all around.

MONEY LESSONS FOR TWEENS AND TEENS

Stretch out their work-pay payments to every two weeks. And add in money for specific expenses you will expect them to cover out of this payment: after-school pizza, movies on the weekend, etc. The idea here is to give them more responsibility for handling money. By paying them every two weeks you are requiring them to make that money last for two weeks. It's an introduction to budgeting. Will they probably run through all of the money in the first week when you start this system? Of course! But don't punish them. Teach them. Agree on extra chores they can take on if they need money before the two weeks are up.

Have them pay the bills. Until your kids see the cost of the gas and electric bill or the credit card bill they have no way of comprehending what it costs just to keep your family going. There's no need to lecture here. Show them. If you don't yet use online bill-pay, get it up and running right now. (It should be free.) Then sit down with your kids once a month, hand over control of the mouse, and have them pay the bills with you. It will be a great conversation starter.

The great utility challenge. Pull out your utility bills and make your kids an offer: If you are able to reduce your monthly costs by at least 15% you will split the savings with them. So if this April's bill is 15% lower than last April they will get 50% of the savings. You will be amazed how quickly the lights are turned off in rooms they are leaving, showers miraculously shorten, and everyone is happy to put on a sweater and cozy pair of socks in the winter so the thermostat can come down a degree or two or three. It's a fun challenge that also connects your child to how it takes money to live, and how they can have an impact on your family's expenses.

Set a seasonal clothing budget. Before you step inside the mall or sit down for some online clothes shopping, give your child a firm dollar amount they can spend. Then have them pull aside everything they want—or put it in the virtual shopping cart—and write down the cost of every item. If you're at the mall, ask the salesperson to put the clothing on a hold rack for a half hour and find a place to grab a drink or snack and talk through the list. Again, this is not a test. Help them decide what they need to let go of to come in at your predetermined budget. This is their first experience with living below your means, but within your needs. If they want more than they need, that's fine. They can either pay for it themselves or you can spell out extra chores and responsibilities they must complete to earn the extra money. If they spend less than the agreed-upon amount, deposit the money they didn't spend into their savings account as a reward.

MONEY LESSONS FOR TEENAGERS HEADING TO COLLEGE

Between the ages of 16 and 18 is when you should start preparing your children for being out on their own. Your child's high school may not have a personal finance curriculum. That means you must step up and make sure your child has a solid grounding in basic money management before heading off to college. I cannot tell you how many young adults today leave college with thousands of dollars in credit card debt and a lousy credit score because no one ever took the time to teach them how to respect and handle money. To make sure your child emerges from college on solid financial footing requires teaching them what they need to know before they leave high school.

Put them on a monthly payment schedule. This is a natural progression from paying them every two weeks when they are a young teen. Set up a checking account at the bank and give your child a debit card. Every month deposit the money into that account. Do not sign up for an overdraft service tied to another bank account. The idea here is to give your child the opportunity to learn how to handle their money. If at the end of the month they have money left over, that's great. If they run out of money with a week to go, well, that's great too; it's an opportunity to learn money management.

Spell out your spending limits. Before each school year, sit down and agree on what expenses you will continue to cover. Be very specific. If they want to upgrade to a new smartphone or an unlimited data plan, they need to pay you for that cost. If they intend to borrow the car every weekend, discuss their responsibility for making sure they return it to you with the same amount of gas in the tank. If they want more clothes than you have budgeted for, they are going to have to come up with that money. Yes, now is the time to talk about getting a part-time job. Please do not tell me they are too busy with schoolwork or after-school programs. That's the attitude that prevents a teenager from becoming financially responsible.

Give them access to your credit card. If your credit score is at least 700, add your teen to all your cards as an authorized user. Your child will begin to build his or her own credit report by piggybacking on your credit history. You need to add them to all your cards in order for this to work. You don't have to tell them you've done this. I'd recommend you give them a debit card (without overdraft protection) or a prepaid card first; let them get used to using it before you entrust them with a credit card that reports to FICO. (Debit cards and prepaid cards do not report to FICO.) When you feel they're ready, give them one of your cards. Have your child use that card at least once a month to make a purchase for the family. If you are out for a dinner, have them handle the bill; don't forget the need to teach proper tipping. The idea here is to familiarize them with how to handle credit cards. Then you are to review your bill with them each month. The most important les-

son here is the information on the statement that shows the interest rate you would owe on any unpaid balance, and how long it
would take you to pay off that balance if you made just the minimum payment. There is no better way to teach than to show. And
the good news is that all monthly credit card statements now include all that important information. Use it as a teaching tool.

If your credit score is below 700 it does not make sense for
your child to piggyback on your card. In that case, I recommend
you either get your child the Approved Card, my new debit card
that reports to a major credit bureau (see box on pages 24–25) or
you can cosign a secured credit card for your child. You will need
to make a deposit to cover the card's charge limit—that's the secured part. I would keep the limit low, say $500 or less. Just make
sure that the card you choose has the lowest possible fees and that
it reports the card's payment history to at least one of the three
main credit bureaus so your child starts to build a credit history.

Beginning in 2010, young adults under the age of 21 cannot be
offered a credit card on their own unless they have the proven income to qualify for the card or if they have an adult cosign for the
card. My recommendation is that you discuss with your child that
you hope they will not try to get their own credit card until they
have graduated from college. That's an important four years where
you can still help them build a strong score and avoid costly mistakes. Give them a wider berth than in high school; decide what
expenses you want them to put on the card while at school and set
a monthly credit card limit. This isn't just about keeping them teth-
ered while in college. The goal here is that at age 21 or 22 they already have four years or more of a solid credit history. And that
will make their transition into the real world so much easier. If
they emerge from college with a solid credit score, it is more likely
they will be able to qualify for a credit card that doesn't charge
outrageous fees, get their own cell phone plan—yes, it will be time
to cut them off of your plan—rent an apartment, and set up their
utility service without having to pay any up-front deposits. It can
also mean they will qualify for a less expensive car loan and car insurance.

HOW TO HANDLE MONEY GIFTS AND SAVINGS

Teaching your children the pleasure of saving is going to be one of your hardest tasks. If you force them to save they might grow to resent it. Rather than see the value of saving, they get stuck on how they can't spend the money that is supposedly theirs. It sends all the wrong messages. There are a few approaches to consider to try to illustrate for them that, while it is indeed fun to spend money, there is satisfaction to be had, too, in putting money aside for later use:

I would first encourage parents—and grandparents—to consider noncash financial gifts as a way to start this education process. I recently had a 13-year-old girl on my show who wanted to spend $8,000 she had received in cash gifts on a Rolex watch. Her family was aghast; they just assumed she would save that money for her future. You can't assume anything. And if you give cash with no strings attached, or you have not actively helped your child learn how to spend, and learn the value of saving, well, what do you expect?

I think money gifts such as U.S. savings bonds or a stock purchase of a company they are familiar with is a good way to introduce the concept of investing. At TreasuryDirect.gov you can learn all about Series EE savings bonds, which make a great gift for young children. For stock purchases, open up an account at a discount brokerage and purchase a few shares of stock; each month sit down and review the statement together. That's a great way to start an ongoing conversation about saving and investing.

That said, at the same time you must also help them learn how to handle money. By the time your child is 10 or so I want you to put your child in charge of how to handle any financial gifts. That's right, I said your child is in charge. As I will explain in a moment, you are going to give them a three-option framework to work from, but you must leave the choices to them. This is an opportunity for you to learn too: How good is your child at making the "right" money choices? You need to give them the room to make those choices, and then if you are not comfortable with how they are handling things, that's when your teaching begins. But first you must give them power over their money. I imagine that sounds very odd to you. But think about it. If you don't give them a true stake in the decisions, you likely won't get their full attention; they won't engage in this very important learning process.

THE THREE-OPTION APPROACH

Sit down with your child and explain that the annual birthday and holiday money they receive is theirs to handle, but that they must tell you with each gift the how and why of what they choose to do with the money. You will frame this conversation by laying out three possible options:

- They save it for a future goal.
- They spend it.
- They share some of it by making a charitable donation.

I would refrain from telling them what you think the proper split of the money should be for all three. And hey, if they look at you and say they want to use 100% to spend, well, Mom and Dad, welcome to your uncomfortable truth. You have some parenting to do on the importance of saving and giving. You really need to focus on what's going on here. As I noted earlier, kids don't simply do as you say, they often do as you do. If your child wants to only spend, I encourage you to consider whether your behavior has on some level "taught" them that this is acceptable. Children, of course, pick up many cues from outside the home—they're influenced by their friends, by what they see on television or online or in magazines—but what they experience at home is probably most influential of all. I am asking you to question whether your own spending habits and behaviors might be sending the wrong message. If you don't like what you see and hear as you start to have these conversations, it's time to recognize the signals you have put out for years that may have created this mindset in your child.

Ultimately I hope your child soon gets into a rhythm where she wants to use her money to save, spend, and donate. All these are important. I'd rather see a child spend some of their money than put 100% in savings or give it all away. The goal here is to teach your child how to handle money, and all three options have a place in our lives.

I want to make sure you really understand the importance of giving your child total control of a spending account: If you prevent your child from being able to use some of their money, to touch it—physically—and use it to buy things—yes, wants are okay!—they will just end up resenting the process and probably rebel when they get older by overspending. Help them learn how to spend responsibly—in moderation—today. That will serve them well as adults.

Some tips on each option:

• **Create an incentive to save.** There is no question that the delayed gratification of saving for a future goal is hard enough on adults—just look at how many people are not saving enough for their retirement—but you should multiply that difficulty factor by 10 to capture the challenge it is for children. When you suggest to an 8-year-old that he should save money for when he is 18 or 22, you are asking him to set a goal that is longer than he has even been alive! That's not exactly an easy concept to grasp. I think you should encourage your child to set short-term goals. No longer than six months, at the start. That's how you keep your child engaged and enthused. That's how you convey the pleasure of savings.

Offering a matching contribution can help a child stay focused on a long-term goal. Just like with your 401(k), you might agree to chip in 25 cents or 50 cents for every dollar your child agrees to set aside in a savings account for a future goal you are all agreed on. And perhaps you offer an even higher match rate for money they set aside for charitable donations. That's a clear telegraphing of what you value most.

• **Spending:** Maybe your child will spend it carefully on treasured items. Maybe it will be thrown away on things that quickly lose their allure. You are not to judge, guide, or control. This is a learning process. We learn as much from our mistakes as our triumphs.

• **Giving:** Ideally your child is already familiar with the concept of giving; as I explained earlier, from a very young age I encourage you to have your child donate unused toys or outgrown clothes to your local charities; have the children be part of the actual transfer of goods. That tangible experience is how you start the conversation simply by doing. Once you introduce the concept of giving money to charities, help them understand their options. You can offer guidance, you can explain how they can help people close to home or on the other side of the world, but ultimately let your child decide.

KEEP A MONEY JOURNAL

I also encourage you to have your children keep a journal of how they choose to use their money. Every time they put money into a savings account, spend it, or donate it, I want them to record their thoughts and feelings in the moment. Be sure to sit down and review the journal after six months or a year. The journal is a written record of your child building a dream of her own. In it, she is beginning to explore and experience what it means to make a choice to consciously spend less than you have, to take pleasure in saving, as well as to enjoy spending.

When you are reviewing the journal you might also ask your child to reexamine her purchases. For example, if your daughter spent $35 on a video game eight months ago, ask her if she had it to do over again, would she rather have that video game or the $35 in cash. This conversation will lay some important groundwork for future conversations. In the coming months when your daughter is contemplating a purchase, you can ask her if she thinks this will be a purchase she will love or regret six months from now. Don't say it in a judgmental way. Your goal here is to simply guide your child through a thought process, not to impose opinions of your own.

LESSON 3. HOW TO CREATE A FINANCIALLY HONEST COLLEGE STRATEGY

College can be one of the best investments you and your child will ever make. The lifetime earnings advantage for a college graduate is about $1 million compared to a high school grad. Moreover, our economy creates more opportunities for college graduates. In late

2011 the unemployment rate among people 25 years or older with a high school degree (and no bachelor's degree) was 9.6%. The unemployment rate among college graduates was 4.4%.

You will get no argument from me that college matters. But there is a very important truth I need each and every family to stand in: Cost matters. Putting your children through college was a cornerstone of the American Dream, particularly for immigrants and first-generation children. But the New American Dream cannot simply be, I want my children to graduate from college. It must be, I want my child to graduate from a college that is affordable for my child, and for me. The fact is, most families don't stop to think through the cost part. Oh sure, you know full well that it is a lot more expensive than you can afford to pay out of your savings. But that hasn't made you truly cost sensitive. You still tell your kids to set their sights on any school and you will figure out the money later. And then you end up making a mess of your other important dreams. You stop saving for retirement, or worse yet, you use money in your retirement accounts to pay the college bills. That is not standing in your truth. It is incumbent on you when your children are young to develop a strategy for how as a family you can send your children to college without compromising your other financial goals.

WHO SHOULD SAVE FOR COLLEGE?

Before you start to save one penny for a child's future college costs, I insist that you have the following financial priorities taken care of:

- You do not have credit card debt.
- You have an eight-month emergency savings fund.
- You have a term life insurance policy.
- You are saving for retirement; aiming to set aside 15% of your gross salary.

Until all of that is in place you are not to think about saving for college. Many of you have heard me say this repeatedly over the years: There is financial aid for college. There are loans for college.

But there is no aid or loans to help you in retirement. There is no aid if you run into a rough patch and you do not have sufficient funds in an emergency savings account to navigate your way out of trouble.

Your first order of business is building a solid financial foundation for your family. Only when that is in place can you begin to save for college. And know full well that there is absolutely no shame if you are not able to save. As I explain later in this chapter, there are affordable ways for your child to obtain a quality education. Trust me on this one: What your kids really need from you is the peace of mind that you have your own retirement plan in place so they will not be asked to support you later on.

THE BEST WAY TO SAVE FOR COLLEGE: 529 PLANS

If you have the ability to save for college, the best way to save is by setting aside money in a 529 college savings plan. The two big advantages of a 529 plan are a series of valuable tax breaks and the fact that just a small percentage of assets (less than 6%) inside your 529 account will be used by college financial aid offices when evaluating your family's request for financial aid.

529 Plan Basics

A 529 plan allows anyone, regardless of their income, to contribute money into a special savings account that works much like an individual retirement account. There is no annual limit to what you can set aside; the lifetime savings limit is typically $300,000. You choose the investments for the account, and while the money is invested in the 529 plan there is no tax bill. Withdrawals from the plan that are used to pay for "qualified" school expenses will be tax-free. Depending on the state you live in and the specific plan you choose, you may also be able to claim some of your contribution as a deduction or credit on your state income tax return.

A 529 plan is, in my opinion, a better way to save for school than an UGMA/UTMA, a Coverdell Education Savings Account, or a Roth IRA.

UGMA/UTMA

These are custodial accounts that adults set up for minor children, as permitted by the Uniform Gifts to Minors and the Uniform Transfers to Minors acts. The child is in fact the "owner" of the account. There are tax benefits to these accounts, but I do not like them for college savings for two important reasons: Once a minor child reaches the age of 18–21 (depending on your state), he or she has complete control over the assets. If your child decides to take the money and head out for a global adventure, you have no legal right to stop her. The other problem is that UGMA and UTMA assets are treated differently than 529 assets when assessing your family's application for financial aid. Less than 6% of assets held in a 529 plan owned by a parent (for the benefit of a child) are used to compute a family's eligibility for aid. By comparison, 20% of assets owned by your child—such as an UGMA or UTMA—are factored into the calculation. In other words, money owned by a child will reduce your eligibility for financial aid, or the level of aid your family qualifies for.

COVERDELL EDUCATION SAVINGS ACCOUNT

There is nothing inherently wrong with a Coverdell (previously known as an Education IRA) but they don't offer any major advantages over a 529. As with a 529, money you invest in a Coverdell grows tax-deferred and withdrawals will be tax-free if used for qualified education expenses. While there is no income test for making contributions to a 529 plan, married couples with income above $220,000 (or $110,000 for single tax filers) are ineligible to contribute to a Coverdell. Moreover, the current annual maximum contribution to a Coverdell—effective through 2012—is just $2,000.

ROTH IRA

It is absolutely true that a Roth IRA can be an interesting way to pay for college costs. No matter your age, money you originally contribute to a Roth IRA can always be withdrawn without penalty or tax. And if you withdraw any of the money you have contributed before age 59½ to pay for college costs, you will not owe the typical 10% early withdrawal penalty, though you will owe income tax on the earnings. (There are special rules for Roth conversion IRAs; see page 229 for details.)

The problem with using a Roth IRA to pay for college costs is that it can compromise your retirement planning. A Roth IRA should not be asked to do double duty: It cannot be a college fund *and* a retirement fund. If that's your strategy you and I both know what is going to happen: Because college costs occur before retirement it is likely you will sharply reduce, if not use up entirely, the money in the account, leaving you high and dry for retirement. You need to resolve not to allow your retirement to be derailed by a competing demand that chronologically happens to occur first; chronologically is not how I want you to prioritize. As I explain in the class on retirement planning in your 20s and 30s, a Roth IRA is my favorite type of retirement account. I just want you to use it for retirement, first and foremost. Now, that said, if you have set up a Roth IRA with the explicit purpose of using it for college costs, that is a different matter. In that instance using your original contributions to the Roth to pay for school—they are not taxed nor do you owe any early withdrawal penalty—is a fine strategy. Just remember to leave the earnings in the account and use that for your retirement. If you were to make an early withdrawal of earnings from a Roth you might be hit with tax.

But please stand in your truth. If you know deep down that the Roth IRA you have is needed first and foremost for your retirement, please do not use it for college.

WHAT IF YOUR CHILD DOESN'T NEED THE 529 MONEY?

There are some important rules you need to understand in the event your child chooses not to go to college or is awarded so much in grants and scholarships that you don't need all the money you have set aside in a 529 plan.

You can transfer the account to another beneficiary. Most 529 plans allow you to switch a beneficiary to another family member, including siblings (and step-siblings), nieces, nephews, first cousins, and in-laws. You could also name yourself the beneficiary and use the money to go back to school.

You can withdraw the money for noneducational purposes. There is no penalty or tax on money you contributed to the account, but if you withdraw earnings from the account and that money is not used for education purposes, it will be subject to income tax as well as a 10% penalty.

HOW TO CHOOSE THE BEST 529 PLAN FOR YOUR FAMILY

There are two flavors of 529 plans: direct sold and advisor sold. I only want you to consider direct-sold plans. The fees for advisor-sold 529 plans are too high, and often the advisor-sold lineup of investment choices does not include low-cost index funds. If you want the advice of a trusted financial advisor on how to handle your college savings, pay the advisor a separate flat fee for his work rather than have him guide you into expensive advisor-sold 529 funds. If your advisor only uses advisor-sold 529 funds I recommend you find a new advisor who is not dependent on commissions. At NAPFA.org you can search for local advisors who work on an hourly or fee basis.

TIP: I highly recommend every family spend some time at Savingforcollege.com. It has wonderful articles and tools to help you make an educated decision about the best 529 plan for your family. Here are some important issues to consider:

Compare your state plan to an out-of-state plan. Every state offers its own 529 savings plan. But please understand that you are not obligated or required to stick with a plan offered by your state. You can in fact invest in any plan from any state and use your money to attend any school in any state. The sole advantage of sticking with your state's plan is if it offers valuable tax breaks or other incentives to residents. For example, contributions you make to any 529 plan are not eligible for a federal tax deduction. But some states allow in-state residents to claim a state tax deduction or a credit on their contributions. That said, there is often a limit on the value of the tax break, and in some states there is an income cutoff to be eligible for the tax break.

At Savingforcollege.com you can find state-by-state information on the tax treatment for in-state residents. This is obviously an important consideration when choosing a 529 plan, but it should not be your only consideration. It makes absolutely no sense to sign up for an in-state plan that has high fees and expensive mutual funds. It can make more sense to pass up the tax breaks and choose a plan offered by another state that has lower fees and better investment choices.

Focus on fees. Similar to how a 401(k) works, when you contribute to a 529 plan you will choose from a menu of investment options. Typically these are mutual funds. Every mutual fund has an embedded annual fee called the expense ratio. This can be as little as 0.20% or so, or it can be 1.5% or more. The more you pay in fees the less your money will go toward paying for college. Before you sign up for a 529 plan make sure it offers mutual funds with annual expense ratios below 1%, and the lower the better.

Check for conservative investment choices. As I explain below, by the time your child is a senior in high school you will want to have the bulk of your account in conservative investments; it is too risky to have your money invested in stocks when you know you will need that money in one to five years. Not all 529 plans offer a money market or certificate of deposit (CD) option. Please stick with a plan that gives you the option of pulling out of stocks as your child nears college age.

Understand beneficiary transfer rules. If you have more than one child and you anticipate you may want to transfer the beneficiary from one child to another, make sure your plan allows this move.

HOW TO INVEST YOUR 529 PLAN

Many parents with children in high school learned a very painful lesson during the 2008 financial crisis when their 529 accounts lost

30% or more because so much of their account was still invested in stocks. Given that they had just a year or two before they would need to start tapping their funds to pay the college bills, they should never have left so much in volatile stocks. And what was most alarming was that many of these parents had left it to the plan to make the decision about how much to have in stocks versus bonds and other conservative investments. A popular feature of many 529 plans is an age-based fund that leaves it to the plan sponsor to alter the mix of stocks and bonds based on the child's age. This works just like a target retirement fund; the idea is that as the child gets closer to college, the portfolio will become more conservative. In fact that's how many plans work, but not all. The bottom line is that you cannot blindly rely on anyone to make your investment choices for you. You are responsible for making sure your money is invested in a way that makes sense for you.

If you investigate an age-based fund within a 529 and are comfortable with how it ratchets down your stock allocation as your child progresses through high school, then that is fine. But please make an informed choice. You can always build your own portfolio by choosing from among the other investment choices offered within the 529 plan.

Here is my suggested allocation:

- **Under age 14:** 80–100% stock mutual funds
- **Age 14:** 75% stock funds
- **Age 15:** 50% stock funds
- **Age 16:** 25% stock funds
- **Age 17:** 0% stock funds

TIP: One absurd restriction imposed on 529 investors is that you are only allowed to change your asset allocation once a year. Please be aware of this rule and make sure you complete all your rebalancing at one time.

If you do not choose the age-based all-in-one fund offered within the 529 (on page 180 I explain why I do not like these all-in-one funds), then the advice on investing your 529 echoes the advice in the retirement chapters: The bulk of your stock allocation—I recommend 85%—belongs in large U.S. blue-chip firms. If you see a fund with the words "S&P 500 index," that is a good choice. Or any fund that is described as investing mostly in "large cap" stocks. The remainder of your stock allocation can be invested in an international stock fund or ETFs. We live in a global economy; while your U.S. blue chips typically derive plenty of their business from foreign markets, it's also smart to have a small portion of your stock portfolio directly invested in an international fund.

For the portion of your portfolio not invested in stock funds, I recommend you stick with the cash or CD option within your 529. As I explain in the Retirement Classes, I have never liked bond funds. And with my expectation that in the coming years interest rates will rise from their current historic lows, bond funds will face especially rough headwinds.

THE COLLEGE TALK EVERY PARENT MUST HAVE WITH A HIGH SCHOOL FRESHMAN

As a family you need to start talking about college finances no later than freshman year in high school and begin to map out a strategy that will make college affordable.

Explain what you expect to be able to contribute to annual costs. Your child deserves to understand exactly what, if anything, you will be able to contribute to his four years of college costs. Waiting until senior year to spring the news that you have little or nothing is unfair. By having the conversation earlier you give your child the opportunity to plan.

Put a financial safety school on your list. Guidance counselors are quick to talk about applying to at least one school your child will easily be accepted into. I would take this strategy one step further and make sure you have a financial safety school: Plan on applying to a public in-state school that you know will be affordable. A public four-year school can cost one-half to one-third what it costs to attend a private four-year college. If your child qualifies for a generous financial aid package at a private school, that's great. But the idea here is that in the event the aid package at an expensive school isn't generous enough, you will have an afford-able option to fall back on.

Strive to make the most of high school. Once you explain your financial situation to a high school freshman or sophomore you give them even more incentive to do well in school. Every A they receive now can help them qualify for financial aid. Advanced Placement classes can also help all of you save on college costs: Many colleges will waive some basic required courses for students who score well on the AP test.

TIP: Mark Kantrowitz, the wizard behind FinAid.org, also has the inside scoop on winning scholarships to offset tuition costs. If you have a child in high school, I would recommend you take a look at his new book, *Secrets to Winning a Scholarship*. The price is under $10 because Mark wants it to be available to everyone, including low-income families who could benefit the most. I approve!

Start the loan conversation. In the next lesson I will explain the best ways to borrow for college. One of the hardest steps in this process is for you and your child to limit what you borrow for school. Just because someone will loan you $40,000 a year—and yes, you can borrow that much or more—does not mean you should. As a family you must stand in the truth that the goal is for your child to emerge from college without anyone in the family being saddled with so much debt that they will not be able to reach their other financial dreams.

BORROWING RULES FOR COLLEGE LOANS

As I stated at the beginning of this lesson, college is a smart in-vestment. And I absolutely believe that college loans are "good debt." But too much of a good thing can become a bad thing. You and your children need to borrow wisely. One of the problems with the college loan system is that there are not any checks and balances to prevent you from borrowing more than you can af-ford. That just makes it all the more important for your entire family to stand in the truth—together—and create a borrowing plan that will allow both student and parent to easily handle the eventual payback of the loans. You need to understand that college debt, whether it is taken out by the student or the parent, is currently not eligible to be discharged in the event you file for bankruptcy. It literally stays with you forever. See what I mean: You need to really be careful in how you borrow for school, and how much you borrow.

Most families will qualify for some amount of need-based financial aid. You can get an estimate of what your family might qualify for here: http://bit.ly/a6VEJ. We all know that it is rare that your child will get a complete "free ride." So your family will need to cover the portion of the bill that exceeds your aid. You can of course use your current income, as well as tapping any college savings funds, such as a 529. But it is also likely you will need to take out loans as well.

This is how you are to approach the loan part of the college financing puzzle:

- Student borrows first using a federal Stafford loan.
- Parent considers borrowing using a federal PLUS loan.
- Neither student nor parent uses a private loan.

Please follow this strategy closely. Federal loans are the only loans you should ever take out. They charge reasonable fixed interest rates, and borrowers have a few different repayment plans to choose from, including plans that will allow you to defer, delay, or reduce your payments if you lose your job or experience financial hardship.

The Risks of Private Loans for College

Private loans offered through banks typically charge a variable interest rate. The starting rate is often higher than the fixed rate on federal loans. And listen to me here: General interest rates in the coming years are likely to move higher. When that happens, the interest rate charged on private student loans will also rise. In 2011 some lenders began to offer fixed-rate private college loans.

Still, I would much rather you stay away from private loans for a very important reason: If you fall into financial trouble once you are in repayment, private lenders have no obligation to help you out with a different payment schedule. What is most galling is that in the event a private loan borrower dies, the debt may still be owed. With federal loans, the debt is forgiven in the event the borrower dies or becomes permanently disabled.

My opinion is that private student loans should never be used. Period. If that means your child needs to consider a less expensive school, then that is the truth your family needs to stand in, united as one.

Alert: What to Do If You Already Have a Private Loan

If you already have a private college loan or you have cosigned for someone who has taken one out, I insist that you take out a term life insurance policy that can cover 125% of the current loan amount. As I just mentioned, in the event someone with a private college loan dies, the loan may not die. It is up to the lender to decide if it will still demand repayment. By purchasing a term life insurance policy, your family—or your cosigners—could use the death benefit on the policy to repay the loan. This is an incredibly cheap way to protect your loved ones. The term policy should be for a minimum of 10 years after the student is scheduled to graduate. Given that many borrowers need even longer to repay their college loans, I would recommend you consider a 15-year or 20-year policy. I also recommend that the amount of your policy be 25% or more than what you currently expect the loan's expected total cost to be. Why? In order to provide some insulation from rising interest rates—remember the private loan is a variable rate—and the fees that the banking industry is expert at finding reasons to charge you. So for example, let's say you have private loans that you expect will end up costing you $50,000 to repay. I would consider a 20-year level term life insurance policy with a death benefit of $62,000 or so. For a 20-year-old male in good health that policy might cost $10 to $12 a month. That's it. Less than $150 a year to protect your loved ones from having to finish paying off your private student loan. And purchasing term life insurance is really simple. You can learn more at the websites of term insurance specialists SelectQuote.com and AccuQuote.com.

HOW TO BORROW FOR SCHOOL

When your child applies to college you should complete the Free Application for Federal Student Aid (FAFSA) form. Schools require the FAFSA form to determine your family's eligibility for financial aid. It is unlikely that grants and scholarscships will cover all your costs. If you can't make up the difference out of your current income or savings, your next move will be to take out loans. Families that meet a low-income test may be able to borrow up to $5,500 a year at a fixed interest rate of 5% through a federal Perkins loan; every school administers Perkins.

Student Borrows First: Stafford Loans

Your child is to borrow for school before you take out a loan. The federal Stafford loan program is hands down the best college financing deal out there that is available to everyone, regardless of need.

There are in fact two types of Stafford loans: subsidized and unsubsidized.

A subsidized Stafford loan is based on financial need. For the 2011–2012 school year the fixed interest rate will be 3.4%. The interest rate for loans taken out in the 2012–2013 school year will be at a fixed interest rate of 6.8% and under current law will remain at that level in subsequent years. The government pays the interest on subsidized Stafford loans while the student is in school and during a six-month grace period after the student graduates (or leaves school). Once the student begins repayment he or she is responsible for the interest payments.

An unsubsidized Stafford loan is available to all students regardless of financial need. The fixed interest rate is 6.8%, and the student is responsible for paying the interest while in school, or the interest can be added to the loan balance. My recommendation is to try to pay that interest while you are in school; a part-time job or maybe some help from mom, dad, or grandparents will help keep the loan balance lower so when repayment begins within six months of leaving school you will have a smaller balance to pay off. At www.direct.ed.gov/student.html you can find more information about Stafford loans, including calculators to help you estimate what your payments may be based on a few different plan options.

STAFFORD LOAN LIMITS

For the 2012–2013 year the student can borrow the following amounts based on their year of school:

	MAXIMUM STAFFORD LOAN LIMIT
Freshman	$5,500 (no more than $3,500 may be subsidized)
Sophomore	$6,500 (no more than $4,500 may be subsidized)
Junior	$7,500 (no more than $5,500 may be subsidized)
Senior	$7,500 (no more than $5,500 may be subsidized)

I am fine with every student borrowing these maximum amounts. Graduating with a total of $27,000 in debt is not an amount that will bury you. A good rule of thumb is to keep your borrowing below what you expect your annual starting salary may be at your first job. Assuming the student has picked a field that pays a starting salary of $30,000 or more, paying back the Staffords is realistic.

Parents Borrow Next: PLUS Loans

If the financial aid package and Stafford loans are not enough to cover the cost of school, your family's next step is to consider the federal loan program for parents of college students: the PLUS program.

Go to The Classroom at www.suzeorman.com: Find guidance on my website about what factors to consider when determining how much young adults can honestly afford to borrow for college.

I think the federal PLUS loan program is terrific. It charges a reasonable fixed interest rate of 7.9%. There is also a 4% fee on the initial amount of the loan. Like Staffords, the PLUS program offers a few different repayment schedules based on your financial needs. Most important, if the parent dies or is permanently disabled, the loan is forgiven.

That said, not every parent should take out PLUS loans to help pay for college. In my opinion, you should meet the following standards:

- You pay off your credit card each month, in full.
- You have an eight-month emergency fund.
- You are on track with your retirement savings.

Please stand in the truth here: If you have not taken care of those financial priorities you are not in a position to borrow for a child's college costs. Your financial security is not yet firmly in place. Borrowing more at this juncture would just put you further away from reaching those more pressing financial goals.

Qualifying Rules for PLUS Loans

Your FICO credit score is not a factor in qualifying for a PLUS loan. Your credit report will, however, be checked to confirm that you are current on all your payments—meaning no payments are ninety days past due—and that you have not declared bankruptcy or gone through a foreclosure in the past five years. (Short sales, however, are okay—you can still get a PLUS.)

If you are not eligible for a PLUS loan, you will want to notify the financial aid office at your child's college; your child may be eligible for more aid from the school and could qualify to borrow more from the Stafford program. When parents are ineligible for a PLUS, the unsubsidized Stafford loan limit rises to $9,500 a year for freshmen, $10,500 for sophomores, and $12,500 a year for juniors and seniors. At FinAid.org, which is run by college financing expert Mark Kantrowitz, you can learn more about all federal loans.

How Much to Borrow in PLUS Loans

One of the flaws of the PLUS program is that it does not set any borrowing limits based on your income. The basic rule is that you can borrow up to the total cost of attending school, minus any aid your child receives. But please, parents, do not tell yourself that you can afford any amount.

My recommendation is to use the calculator at the College Board website (www.collegeboard.com) to get an estimate of what your payments would be. You are to borrow only an amount that you are confident you can repay out of your monthly cash flow and within 10 years of your child leaving school.

For parents who may have used a PLUS loan in the past, I want to point out that an important change was instituted in 2008. Instead of being required to start your repayment of the PLUS loan within six months of receiving the loan, you can now defer your payments until your child leaves school. This can make it easier to pay some costs while your child is in school, and then handle the repayment after school. It also means that your child will be out of school and may be able to chip in some money to help get your PLUS loan paid off sooner rather than later.

HOW TO CHOOSE THE RIGHT SCHOOL

Okay, let's pull this all together. When your child is accepted to colleges, you will be given your aid package and what your family's contribution is expected to be. I am not exaggerating here:

This could be the biggest stand-in-the-truth moment for all of you. I need you to understand what I mean by "the right school." The right school is the best school that is also affordable. That means you and your child can swing the tuition from a combination of current income, 529 savings, Staffords, and borrowing a reasonable amount in a PLUS.

If you find yourself contemplating borrowing more from a PLUS, or you or your child is considering a private student loan, please stop yourself right there. Take a deep breath and stand in the truth. You are about to make a financially dishonest choice that could undermine your family's long-term financial stability. Remember, cost matters. The annual cost for a four-year state school for an in-state resident was about $17,000 in 2011–2012. For an out-of-state student attending a public school the average cost was $29,700. At a private four-year school the average cost was more than $38,600. If the more expensive schools do not offer you enough financial aid, the honest move is to consider the school that will not hijack your ability to realize all of your family's financial dreams, not just paying for college.

And if the cost of an in-state school is still too high, you and your child should consider having him start at a community college. Your child could live at home—a big cost savings—and then after the first year or two, he can look into transferring to the in-state school.

LESSON 4. HOW TO HELP ADULT CHILDREN FACING FINANCIAL CHALLENGES

The empty nest isn't what it used to be. Life postcrisis shows that more college graduates are moving back home with Mom and Dad, sometimes out of necessity if they have yet to find a job, but also because they know that the house they grew up in is going to be a lot nicer than what they could afford on their own. And having to move back with your parents doesn't carry the same stigma as it did years ago. A survey by Monster.com reported that 52% of 2010 college graduates *who have a job* had nonetheless moved back in with a parent or guardian. At the same time, many adult children who have been independent for years are now facing financial challenges—a layoff, a too expensive mortgage—that have them turning to their parents (and grandparents) for help.

The truth is, there is no age when a parent stops worrying about the welfare of a child. And the instinct is always there to step in and ease the pain. But it is very important for both parent and adult child to navigate these new family dynamics with care and respect for each other's financial well-being. To that end, I would encourage you and your children to proceed with a few ground rules:

Every child who moves back home must pay rent. Even if they have yet to find a full-time job, I think it is important that they contribute to the family finances. If you want to give them a six-month grace period while they adjust, that's fine. But then start charging rent. Look, they need to understand they are no longer your babies; you are helping them start to make the transition to being an independent adult. This is not about whether you can afford to take care of them or not. You will be helping them stand in their truth if you treat them like the adults they are.

One idea for those of you who are squirming at charging your kids is to quietly—without your child's knowledge—put their rent into a separate savings account. Once they are ready to step out on their own you can return all that money to them.

Make sure they have health insurance. Young people get sick and have accidents. If they do not yet have a job with health insurance coverage you have two options for getting them insured:

- **Consider adding them to your employer-provided plan.** A feature of the 2010 health reform was to allow children to stay on parents' health plans until they turn 26. (If your child is in fact living in another state, adding them to your policy may not make sense if your company's health insurer offers the best terms only to in-state providers. You could find yourself paying more out of pocket if your child needs to use an out-of-plan provider.)
- **Shop for an individual plan.** Young adults in good health can often qualify for an inexpensive plan. You can shop for coverage at ehealthinsurance.com.

Get them on schedule with their student loan repayments. After a six-month grace period upon leaving school, all students must start repaying their federal student loans. If they have yet to find a job they will be able to apply for a deferment on federal loans. But they cannot afford to ignore their loans. Fees and penalties will just make matters worse, and they could end up having part of their salary—once they get a job—siphoned off to repay the loan. I also want you to make sure your college graduate understands that even if they were to someday declare bankruptcy, their student loan debt would not be forgiven. Please make sure your child stays on top of this debt. Their school's financial aid office should have given them a lecture on all of this before they left school. If not, they—and you—can learn more at www.studentaid.ed.gov.

How to Handle Student Loans That Are in Default

If you have existing student loans that have already fallen into default—that is, you have not made your payments, for whatever reason—then I am asking you now to face up to the consequences of these actions with all the courage you can muster. You must do everything you can to get your loans out of default. If you fail to work out a payment plan, you may find your wages garnished up to 15% to settle your debts, and your credit score will be such a mess you will find it hard to borrow for a home or car at an affordable rate. That's right, take a deep breath. I urge you to deal with this problem now, because no matter what you may be thinking, you cannot outrun it.

Here are some resources to help you figure out your options:

• If you have a federal loan, start at the Department of Education's website (www.ed.gov), which explains your options for getting back on track with a defaulted loan.

• The FinAid.org website, run by student loan expert Mark Kantrowitz, has a clear explanation of what's at stake and how to address a default: www.finaid.org/loans/default.phtml.

> • The website for Student Loan Borrower Assistance (www
> .studentloanborrowerassistance.org) has terrific advice on deal-
> ing with defaults, loan servicers, and collection agencies from a
> place of strength. Click on the "Default and Delinquency" tab on
> the right side of the site's homepage.

HOW AND WHEN TO HELP INDEPENDENT CHILDREN WHO ARE IN FINANCIAL TROUBLE

It is a fact of the times we live in that many young families that might have been doing just fine are now in dire straits because of lingering damage from the financial crisis. If your grown children come to you asking for financial help I need you first of all to stand in two truths: yours and theirs.

Your truth: Can you afford to offer financial assistance? I am asking you for just one moment to suspend your parental instinct to help without hesitation. I need you to do a financial accounting of what you can honestly afford to give them without putting yourself at risk. I understand how hard this is, but if you end up on shaky financial ground, and they are on shaky financial ground, you haven't helped anyone but have only increased your family's financial problems.

Their truth: Is their financial problem short-term or long-term? If they need your help to bridge a short-term problem, then by all means, if you have the ability to give them money, go right ahead. But in many instances I think you will find that your children have a bigger, more persistent issue causing the hardship and that might well require more than just the immediate boost that a gift or loan from you can provide.

For example, if your daughter and son-in-law cannot afford their mortgage and are hoping to get a loan modification, I would tell you to resist giving them money to float them while they go explore this option. As I explain in the Home Class, very few borrowers are able to qualify for a loan modification. It makes no sense to give money when the sooner they can accept the truth, the better: They probably need to walk away from that home. The same is true if your child's family is coping with a layoff. I understand help-ing out for a few months, but you need to clearly define how long you will be able to offer help. You—and they—also need to stand in the truth that even once they find a new job, in this economy, it may not necessarily pay as well as their prior job. If that means they can't afford to maintain their current living costs, the solution should be for them to find ways to reduce their living costs.

Cosigning Loans: Be Very Careful

When your adult child asks you to cosign a loan I need you to promise me—and yourself—that you will make your decision once you are firmly standing in some very crucial truths. Begin by considering the following matters:

• **Why is your child asking for your help?** If it is because a lender doesn't think your child is qualified to handle this loan, then you should be cautious as well. Is the issue that your child is trying to spend too much money? If he were to lower the price tag of the car or home he has his eye on, would he be able to qualify on his own? If so, that is the far better move. I know you only want to help; but encouraging self-sufficiency is incredibly helpful. And if the lender is hesitant because your child has a low FICO credit score, well, that should be a big warning signal. Look, if your child has a bad score because of one inadvertent slipup, that's okay; maybe they were slow to grasp how important it was to be on schedule with their student loan repayments, but are now doing great, making timely payments. But if your child has a low credit score because of poor credit card management that's a different story. That tells me she hasn't yet learned how to be financially responsible. By cosigning the loan you are not just po-tentially walking into a money pit of a deal, but you are enabling your child to continue her irresponsible behavior. I am not saying you can never cosign for her. But how about waiting a year and in the interim, you work with your child to help her get a firm grasp of what it takes to be financially responsible?

- **Can you truthfully afford to cosign?** Mom and Dad, the minute you cosign you are committing to making good on the entire amount of the loan if your child falls behind in the payments. I know your child is wonderful. I know how much you love her. And I am not even suggesting she is actually irresponsible. But what if she is laid off? And the next job doesn't pay as well? Or an illness prevents her from continuing at the same job? Life happens. To all of us. I am asking you to consider how prepared you would be to take over the loan if your child were not able to handle it on her own, for reasons completely beyond her control.

  I want you to ask yourself: If I had to make the monthly payments—for the life of the loan—would it in any way impact my financial goals? If making those payments would eat into your emergency savings, or cause you to scale back or stop saving for retirement, then you must stand in your financial truth first. That is not selfish. Putting your own financial stability at risk is never a good idea, for all parties. I also want you to think this through for the life of the loan. If you are 50 years old and your child asks you to cosign a 30-year mortgage, could you in fact handle the payments once you retire?

- **Rules for cosigning:** If you can in fact afford to cosign, go right ahead. But I hope you will also require that you receive formal confirmation each month that the payment was made on time. Your child can arrange for you to receive a duplicate statement or email alert that confirms the payment. Think that's invasive and infantilizes your adult child? I don't. If your child is standing in his truth he would volunteer to do this without your even having to ask. You have just taken on a huge financial responsibility. I think the least your child can do is show you he respects that gift and wants to give you peace of mind that he is on top of the payments.

  And if you are cosigning a loan for a child who has struggled with on-time bill payments, I would go as far as having your child

> pay you the amount of the monthly payment—at least 10 business days before the payment is due—and then you can be the one to make the payment to the lender. This isn't just about your kid; this is about protecting your FICO credit score.

LESSON 5. THE CONVERSATION EVERY ADULT CHILD SHOULD HAVE WITH HIS OR HER PARENTS

If your parents are in their 50s, you probably planned on skipping the Retirement Class aimed at people in their 40s and 50s, not to mention the class on living in retirement. But guess what: I am going to ask you to read those classes too because they contain a few important lessons. There are some defining conversations you should have with your parents while they are still young (yes, parents in their 50s and even early 60s are young by my standards). As I explain in that class, there are some critical measures to be considered and acted on in your 50s to help ensure your financial security in your 70s, 80s, and beyond.

Too often, families avoid these conversations about the inevitable road ahead. Then when the parents are in their 70s and not in great financial shape, they turn to their child for help, and at that point there is less time and opportunity for either the parents or the child to deal with things effectively. If you have this conversation sooner rather than later, you will both be better off. This isn't an attempt to accelerate a type of role reversal; this is about adults—children and parents—coming together to work out a plan for the future.

So go to the Retirement Class and "audit" that class; know what your parents are facing. And when you're ready to have the talk, here is a short list of topics you will want to cover:

Will they be able to retire mortgage-free? Whether they plan on staying in their current home or relocating, their goal should be to have no mortgage costs in retirement.

Have they considered long-term care insurance? If your parents cannot afford a policy on their own, you (and your siblings) should consider whether you can help with the premium cost for a policy. Spending a hundred dollars or so a month now to help with LTC premium payments could save you tens of thousands of dollars decades from now if your parents will require nursing care or assistance with daily activities when they are elderly.

Have they carefully run the numbers on their retirement income? If your parents are considering retiring before age 66 or so, do they feel confident that they will have enough retirement income to support themselves for 25 to 30 years? In the Retirement Classes, I discuss strategies that can deliver more income in retirement, from delaying retirement, to waiting until at least age 66 or 67 to begin receiving Social Security, to choosing the right payout option if they are entitled to an old-fashioned pension.

Building Family Financial Security Under One Roof

For most households, the monthly expense of the mortgage or rent, and all the other costs that come with maintaining a home, are the biggest line item in the budget. If you look down the road and find that your dreams require a dramatic reduction in living costs, then quite possibly your next conversation should be about whether it makes sense to combine households. Yes, I am talking about multiple generations living under one roof.

Of course, you know best whether family dynamics would doom this to fail or could make it a brilliant move. But if you are a close-knit family and the thought of moving in with your parents, or having them move in with you, doesn't set off your stress receptors, then I am here to tell you that combining households is a phenomenal idea. Interestingly, even before the recent recession took hold, a survey by the Pew Research Center found 16% of households—accounting for 49 million Americans—had at least two adult generations present. That's up from 12% in the 1980s. I fully expect that that percentage is higher today, simply because of the vast number of families that have lost their homes or are struggling with long-term unemployment.

But I don't think extreme financial hardship is all that is at play here either. Part of the New American Dream is a shift in emphasis. Overextending ourselves to buy more or own more has lost some of its cachet. Sure, we still want to live well and have our creature comforts. But I sense we are also rethinking the extent to which our material possessions matter, and recognizing—or remembering—that it is relationships that matter most.

Now, of course, not every family can pull this off. Personalities will dictate what is possible for your family. But I ask those of you who can envision combining households not to be shy about raising this possibility and starting the conversation. I think for many families—across generations—it could be the path toward ensuring everyone's new dreams are realized, together.

Do your parents have their essential legal documents updated? It's not enough that they drew up a will or revocable living trust 10 or 20 years ago. They—and you—need to make sure that those documents are up to date. If there has been a death, divorce, or remarriage, they might inadvertently be disinheriting you.

Make sure, too, that your parents have an advance directive that spells out what level of medical intervention they want if they ever become too incapacitated to speak for themselves—and that they give you a copy. Without that document, adult children are exposed to unnecessary heartache, and often irreparable sibling arguments, about how to handle end-of-life decisions. The parent can make sure it never comes to that, by having this document in place.

Go to The Classroom at www.suzeorman.com: I have written extensively in the past on the essential documents every adult must have. On my website you can find articles on why a simple will is often not nearly enough protection for you and your loved ones, and on how to put together the key essential documents: a will, a revocable living trust, and an advance directive.

When a Parent Remarries

We tend to think of the impact of blended families mainly in terms of small children, but the truth is, adult children need to pay attention here too. Very often when a parent remarries, he or she moves into a new home and takes ownership as joint tenant with right of survivorship (JTWROS). That means that when one co-owner dies the other inherits full control of the home. So let's say your mom remarries and puts money down for a new home she moves into with your stepfather. He is a great guy, don't get me wrong. But if Mom and Stepdad own the home as JTWROS, and she dies first, your stepdad has full ownership of the home, with no legal obligation to leave you any portion of the home when he passes. Mom didn't mean to disinherit you, but it can happen nonetheless. Please understand that even if Mom's will or trust says you are to inherit her stake, it doesn't matter. How the home is owned—the title—overrides what is in a will or trust. What your mom and stepdad should have done is take title as Tenants-in-Common; at either's death, their portion of the home would pass to their heirs, not the surviving spouse. (At that point the heirs could then make arrangements, if they chose, to allow the surviving spouse to remain in the home until his/her death.) In The Classroom on my website I review the various ways you can take title to property.

So while you're having those very adult conversations with your parents, you might want to touch on the matter of how their house is owned and what they would like to happen to it in the event of their passing. And then make sure their will and trust reflect their wishes.

I recognize that these may not be the easiest of conversations to initiate, but bring the right energy to the task and I think you may be surprised by how cathartic this could be for everyone. The goal here is to establish that your parents have what they need for a comfortable and secure retirement. In my opinion, it is a great way to honor your parents—to show them they have raised responsible, thoughtful, farsighted children with their best interests at heart. What a powerful legacy that is.

LESSON 6. ADVICE FOR GRANDPARENTS: HOW TO BUILD A LASTING LEGACY

According to a poll by the MetLife insurance company, grandparents bestowed $370 billion in financial support on their grandchildren from 2003 through 2008. The median gift was $3,000, and nearly 4 in 10 grandparents with a college degree were contributing to a grandchild's education.

The beating heart at the core of all that giving is, without a doubt, love. Every grandparent I know yearns for their grandchildren to have the resources and opportunity to live a wonderful life. That is a universal dream. But in the years since that survey was taken, the financial gifts grandparents can provide have taken on a new importance. As parents struggle to retool their financial plans, assistance from grandparents can be a huge help. In the MetLife survey, more than 80% of gifts were made in cash. I don't think that's smart. The money you give today funds the dreams of your grandchildren. Do you hear that? Grandparents: You are the dream makers for your grandchildren! In the lesson that follows I will share strategies that will help you help your grandchildren make the most of your giving.

The benefits to your grandchildren aside, it also happens to be a smart way to shift assets out of your estate. In 2012 any individual can gift up to $13,000 to any other individual without running afoul of gift tax laws.

Here are a few different ways to consider how to gift money for dreams:

Follow the parents' lead. Ask your kids if they have instituted any savings programs within the family. As I explained earlier for parents raising kids, I recommend encouraging children from an early age to set aside some money for savings and charitable giving. Grandparents can participate in the plan that is already in place and you can institute your own matching policy.

529 college savings plans. Ask your kids if they have set up a 529 college savings plan for their children. You can make contributions directly into that plan.

Set up a Roth IRA for a teenage grandchild who has a part-time job. As long as your grandchild has earned income you can fund a Roth IRA for them. So let's say your grandson made $2,000 last year in a summer job. You could give him $2,000 to open a Roth IRA; he doesn't have to invest his own money. As long as he made $2,000 you can bankroll the IRA contribution. In fact, if your grandchild earned at least $5,000, you can give him that much in 2012 for a Roth IRA; $5,000 is the 2012 maximum annual contribution limit to Roth IRAs for anyone under the age of 50.

Here's where the legacy part comes into vivid display: Let's say you contribute $2,000 a year to your grandson's Roth IRA each year from the age of 15 to 25. So you have contributed a total of $20,000 over 10 years. Now let's assume that money grows at an annualized 6% all the way until your grandson turns 70. Your $20,000 in Roth IRA gifts could be worth nearly $400,000. And as I explain in the Retirement classes, contributions to Roth IRAs can be withdrawn at any time without owing a penny in tax. Wow—I wish someone started an IRA for me when I worked my first job as a counter girl making sandwiches in my dad's delicatessen when I was a teenager. That's quite a legacy to put in place.

Help them save for a car and/or home. Notice I said "help." I think it is very important that your grandchildren—and your children, for that matter—make the commitment to save on their own for big-ticket purchases. If they lack the resolve and the resources to save for a long-term goal, then they are probably not yet responsible enough to make that purchase. I think it is great if you contribute to their goals, but I do not want you to bankroll anything in full. Sit down with your grandchild and ask him what he hopes to save up for in the future and then offer to become his co-saver. Think of this like a 401(k) match. Maybe for every dollar he puts in the down payment fund you can match 25 cents, or a dollar, or $5.

Give experiences, not things. Recent studies have shown that happiness comes more from pleasurable experiences than from buying things. I think that's a great opportunity for grandparents. Focus on gifts that you can experience together, whether it's tickets to a ball game, a weekend jaunt to the city to hit museums and the theater, or a weekend getaway at your home just to spend some time together. In addition to the fun of the here and now of the experience, you are also building memories, and maybe passing along some legacies as well. That, after all, is the most precious gift you can ever give.

LESSON RECAP

- Stand in the truth together, as a family. The more you talk and share, the greater your ability to reach your new dreams.
- Raise your children to be financially honest. Teach the value of saving, but give them the space to spend as well.
- Choose a college that is a great financial fit. Cost matters.
- Know how best to help a family member in need. Are you solving a problem or providing a temporary patch that just delays the inevitable?
- Pay it forward. Grandparents can seed the dreams of grandchildren.

CLASS

HOME

THE TRUTH OF THE MATTER

There is no aspect more fundamental to the classic notion of the American Dream than homeownership. Ask anyone their definition of the American Dream and I have no doubt that the first thing out of their mouth will be "Home." The postwar boom years of the last century and the rise of suburban life ingrained this notion in us that homeownership is not only something to strive for as an American but very nearly our right. There is no single image that speaks to our security so much as a family home. And there is no greater manifestation of how each successive generation has fared better than the previous one—that very American promise—than the way we've traditionally "traded up" in the area of real estate. And why shouldn't we have come to believe in this? After all, as a general rule, home values have historically risen over time. Your parents or grandparents most likely bought their first house for less than what you might spend today on a new car, and that house probably increased in value dramatically over the years. No surprise, then, that we grew to expect that you would buy a house that in time would be worth significantly more than what you paid for it, and that house would provide for you and your children. The equity you had in the house would be a safety net, a way to help fund college costs, to bridge a shortfall, to ease some of the anxiety of an underfunded retirement account. And then overnight, everything seemed to change.

The implosion of the housing market has already resulted in more than five million foreclosure notices in 2008 and 2009, 2.8 million in 2010, and 1.6 million more in the first nine months of 2011, according to RealtyTrac. To be sure, the epic proportions of this disaster were the result of lax lending standards that allowed unqualified borrowers to become homeowners. But also to blame was a kind of entitlement gone wild—the American Dream careening out of control, fueled by greed and recklessness and untethered to a genuine sense of fiscal responsibility. I'm not going to lecture and point fingers—I did that in my 2009 book, *Action Plan;* we all know what went into making that perfect storm and we know all too well that the damage and repercussions are far from over. But I will point out that the housing crisis has ruptured and twisted our view of the American Dream like nothing else in my lifetime.

And the truth is, greed is not the entire story. Many families that didn't overreach during the bubble years are nonetheless suffering as well. As I write, more than six million Americans have been unemployed for more than six months. Nearly one in five of us is either unemployed or working part-time, because we can't find a full-time position. Continuing to make a monthly mortgage payment under those circumstances is proving painfully difficult given those harsh realities and the jobless recovery that we are told is under way. The federal government's mortgage modification program has been a massive disappointment; from its start in the spring of 2009 through mid-2011 less than one-third of homeowners who were eligible for the Home Affordable Modification Program (HAMP) were granted permanent modifications.

And let's not forget that millions of people who have dutifully and responsibly made their mortgage payments have been direly affected as well. Deflated home values have put an end to the prospect of a home as retirement fund or college fund and raised the question of whether homeownership in fact even makes sense anymore. I am shocked by the number of people I talk to who view their home as an albatross, who are underwater, owe more than their home is worth, and regret the day they thought a home purchase was a great idea. It still surprises me to hear so many of you tell me you can't wait until you can unload your house, that you long for the days when you sent your landlord a rent check and slept soundly at night. I guess my surprise is a measure of how ingrained the desire to be a homeowner is in every one of us. Even those of us who know the steep costs and the pitfalls of buying real estate, can't help but feel some sense of betrayal, deep down, that this form of security has been taken from us.

So where does that leave the American Dream? In desperate need of revision, I'll tell you that much. If your home is no longer the rock-solid financial foundation of your net worth, then it is time to rebuild that dream from the ground up. And guess where we start? You got it: by letting go of beliefs and platitudes that may no longer be a part of your reality, looking deep inside, locating your truth, and standing firmly in it.

If we are going to create together a New American Dream that defines us and sets down values that are durable, crystal clear, and unimpeachable, for generations to come, then we need to agree on some fundamental truths at the outset. Interestingly, you'll see that many of these ground rules are ones your grandparents would have embraced—another case of going back to the future. So maybe in the end, we are not rewriting the American Dream so drastically after all; we are just getting back in touch with it in its purest form.

Before we begin this class in earnest, I would like us to walk through some governing principles, to make sure we are in step in our views about real estate:

- **A home is not a stock.** Investing in a home because you think it will rise in value enough to finance other financial goals—your retirement, college tuition, expensive annual vacations—was never wise. I appreciate that for a decade or so, watching your home's value rise at a double-digit annual pace and being able to tap into those gains with a home equity line of credit was simply too irresistible for many. But we now know where all that financial dishonesty led and we are not going back there.

As I will explain in this class, homeownership is still a viable and smart step for many families. But it must not be viewed exclusively in terms of an investment. It is a place to live, first and foremost, a place to raise your family. That is its primary function. And when purchased with the right financial strategy and expectations it will also be a solid investment. It is a long-term savings vehicle you live in, not a short-term asset you flip to pay for other financial goals.

• **Renting may work best for many Americans.** While the old American Dream was rooted in the notion that it always made sense to buy once you could afford a home, the new dream requires a more complex analysis of what honestly makes sense given your career and family situation.

• **Financing is cheap, but not easy.** As I write this in late 2011, mortgage rates are remarkably low. The fact that you can lock in a 4.1% interest rate on a 30-year mortgage and 3.3% for a 15-year fixed is an incredibly great deal. But qualifying for that great deal is no easy task as lenders have tightened their standards. To obtain a conventional mortgage you must now come to the lending table with a higher credit score, a higher down payment, proof that you have ample savings to be able to keep paying the mortgage if you are laid off, as well as full documentation of all your income and assets. Refinancing now requires having at least 20 to 30% equity in your home; just a few years ago you could refinance with no equity.

For those of you looking at today's low prices and thinking it may be a smart time to buy, I ask you to stand in the truth of whether it may make more sense for you to rent. For homeowners who are struggling to keep up with a mortgage I ask you to stand in the truth that letting go may be the most honorable way of moving your family forward. And for all of us, we must adapt to the fact that a home is not a liquid investment whose value will rise at a fast and furious pace. I want to be clear: I still think that home-ownership can make great sense for many of you. But you must have a clear-eyed understanding of what a home is and what it isn't. I ask you to read every word of this class carefully and leave your assumptions behind. The work of this class is absolutely critical to shaping our notion of what truly constitutes your New American Dream.

I have organized the Home Class into the following lessons:

- The Truth About Home Values
- When It Makes Sense to Rent
- The New Rules of Buying a Home
- What to Do If You Are Underwater
- How to Reduce Mortgage Costs
- The Dangers of Home Equity Lines of Credit
- Reverse Mortgages
- Investing in Real Estate

LESSON I. THE TRUTH ABOUT HOME VALUES

If all you know about the housing market is based on what happened during the past 10 years, then the truth is you know very little. The extreme gyrations in the market since 2000 are in fact exceptional. Therefore, this lesson must begin by making sure you understand that recent history was completely disconnected from the longer-term story. Whether you are a renter thinking of buying or an owner deciding whether to stay put, trade up, or trade down, understanding what happened during the housing bubble and its costly aftermath is the foundation of this lesson.

A DECADE OF EXTREMES

From 2000 through the spring of 2006, the S&P/Case-Shiller index of home values in twenty metropolitan areas more than doubled. The average annual gain of 12% during that stretch exceeded the 10% long-term average for stocks. But since that peak, the same index has shed more than one-third of its value through the summer of 2011.

I am here to tell you that neither double-digit annual gains nor double-digit annual losses is in any way normal. The ride up was fueled by a confluence of unprecedented events we all know are unlikely—I hope—to ever occur again. Lax lending standards allowed otherwise unqualified borrowers to become homeowners, and many more qualified buyers to purchase more house than they could actually afford. And don't get me started on the role of Wall Street and regulators in aiding and abetting the dishonesty.

The ride down of the past four years is the painful process of coming back to the truth. That truth, over many decades, is that home values rise at an average annual rate that matches or slightly exceeds the long-term average annual 3.5–4% rate of inflation. For all the pain of the bubble bursting I find it so interesting that the same housing index today is 41% above where it stood in 2000. That works out to about a 3.0% annualized rate. Not too far off the long-term rate, is it?

Of course, national averages do not tell the real story of what is happening in your area. In the regions that had the biggest boom, the bust has been the most painful, and it may be a few more years before we see prices stabilize in those areas, since the backlog of foreclosures must be winnowed down. But the point here is that whatever has happened to your market, whenever it reaches its bottom, I want you to know what you can rationally expect to happen going forward. And that is why I want you to focus on a rate of 3.5% or so, on average.

STAND IN THE TRUTH

That brings us to our central stand-in-the-truth moment for the Home Class: Be realistic about what your home is worth today and be realistic about what it may be worth five, 10, 20 years from now. A $300,000 home in 2006 that is now worth $200,000 might "get back" to $300,000 in about 12 years, assuming an average price gain of 3.5%. Even at a very strong 6% rate it would take more than six years to get back to 2006 levels.

The decisions you need to make—the housing dream you are in charge of re-creating—must be grounded in your personal truth of what you have today, not what you had at the peak of the housing bubble in 2006. And I am asking you to look toward the future with an expectation that housing prices will, at best, post gains that are more in line with their long-term historical trend of keeping pace with inflation. This brings me back to a point I introduced at the outset of this class:

A HOME IS A SAVINGS ACCOUNT, NOT A HOT STOCK

Even though a home can still be a very solid investment that over time should grow in value, it is never ever to be mistaken for a liquid investment. Your emergency fund at your bank or credit union is liquid; you have access to it 24/7 and you know exactly what it is worth. A stock or bond investment is also fairly liquid; you can sell it five days a week and have the money in your account typically within a few days.

Your home, on the other hand, is an illiquid investment. If you wake up tomorrow and decide to sell, the best-case scenario is that you might have the cash deposited in your bank account in sixty days, and that's me being highly optimistic. In late 2011 the average time it takes to sell a home is three to six months in many markets. That's a long time to wait for your money.

What about a home equity line of credit (HELOC)? As far as I am concerned the rise of the HELOC is one of the most costly tricks the financial services industry played on willing homeowners. I never advocated turning your home equity into an ATM you could tap at any time. And as I explain later in this chapter, I think HELOCs could be especially dangerous in the coming years.

So do I think owning a home is still a viable dream given my insistence on expecting moderate appreciation going forward? Absolutely. But so too is renting. Remember what I explained in the very first chapter of this book: The way you create lasting security for you and your family is to focus on creating entirely personal dreams that reflect what is right and honest for you and you alone.

LESSON 2. WHEN IT MAKES SENSE TO RENT

It used to be, not all that long ago, that renting was something you settled for if you couldn't afford to buy a home. Renting was a way station en route to buying, a rite of passage. My, how times have changed.

These days, in my opinion, renting can be the end in itself, a far better move, depending on your personal circumstances.

To those of you currently renting who are wondering if now is a smart time to buy because you can get a good deal on a house, I want you to first make sure you can answer yes to every item in my checklist:

- Do you intend to live in your home for a minimum of five to seven years?
- If you lost your job—or wanted a new job to advance your career—could you reasonably expect to find a comparable job locally (i.e., one that would not require that you relocate)?
- Can you afford a 20% down payment?
- Do you place a high value on knowing you don't have to answer to the whims of a landlord?

My 5-to-7-year rule is to help you avoid the likelihood that you would someday sell your home and have less in your pocket than what you paid. What you must realize is that when you go to sell you will need to spend about 8% to 10% on settling all your selling costs. The way the real estate system works, the seller pays all of the agents' fees; typically that is 6%. On top of that you may have to pay a transfer tax to your state or county that might be 1% or more of the sale price. If you live in a condominium, cooperative, or other development that has a homeowners' association, you could even encounter a fee when you sell; this practice has become more common as a way to discourage investors who buy with the intention of flipping a property. Then there is the cost of moving. Add it all up and you can see why I say you need to plan on giving up 8% to 10% of your sales price to make the move. Given that we may still have a few years ahead of us before the market stabilizes, I think buying today with anything less than a 5-year to 7-year time horizon is risky. Over a shorter period we can't confidently assume you will get anywhere near enough price appreciation to cover the 8% to 10% cost of selling.

Your job outlook is another important factor as well. If you have any reason to expect you might need or want to relocate within the next five to seven years, then renting can in fact be the far better option for now.

I also think renting is smart if you have yet to save up a 20% down payment. I am well aware that loans insured by the Federal Housing Administration (FHA) come with very low down payments. But as I explain later in this chapter, your housing dream will be more sustainable if you can make a 20% down payment.

Another important consideration is whether you really, truly, deep down yearn to be a homeowner. Don't listen to anyone else. Do not feel like it is something you should do. Your new dreams must be as firmly rooted in emotional truths as in financial truths. If you are scared of buying, then embrace the truth that you are meant to rent. If you don't really care that you can't renovate the kitchen or that you might have to move in a few years if the landlord raises your rent too high, then renting is right for you. Respect your feelings; they have as much sway here as your finances.

THE MATH OF RENT VS. BUY

There are of course many factors that come into play when deciding whether it makes financial sense to buy or rent. At the top of the list is what it would cost you to rent a comparable home that you are considering buying. Then you need to factor in the purchase costs (closing costs on your mortgage can equal 5% or more of your purchase price) and the eventual cost of selling as well. While you are an owner you will have the benefit of some tax breaks, as well as full responsibility for maintenance and property tax.

At the same time, I want to make sure that renting is not overplayed as the "best" solution. As with all financial decisions there are trade-offs. And with renting you must prepare—and budget—

for the possibility that the landlord will raise your rent, or decide to sell the home, and the new owner imposes a big rate hike at the next renewal. And you must put a personal price on how important or unimportant it may be to you to know you can stay put and renovate the home to your choosing.

The Best Buy vs. Rent Calculator: *The New York Times* has a free online calculator that allows you to build a very customized calculation based on your personal circumstances. The calculator will show you an expected break-even date where the cost of buying (and eventually selling) makes more sense than renting. No calculator can perfectly capture every nuance of each individual situation, but this calculator does an excellent job of making sure key costs are accounted for. Give it a spin and see how long you would have to stay put before the cost of buying would be worthwhile. Go to www.nytimes.com/interactive/business/buy-rent-calculator.html.

Tips for Using the Calculator

- Base your purchase information on making a 20% down payment.
- Plug in the current rate for a 30-year fixed-rate mortgage.
- Check your local newspaper or ask a real estate agent for an estimate of what comparable homes rent for in your area.
- Assume that both home prices and rents will rise at either 3% or 4% a year.
- If you are considering buying a condo, please click the "Advanced" settings button so you can input the fees you may likely pay.

ADVICE FOR OWNERS WHO NOW WANT TO RENT

I know that many of you who own a home are questioning whether it makes sense to sell and go back to renting. In the "What to Do if You Are Underwater" lesson later in the chapter I share strategies for homeowners who now have a mortgage that exceeds the current value of their home. But I also want to address those of you who have equity in your home but are now wondering if it makes more sense to sell and rent. Again, I am going to come back to the fact that you must shape and follow your own personal dream. If you are considering a move because of a life change—the kids moving out, you're ready to retire and downsize, or you recently ended a relationship—then by all means it makes sense to run the numbers and see if renting is right for you. But do not gloss over the potential drawbacks of renting as well. Think through the trade-offs and make an informed choice.

If your issue is that you just feel overwhelmed by the cost of the mortgage and maintenance and you know you can indeed save more by renting, then you are absolutely to stand in that truth. There is nothing wrong with changing your mind; if your new dream is to rent rather than own, then that is the right dream for you. Just promise me you will factor in the 8% to 10% cost of moving. That is not a reason to stay put, but if it adds up to more than you can cover from the gain on the sale, I want you to plan for how you will cover the costs. You may need to head back to chapter 2 to find ways to boost your savings for the next six months or year so you can cover the cost of the move.

LESSON 3. THE NEW RULES OF BUYING A HOME

For renters who are eager to buy now that prices have come down, and for owners who are looking to make a move, I have rules I want you to follow so your new housing dream will give you security, not stress.

SET A BUDGET THAT SATISFIES YOUR NEEDS

Remember the credo of chapter 2? *Live below your means but within your needs.* Now is the time to embrace that phrase and make it a governing principle of your life. I do not want you listening to a mortgage lender who tells you what you will be allowed to borrow, nor do I want you to follow the advice of a real estate agent who insists the bigger, more expensive house is a better value. Listen only to yourself. This is your dream, and so it must be rooted in what makes sense for you. I want you to seriously think through how much space you need. The size of new homes has increased about 35% over the past three decades, yet household size has declined. I want you to be comfortable, I want you to enjoy your house. But a smaller home that fits your needs means a more manageable mortgage, a lower property tax bill, lower utility costs, and likely less time and effort to maintain. And lower housing costs leave more income for your other important dreams, including funding your retirement or saving for a child's college education.

KNOW YOUR INCOME LIMITS

Lenders are now back to calculating how big a loan they will offer you based on your income, a practice all but abandoned during the housing bubble. The two standard calculations are:

- Your mortgage, property tax, and insurance (called PITI) should not exceed 25% of your gross (pre-tax) monthly income.
- Your PITI and all other debts should not exceed 36% of your gross monthly income.

There is leeway in those numbers; if you have other assets or make a big down payment you may be able to run past those limits. And in high-cost areas, the 36% debt-income ratio often is stretched past 40%.

My recommendation is that you never exceed the 25/36 rule. If you think that's impossible, then I ask you to return to another tenet from an earlier lesson: *Sometimes when we feel stuck we must change our perspective.* If 25/36 seems out of your reach then you have two choices: Hold off purchasing until your finances make 25/36 doable, or shop for a less expensive home. The quickest way to buy an affordable home that meets the 25/36 test is to lower the price tag. That is the essence of living below your means but within your needs.

First-time homebuyer alert: Please do not think that you can afford a monthly mortgage that is equal to your current rent. There are many additional costs that come with home-ownership that can add 30% or more to your monthly base mortgage rate. In The Classroom at my website you will find information on how to figure out the true cost of homeowner-ship and how to test whether you can honestly afford to buy. Go to www.suzeorman.com.

AIM TO MAKE A 20% DOWN PAYMENT

Are you thinking that sounds crazy given that we all know you can get an FHA-insured loan with a 3.5% down payment? So why, you are wondering, should your dream of homeownership be delayed by that 20% obstacle? I know all about the FHA program. I am well aware of what you can get these days. My job is to teach you what I think is best for your long-term security. In my opinion, if you cannot afford a 20% down payment, you cannot honestly afford to buy a home. During the 2000–2006 stretch, if sizable down payments had been required we would not have had such an inflated bubble and its painful deflation. Down payments below 20% also mean you must purchase mortgage insurance; whether through the FHA-insured program or private mortgage insurance, this adds to your housing costs.

A SPECIAL NOTE ABOUT FHA-INSURED LOANS

Before the financial crisis, mortgages insured by the FHA accounted for about 5% of the new loans doled out in any given year. In early 2011 the FHA insurance program accounted for about 30% of loans for home purchases. How come? Well, lenders are making it tougher to qualify for a conventional mortgage and are all too happy to steer clients into FHA-insured loans given the fact that the federal government is in fact *insuring* that it will pay off the loan if the borrower runs into trouble.

I have to say that I am not a huge fan of FHA-insured loans.

The fact is, they perpetuate many of the problems that got us into this housing mess. For starters, until 2010, the FHA didn't require a minimum FICO credit score to be eligible for a mortgage. And it wasn't until last year that it set a FICO credit score floor. But that floor is a score of 500! If you can make a down payment of at least 10% and your FICO credit score is between 500 and 580, that's good enough for the FHA. And if you have a score above 580 you are eligible for an FHA-insured mortgage that requires just a 3.5% down payment. That said, many lenders that offer FHA-insured mortgages are applying their own FICO score rules, and require a FICO score of at least 620–640. In my opinion any FICO credit score below 700 is in fact a sign that you have some financial issues to address.

And a 3.5% down payment just strikes me as dangerously low. When you put down 10% or 20% the simple truth is that you will think longer and harder about what you are doing. Putting so much of your own money on the line forces you to stand more solidly in your truth. And that large down payment gives you downside protection if, God forbid, anything were to happen and you needed to sell the home at potentially less than your current mortgage balance. Let's say you made a 20% down payment and values are 5% lower when you go to sell. Well, you still walk away with 15% equity; that's more than enough to cover your closing costs and the agent's fee. But if you put down just 3.5% to 5%, you will find yourself owing the bank money to move, or face the foreclosure or short-sale process. As I explain below, that's not a scenario you want to find yourself in.

I also want potential borrowers to understand the cost of an FHA-insured loan. At the time of the loan you will owe an up-front insurance fee equal to 1% of the loan amount, and then there is an ongoing annual insurance premium equal to 0.90% of your loan amount. You owe that ongoing fee until your equity in the home reaches 22%. As we discussed earlier, that could be many years, given that appreciation rates over the long term will likely be modest.

So am I against FHA-insured loans? It depends. If you are considering an FHA-insured loan because your FICO credit score is low due to your own self-induced overspending or poor payment habits, then I absolutely will not condone buying a home with an FHA-insured mortgage. Just because you can do something does not mean you should. And please don't hide behind the notion that because the federal government says it is okay, it is. Look, the federal government has its own agenda: By expanding the FHA-insured loan program, it is trying to keep the battered housing market from bigger losses. But your agenda is to stand in your truth and make financially sound decisions. If you can't get a conventional mortgage because of your own poor choices, then the only honest action to take is to wait until you repair your credit score, or save up enough for a bigger down payment so you can in fact qualify for a regular loan.

Now, that said, I think the FHA-insured mortgage can be a viable option for those of you who are rebuilding your life after divorce, or a financial setback such as a long layoff. Those are circumstances where a poor FICO credit score is not a sign of a lack of financial responsibility, but rather an indication that you have undergone a disruptive life event beyond your control. But even here I ask you to stand in your truth. I would feel so much better if you waited until you had the money to make a down payment of 10 to 20%. Being able to save that much is a sign that you have the strength and tenacity to make the right financial choices. And with a more sizable down payment you will be that much closer to the 22% home equity you need to have the 0.90% insurance fee dropped from your payment.

Special Buying Rules for Condos and Co-ops

If you are considering buying a condominium or cooperative, please be very very careful. In some of the most overdeveloped markets that have been hardest hit, condo prices can, at first glance, look like an incredible steal. But when you purchase a condo or co-op you are purchasing more than four walls; you are buying a piece of an entire development, and that means you have to make sure the development itself is a good investment. Here are the questions to ask:

• **What percentage of the units are owner-occupied as a primary residence?** Lenders and the FHA are cautious about offering mortgages for properties that are in developments full of vacation or investment-property owners. And if a development is full of renters, that can impact your future resale value as well; unless it is a hot market for investment properties, you might have a hard time selling at a top price when everyone else around you is renting out their units. My advice: Stick with developments that are at least 90% owner-occupied.

• **How many units have been foreclosed on in the past three years?** If the answer is more than 3%, that is a sign of potential trouble, if you ask me; if there are more foreclosures you will likely see your home's value drop.

• **What is the homeowners' association or condo fee for each of the past five years?** You do know that in addition to your mortgage payment, you also will owe a monthly maintenance or common charges fee, right? I am asking because I am surprised at how many people come up to me so excited about a great condo deal, and then when I ask about the common charges they give me a blank stare. These monthly fees go toward paying the general maintenance costs of the development or building—landscaping, security, etc. And a portion of your monthly fee should also be set aside in a longer-term reserve fund that is tapped when the development needs to make an assessment for a major repair or upgrade, such as a new roof. I would be very wary of any development whose association fees have increased more than the general rate of inflation— about 3.5% or so. That's a sign that the development doesn't have a good grip on its costs, which would likely mean more big adjustments going forward. I also think you need to be extremely careful about buying into a development with many unoccupied units; if those units aren't sold or rented quickly it's likely the existing owners will be stuck with higher monthly fees.

• **What percentage of current owners have not made their monthly condo/association fee payments in the past three months?** If it is more than 3% take that as a warning sign that everyone else—including you—may be asked to make up the shortfall.

• **How large is the reserve fund?** All the owners, collectively, are on the hook for any big-ticket repairs or upgrades to the development. Ideally, you want to hear that the condo's roof is 15 months old, not 15 years! You must insist on reviewing the financial statements for the development, including how much money is currently set aside in the reserve fund. At a minimum, at least 10 percent of a condo association's annual operating budget should be set aside for the reserve fund. For older developments that are more likely to need maintenance, it would be great to see even more dedicated to the reserve fund. It's obviously your best bet to focus your sights on developments in good physical shape, but if you have your heart set on a unit in a building that will likely need a new roof or other capital repairs in the next few years, be sure the reserve fund can handle that cost. Otherwise you could be hit with budget-busting special assessments that can cost you thousands of dollars.

Now, if all of that checks out, I then want you to do a full 360-degree inspection of your unit. Look, you are going to be living with neighbors quite near. So you better make sure you will be content amid all that closeness. Spend some time walking around the development and talk up as many residents as possible; are they effusive or complaining? You also want to do a noise check: If it's a multilevel unit, I would ask to have someone walk around the unit above you; I personally would never go near a place where I could hear my neighbor's every move. Same goes for any attached units nearby. Are the walls soundproof? And if you are highly sensitive to cigarette or cigar smoke, try to find out if neighbors you will be sharing ventilation systems with are smokers; in many buildings that smoke could end up wafting into your unit. And be sure to visit at a few different times, especially a weekend night. If you enjoy peace and quiet, it is better to know now if your neighbors tend to be more outgoing—and noisy—party types.

WHERE TO COME UP WITH THE DOWN PAYMENT

As discussed in "Stand in Your Truth," the way to save for capital purchases is to create automated savings accounts so you can add to your dream funds every month. Set up a separate account for your down payment. The money should be kept in a stable bank or credit union account; money you expect to need within 10 years should never be invested in stocks.

DO NOT TOUCH YOUR RETIREMENT SAVINGS

In the past I have given first-time buyers the option of taking money out of their retirement savings for a home down payment. There is indeed a special rule that allows first-time buyers to withdraw up to $10,000 from a traditional IRA for a down payment, and be exempt from the 10% early withdrawal penalty levied when you are younger than 59½. (Though you still will owe income tax on the withdrawal.) Roth IRAs are another down payment source; you can always access money you contributed to a Roth without any tax or penalty, and first-time buyers can take $10,000 of earnings without paying the early withdrawal penalty. Income tax is only charged if the account is less than five years old.

However, I do not subscribe to that advice anymore. Given the struggles so many of you are having saving for retirement I am going to insist that you leave every penny of your retirement money invested for retirement. If that means you need to spend a year or two saving up for a down payment, that's the truth I am asking you to stand in. Remember, the New American Dream is not just about sensible homeownership, but about retiring with security as well.

I also do not advocate borrowing large sums from your family for the down payment. This is primarily a lesson in personal accountability. I want you to be responsible for what likely will be your single biggest investment ever. For a 20% down payment I do not want your family chipping in more than one-quarter of that amount, or 5%. And it is your responsibility to make sure your family members are standing in their truth. They must never give you money if it compromises their own financial security.

MAINTAIN AN EIGHT-MONTH EMERGENCY SAVINGS FUND

In late 2011, more than 40% of unemployed Americans had been out of work for at least six months. That statistic alone should make it obvious why I insist you have ample savings set aside so you can continue to cover your mortgage and other housing costs in the event of a layoff or furlough. In fact, mortgage lenders will be looking at your savings when evaluating your application. Without at least four or five months' worth of mortgage payments saved up you may find it hard to land a deal.

GET A STEAL OF A DEAL

An all-too-common trap I have seen people fall into is to look at a home's list price relative to what that home might have been worth several years ago. What happens is they see a $200,000 price tag on a home that might have cost $350,000 three years ago and they think they have found an incredible deal. Not so fast. Please do not get blinded by comparing current prices to pre-bust values. What matters—in fact, the only thing that matters—is whether you are getting a deal based on current market trends. If you end up paying $200,000 for a home today when similar homes in the area are selling for $180,000, that's not a deal. You have overpaid. Please promise me you will make your offer based on a careful analysis of current price trends in your area and block out any thoughts about what that home might have sold for during the real estate bubble. Not only does that old value have nothing to do with its current fair value, there is no guarantee that it will ever reach bubble prices anytime soon. You've got to keep your feet on the ground and stand in the truth.

OPT FOR A 30-YEAR FIXED-RATE MORTGAGE

As I write this in late 2011, a 30-year fixed-rate mortgage for a well-qualified buyer is 4.1%. I can't tell you how seriously great that is. When you can lock in a low rate and you never have to worry about it changing, you must grab that deal. Yes, I know five-year and seven-year adjustable-rate mortgages have even lower rates, but they also come with risk as well. Haven't we all learned the risks that come with adjustable-rate mortgages? Many of today's foreclosures came about because people took out adjustable mortgages during the bubble that they assumed they would be able to refinance out of before the rate adjusted. When that didn't pan out as expected the troubles began. And given that interest rates are currently at historic lows, the trend going forward is for rates to rise, not fall. All the more reason to lock in a safe-not-sorry 30-year fixed-rate mortgage.

TIP: Consider a 15-year mortgage if you are at least 45 years old. As I explain in the retirement chapter, I think one of the best retirement strategies is to get your mortgage paid off before you retire. So if you are purchasing a house today that you anticipate you will retire in, and retirement is within 15 to 20 years, I want you to consider taking out a 15-year mortgage. Yes, that means your monthly payments will indeed be higher, but at today's super low interest rate—3.3% as of late 2011—a 15-year is incredibly affordable. If you have the income and savings to be able to handle the higher monthly payments you will save tens of thousands of dollars in total interest payments as well as arrive at retirement mortgage-free.

And if you are confident you can afford the higher required payments with the 15-year loan, it is the better strategy than just settling for a 30-year mortgage that you intend to pay off in 15 years. The interest rate on a 15-year mortgage is typically about a half a percentage point lower than the rate on a 30-year loan. That helps keep your overall interest costs lower. The website Bankrate.com has a calculator that will walk you through the math of a 15-year vs. 30-year mortgage.

UNDERSTAND THE RISK OF DISTRESSED PROPERTY

In most parts of the country, foreclosed homes and homes that are listed as short sales account for one-quarter or more of the homes for sale. These so-called distressed properties often sell for below-market rates, but you need to be extra careful if you are considering bidding on either type.

A **short sale** is when a lender agrees to let a homeowner sell a home for less than the current balance left on the mortgage. The lender is essentially agreeing to take a loss on that shortfall. As a buyer you must understand that you have two sellers in a short sale: the homeowner who is listing the home, and the lender. When you make a bid, even if the seller accepts, you then must wait to hear if the lender agrees to the terms. That can take months. And if the seller has a second mortgage on the home the process becomes even more difficult; the sale can't go through without the approval of the second-mortgage lender, and that is not something that happens easily or quickly.

A **foreclosure** is when a lender has already taken back possession of a home from a borrower. Sales of foreclosed homes can move much more quickly; once the bank puts the property on the market it is eager to make a deal. But I don't have to tell you about all the problems rocking the foreclosure market, including revelations that many lenders may have foreclosed on homes without going through the proper steps. More troubling is the concern that many lenders lack the proper documentation to prove they in fact have title (ownership) of the home. This is clogging the foreclosure process for months as banks—prodded by regulations and lawsuits—are scrambling to prove their paperwork is in place. Given the turmoil in the foreclosure market I advise you to think very long and hard and ask yourself if you are up for navigating your way through the maze. It can take months. And you must work with a real estate agent with experience in foreclosures, as well as a real estate lawyer well equipped to review all documents. You need legal proof that a title search has been conducted and that you will indeed have free and clear title to the property.

TIP: Title Insurance on Foreclosed Homes. If you are purchasing a foreclosed home and you anticipate making sizable renovations to the property, ask your title insurer for a policy that includes a special rider that would cover not just your purchase price, but also the future value after renovations as well. In the event the foreclosure documentation mess escalates and your ownership is questioned in the future, you want to know at the very least that your title insurance policy will provide ample reimbursement for the renovated value of your home.

I recognize that there are some seriously great prices available on foreclosed properties, but I want you to be very careful if you decide to focus on foreclosed property. The buying process can be lengthy and full of pitfalls, and the current legal issues swirling around add a dose of uncertainty. Please stand in your truth: Maybe paying a slightly higher price for a home that is not a foreclosure is in fact the better deal for your family.

LESSON 4. WHAT TO DO IF YOU ARE UNDERWATER

The steep fall in home prices in many parts of the country means that many homeowners who purchased a home during the bubble—often with little or no down payment cushion—currently have a mortgage that is higher than the market value of their home. According to housing data firm CoreLogic, more than 20% of homes with a mortgage in the second quarter of 2011 were underwater. Arizona, California, Florida, Michigan, and Nevada have the highest concentrations of underwater homeowners.

In this lesson I want to address separate strategies for two very different types of underwater households: those that can't afford their mortgage and those that can. If you can't afford your mortgage and you are in fact underwater, I want you to stand in the truth that walking away may in fact be the right and honest move for you and your family.

If you are underwater and can still afford your home, the math and the ethical questions require a different strategy.

IF YOU ARE UNDERWATER AND CANNOT AFFORD YOUR MORTGAGE

I need to start this lesson by telling you what I absolutely do not want you to do, ever: You are never to touch your retirement savings to keep up with a mortgage you can no longer afford. You must respect your retirement truth as much as your housing dream: You will need to have savings to support yourself in retirement. Using that money today to cover your housing costs raises the risk you will permanently doom your retirement dream.

I know this is such a painful truth to face, but it is the right truth. Please try to step back for a moment and think through the outcome of using retirement funds to cover a mortgage payment: All money withdrawn from a traditional 401(k) or IRA will be taxable, and there may be a 10% early withdrawal penalty as well. That reduces what you will have to put toward your housing costs. And whether the tapped funds are taxed or not, the more important issue is that they are being used at all. What's most upsetting for me is when families withdraw money from their retirement funds to cover a mortgage, and then when those savings are used up they still can't afford the mortgage. They depleted their retirement savings to do nothing more than delay the inevitable: They can't afford that mortgage, period.

And as I explain on page 188 in the retirement chapter, I do not recommend you ever take out a 401(k) loan. So please read that advice before you make this costly mistake.

That brings us to the right strategies to pursue if you have a mortgage you can no longer afford. I am not going to sugarcoat anything here. The very sad truth is that banks have, on the whole, been incredibly unresponsive in working with homeowners who cannot afford their mortgages. The help that was promised, I'm sorry to say, did not materialize for so many of you. The federal government's programs have proven to be woefully ineffective, in large part because lenders are asked—asked, but not mandated— to participate. So far, banks haven't shown much enthusiasm for helping. I mention all of this to make sure you understand the resolve and tenacity that is required to try to negotiate a deal with a lender.

There are four basic options for dealing with your predicament; I list them here in order of their appeal for distressed homeowners.

- **Loan Modification:** Your lender agrees to reduce your payments to an affordable level.
- **Short Sale:** The lender agrees that you will sell your home for whatever it can get in today's market. If the sale price is less than the outstanding balance of your mortgage, the lender will forgive that amount.
- **Deed in Lieu of Foreclosure:** You hand the house back to the lender, and the lender agrees to not go through the foreclosure process. A lender will typically require you to attempt a short sale before considering a deed in lieu of foreclosure.
- **Foreclosure:** The lender takes back your house and sells it. Depending on your state the lender may be able to sue you for any loss it incurs if the sale price is less than the outstanding mortgage balance.

Please understand that the lender, not you, is in the driver's seat here. What you want is irrelevant; this is all about what a lender is willing to offer you. Let's walk through each option in detail.

Loan Modification

If you can prove you have financial hardship, a lender may be willing to reduce your current monthly payment to a more affordable level. I want to stress that this does not mean your principal balance will be reduced. While that is possible, banks have been loath to offer this relief. What is more likely—if you can even win a modification—is that your interest rate will be reduced to lower your payment.

The federal Home Affordable Modification Program (HAMP) offers lenders incentives to reduce the mortgage payments for qualified borrowers. Some lenders may have their own modification programs as well. The bottom line is that you want to start working with your lender as soon as you have any inkling you are headed for trouble. You do not need to be behind on your payments to qualify for the HAMP program; if you can prove financial hardship, such as a drop in your income due to a layoff, or the fact that your mortgage payment is adjusting to a new, higher cost that will make it hard to pay the loan, you may be able to win a reduction.

HAMP Basics

To be eligible for HAMP:

- The mortgage must be for a primary residence that was obtained before January 1, 2009. Vacation homes and investment properties are not eligible.
- The mortgage amount must be $729,750 or less.
- You must be able to prove financial hardship: Either your mortgage has increased or your income has decreased.
- Your monthly mortgage payment (including property tax, insurance, and homeowners' association fees if applicable) must be more than 31% of your current gross income.

TIP: In the summer of 2010 the Treasury Department, which oversees HAMP, introduced a new variation specifically for households in which a layoff has made it hard to keep up with the mortgage payment. The Home Affordable Unemployment Program (HAUP) offers a reduced payment for a short period while the household looks for reemployment. As with all of these programs, lenders are not required to participate, and so far it does not seem to be widely adopted. But please check with your lender to see if it may be willing to use HAUP to give you a temporary reduction in your mortgage cost.

If you meet all those criteria you may be able to win a mortgage reduction that brings your monthly payment down to 31% of your gross income. The HAMP website has a calculator that will show you an estimate of what your monthly payment could be if you win a modification: www.makinghomeaffordable.gov.

I need to be very honest here: To date this program, launched in early 2009, has been a huge disappointment. Early on, people who were put into a trial modification program were then strung along for a year or more before learning whether they had been approved for a permanent modification. Program changes instituted in mid-2010 have shortened the wait considerably, to about four months. Better still, the majority of people who get through the trial modification are now being granted permanent modifications. But you still need to understand the consequences if you do not ultimately qualify for a permanent modification.

The Risks of Asking for a Trial Modification

When a lender offers you a trial modification, your monthly payment will be reduced. That's the good news. The bad news is that this will have a negative impact on your credit score. Why is this? Because even though the bank agrees to lower the payment, it must still report the fact that you are no longer paying the full amount due. So if you have been current on your mortgage and other payments, and you enter into a trial modification, be aware that your credit score is going to take a tumble. The hit your score takes will depend on your score prior to the modification. Unfair as it may be, a high score will actually fall more—possibly 100 points or so—while a lower score will not see as much impact.

The second risk is what happens if you are turned down for a permanent modification, a fact of life for more than two-thirds of borrowers who had gone through HAMP as of the summer of 2010. If you are deemed ineligible for a permanent modification, the lender can turn around and demand repayment for the difference between your regular payment and the trial payment.

Here's an example: Let's say you had a $2,000 monthly mort-
gage payment that was reduced to $1,500 during a 10-month trial
period. Then the lender decides you do not qualify for the permanent modification. It can then demand that you repay the $500
monthly reduction you had for the 10 months. Suddenly you find
yourself back at owing $2,000 to cover the monthly mortgage *and*
you have a $5,000 balloon payment you must pay pronto. If you
can't handle both of those costs, the bank then starts the foreclosure process.

In the meantime, I want anyone considering a modification to
be very aware of what they may be walking into. Before you agree
to a trial modification I recommend you get the lender to answer—
in writing—the following questions:

- Do I meet the financial requirements to be eligible for a permanent modification?
- When will you decide on making my modification permanent? (It is supposed to be three months, but the average
  wait time has been four times as long.)
- If I am denied a permanent modification, will I owe any balloon payment? If so, how fast must I pay back that balloon
  payment?

I then want you to stand in the truth. Given the sorry statistics
on how many homeowners in trial modifications are turned down
for a permanent modification, I want you to ask yourself whether
the better move—the one that allows your family to in fact move
forward—is to walk away from the house.

**TIP: Tax Break for Short Sales and Foreclosures Before January 1,
2013.** Before the financial crisis, if you walked away from a mortgage and your lender forgave you the difference between the sale
price and the mortgage balance, you still had a potential federal
tax bill. The amount of the forgiven amount was reported as "income" given to you and you would owe tax on that income. But a
special law passed in 2008—the Mortgage Debt Relief Act—
temporarily does away with this tax bill. Through December 31,
2012, any short sale or foreclosure in which the lender forgives

any unpaid portion of your mortgage not covered by the sale price is exempt from the tax. The mortgage must have been taken out before January 1, 2009, for a primary residence, and the maximum loan amount covered is $2 million. For those of you who are considering a loan modification, I want you to be aware of the expiration date for this tax break. If you have any doubt whether you will qualify for a permanent modification, or whether even with the modification you will be able to hold on to the home, the wise move may be to let go of the home and have it sold/foreclosed before the end of 2012. If you wait longer and you ultimately need to give up the home, you may not be able to take advantage of this important debt forgiveness regulation.

Short Sale

In a short sale your lender agrees to let you sell your home for a price that is less than the outstanding balance on your mortgage, and the lender will not require you to pay the difference. Lenders know they are likely to get a higher sale price through a short sale than if they have to foreclose on a home and incur all the costs of that process, including selling the house. That's their incentive for considering a short sale. But a lender will not extend a short sale option to anyone who merely doesn't want to pay their mortgage. Please respect the truth that your mortgage is a legal obligation; you promised to make a payment. If you no longer want to make the payment that is not nearly a good enough reason for the lender to agree to a short sale. You must exhibit a financial need for the short sale, such as a change in your household income, or an adjustable mortgage that has adjusted to the point of being unaffordable.

If your lender agrees to a short sale it will have the final say on accepting a buyer's offer. That is, the lender can turn down a buyer's offer if it decides it is too low, even if that means the lender will then start the foreclosure process on your home.

Deed in Lieu of Foreclosure

In some instances, lenders may be willing to work out a deal for you to hand over ownership of the home to the lender without having to go through the formal foreclosure process. It is entirely up to a lender whether it wants to go this route, and typically this will be offered only if a short sale was not successful.

Foreclosure

This should be your last-resort option if you must walk away from a home and you have been unable to work out a modification, short sale, or deed in lieu of foreclosure with your lender.

In a foreclosure the lender takes back ownership of the home and assumes responsibility for selling the property. In twenty-three states this process must go through the court system; in all other states there is no requirement for judicial review.

The behavior of the banks and mortgage servicing companies in handling foreclosures has been awful. We have a massive backlog in the system, compounded by revelations in early 2011 that mortgage servicers and lenders were cutting corners on documentation, or in some cases couldn't even prove they had title to the properties. We are still waiting for that mess to be resolved. But I do not want any of you who are in foreclosure because you have not been able to pay your mortgage to think that this is some sort of reprieve and you will be able to win back your home. If you cannot afford your home, you cannot afford your home, regardless of the paperwork mess. That said, you may be able to use the debacle to your advantage; to the extent it slows down the foreclosure process that gives you more time to think through your next step. The healthiest thing you can do is move out as soon as possible, but if you are not paying the mortgage, staying put while the foreclosure process plays out can give you a few more months—maybe even a year or more—to save money so you can secure a rental once you do move out. The fact that you are in foreclosure means your credit score has already taken a hit; so having more money to make a larger security deposit on a rental may be necessary to convince a landlord to rent to you.

Now, I am not blind to the controversy in suggesting that strategy. But if you have in fact done your very best to work out a solution—and despite your good-faith efforts (see the modification problems I just detailed above) you are still tossed into the foreclosure process—I have no problem suggesting you use the time it takes for the bank to formalize the foreclosure to save as much as you can.

Tax Breaks on Foreclosures

As I mentioned above, through 2012 any foreclosures or short sales of a primary residence that result in a home being sold for less than the mortgage balance are eligible for an important tax break: The amount of the shortfall, which typically is treated as taxable income by the IRS, will not be taxed.

But that does not mean you are free and clear of all obligations.

In certain states, under certain circumstances, a lender or a collection agency can seek a "deficiency judgment" that would require you to repay the difference between the mortgage balance at the time of the foreclosure and the market value of the home. Please understand that just because you "walk away" from the home through a foreclosure, you could indeed still be on the hook for at least a portion of the unpaid balance of the loan. And depending on the state, you could be hit with a deficiency judgment four or five years after the foreclosure! What you may be liable for depends on what type of mortgage you have, and your state. If you have what is called a *recourse* loan, that means the lender, in certain circumstances and in certain states, may have the right (recourse) to sue you for the unpaid portion of the mortgage. If your mortgage is nonrecourse that means the lender doesn't have the right to seek payment for the unpaid balance.

The best investment you can make at this juncture is to talk to a real estate attorney with foreclosure experience so you can understand what may happen to you *after* the foreclosure. Please don't assume that just because you live in one of the nonrecourse states, your loan or the specific nature of your mortgage protects you from a deficiency judgment. (Nonrecourse states that prohibit deficiency for most home mortgages are Alaska, Arizona, California, Minnesota, Montana, North Carolina, North Dakota, Oklahoma, Oregon, and Washington. Please note, other states impose restrictions on lenders' ability to seek deficiency judgments. As I said, retaining a lawyer well versed in your state's foreclosure laws is very important.) While nonrecourse means that you are generally protected from any deficiency judgments, you need to know if your actual mortgage is recourse or nonrecourse. And even if it is nonrecourse you could under some circumstances still be liable for a deficiency judgment. For example, only mortgages for a primary residence are generally protected. Any foreclosure on an investment property or HELOC loans is not protected from a deficiency judgment. And in some nonrecourse states, if the lender was granted the foreclosure through a judicial proceeding it can then seek a deficiency judgment.

I can't emphasize enough how important it is to sit down with a real estate attorney who can spell out the rules and regulations in your state. I want you to go into the process with eyes wide open. Sadly, some people who "walked away" are now finding they must declare bankruptcy after the fact to deal with a deficiency judgment they can't afford.

UNDERWATER BUT YOU CAN AFFORD THE MORTGAGE

For those of you who are underwater on a mortgage but can still afford the payment, your decision involves more than financial issues.

I want to be absolutely clear about what I believe is the right thing to do. If you are 5%, 10%, even 20% underwater, and you can afford the mortgage, I cannot condone walking away. I don't care if rents are cheaper. That mortgage is a legal document; you do not walk away from it out of convenience. If you want out, then sell the home and use your savings to make up any difference between the sale price and your remaining balance. That is what I call being financially responsible.

I also hope that if you are only marginally underwater, you retain the perspective on what your home is. If your family loves that house, if it is the refuge and centerpiece of your family, and you can afford the mortgage, then don't get caught up in its current value. We are most likely through the worst of home price losses.

Enjoy your home for the shelter it provides today, and over time—
it might take ten or more years—you will likely see its value re-
bound.

Now, that said, I do indeed respect that some of you who
bought at the peak of the bubble in the most inflated markets—
Florida, Arizona, and Nevada among them—may now be 50% or
more underwater. And in those instances I understand the rationale of walking away. For example, I have a dear friend who made
a $140,000 down payment on a $700,000 home in Tampa,
Florida, in 2007. She certainly met my stand-in-the-truth test of a
20% down payment. But since then, not only has the value of her
home sunk to $150,000—that is what identical homes are selling
for—but also her association fees have gone through the roof because so many of her neighbors have stopped their payments, or
have already foreclosed. And she's actually lucky; at least her
neighborhood remains safe; I know so many of you who are
deeply underwater are now surrounded by empty homes. That's
not just spooky, it is easy pickings for burglars. So I get it. My
friend ended up walking away and having to declare bankruptcy—
she had a recourse loan. There was no triumph in this. But there
was relief from an awful situation where no one would work with
her to come up with a modification.

The hard truth my friend stood in, and the hard truth some of
you must face, is that it could be decades, if ever, until you will see
home values return to their pre-crash levels in these hardest-hit
areas, especially if your neighborhood and region is currently overwhelmed with foreclosures. In those instances you must dig deep
and decide what is the right financial move for you.

HOW LOAN MODIFICATIONS, FORECLOSURES, SHORT SALES, AND DEEDS IN LIEU OF FORECLOSURE AFFECT YOUR ABILITY TO GET A MORTGAGE IN THE FUTURE

When you do not fulfill your obligation to repay your original
mortgage in full—even if the lender has agreed to a workout—
your credit report will note the underpayment. According to

FICO, the leading resource for credit scores derived from your credit report, a loan modification, short sale, deed in lieu of foreclosure, and foreclosure are all treated the same in terms of your credit score. One is no better, or worse, than the other. Once the underpayment shows up on your credit report it will remain there for seven years. How much it will hurt your score varies; if you had a high score before, it will have a larger impact; if your score was already low, it will have a smaller impact. The impact of this demerit declines over time; it will have less impact six months from now than it does today, and its impact three years from now will be less than two years from now. If you focus on the steps that help your credit profile—on-time payments, for example, and keeping your debt level low relative to your available credit—you can in fact repair a lot of the damage in less than seven years.

While FICO does not differentiate between the various types of loan workouts, mortgage lenders do. I know this might sound a bit crazy when we are talking about walking away from your house, but it is important to understand how your ability to buy another house in the future will be impacted by how you walk away from your current home.

The vast majority of lenders follow the rules laid down by Fannie Mae and Freddie Mac. These two agencies either guarantee or buy up most of the mortgages that lenders make; thus lenders are careful to make sure they follow the guidelines for what qualifies to be bought or guaranteed by either government agency.

If you go through a formal foreclosure, you may need to wait five years to qualify for a new mortgage that is backed by Fannie Mae. The wait can be less if you can document that the foreclosure was due to an "extenuating circumstance," such as a divorce or losing a job. But if you walk away through a short sale or deed in lieu of foreclosure, you may be eligible for a Fannie Mae–backed mortgage in just two years if you have a 20% down payment, or four years for a 10% down payment. This rule presumes you are able to meet all other credit and income qualifications for the mortgage.

LESSON 5. HOW TO REDUCE MORTGAGE COSTS

Despite all the headlines this rash of foreclosures is getting, the truth is that the vast majority of homeowners can in fact afford to stay in their homes—and want to stay in their homes. But those of you who are in this category have a new dream to consider as well. Whereas borrowing as much as possible to buy the biggest home possible was a centerpiece of the old American Dream, for many of you, your new home dream is to get your mortgage paid off as quickly as possible, or to take advantage of the current low mortgage rates and refinance into a less costly loan.

WHEN IT MAKES SENSE TO PAY OFF A LOAN AHEAD OF SCHEDULE

As I explain in great depth in the class about planning for retirement in your 40s and 50s, I think one of the best retirement strategies to put in place is to have your mortgage paid off before you retire. So for anyone who is at least 50 years old and is absolutely sure they will stay in their home through retirement, I am all for accelerating your loan payments so you get the mortgage paid off. If you want to learn more about my reasoning and my recommendations for how to accomplish this, please see pages 196–205.

THE NEW REALITIES OF REFINANCING

For those of you eager to reduce your mortgage costs, today's record low mortgage rates offer an incredible deal. As of late 2011, the 30-year fixed-rate mortgage has an average interest rate below 5%; creditworthy borrowers may be able to grab a rate as low as 4.1%. And a 15-year mortgage has a 3.3% rate.

But to be able to refinance you will likely need to have at least 20% equity in your home. If you don't have that much equity, you will need to bring cash to the deal to reduce your loan amount to the magic 20% level. This is what is known as a cash-in refinance, and in 2011 it accounted for about one-quarter of all refinancings.

I think a cash-in that helps you lock in a lower rate can make tremendous sense if you have the savings to bring to the closing. I do not want you tapping your emergency savings fund for this, nor are you to touch your retirement savings. If you want to do a cash-in, you must have extra savings you can use to pay down your loan to the 80% level.

Whether you are doing a straight refinance or a cash-in refinance, please heed the following.

REFINANCING RULES

Never Extend Your Loan Term

If you have 20 years left on a 30-year mortgage, you are never to take out a new 30-year loan. That will extend your total loan term to 40 years. The goal should always be to maintain or reduce your total loan term when you add the time you have already paid on your current mortgage to the length of the new mortgage. So if you are 10 years into a 30-year mortgage, your refinanced mortgage should be for no more than 20 years. In fact, as I explained earlier, I would root you on if you could handle refinancing into a 15-year mortgage. The whole point is to get the mortgage paid off sooner rather than later.

Calculate the Cost of the Refinancing

There are fees to pay when you refinance. Those can be 1% to 2% or more of the loan amount. Ideally you will pay the fees in cash up front. But if you can't swing that right now, then go ahead and roll the refinancing fees into the new mortgage; yes, your monthly costs will be slightly higher, but if this move does indeed ensure you can get the home paid off faster, and ahead of your retirement, then that's the big-picture goal we need to focus on here. However, you need to understand how long it will take for the lower cost of the new mortgage to offset the fees you paid for the refinance. At Bankrate.com you can use a calculator to compute how many months it will take you to recoup your costs. If you anticipate you might move before then, think twice about the refinance.

Consider a 15-Year Mortgage

The interest rate on a 15-year fixed-rate loan is typically about 0.5% less than the rate on a 30-year. In late 2011 the spread was even greater, about 0.8%. If you are refinancing a mortgage with 20 or more years left, run the numbers to see if you can afford to go with a 15-year mortgage. The 15-year will always have a higher monthly payment than a longer-term loan, but you will spend thousands less in interest payments, and you also have the satisfaction and security of getting the loan paid off sooner rather than later. But don't overstretch to make a 15-year work. This only makes sense if you have the available cash each month to easily handle the payments. And you must still continue to contribute to your retirement savings. If you are in your 30s and 40s I don't think paying off your mortgage should be your highest priority just yet; focus on retirement savings, your emergency fund, and if you want, putting away some money for the kids' college education.

For those of you in your 50s, here's an example of how the 15-year can pay off:

Let's say you took out a $300,000 30-year fixed-rate loan in 2003 at 6.5%. The monthly cost is about $1,900. Now you want to refinance to take advantage of lower interest rates. After nine years you would have a balance of about $260,000 to pay off. If you choose a 21-year loan term (to keep your total payment period at 30 years), your loan payment assuming a 4.1% fixed rate would be about $1,540 a month. So you lower your monthly costs by $360 a month. Pretty good.

Now let's consider choosing the 15-year mortgage instead. At a 3.3% interest rate your monthly payment would be a little less than your current mortgage, $1,833. And of course it is $300 more a month than if you refinanced into a new 21-year mortgage. But remember, with the longer loan you would be paying that $1,540 a month—$18,480 a year—for six years longer than your payments on the 15-year loan. With the 15-year loan, you will not only have the loan paid off six years faster, which can be a huge boost come retirement, but also your total interest payments with the 15-year loan will be about $70,000, compared to $128,000 for the 21-year loan. That's a savings of $58,000.

LOWER YOUR MORTGAGE COSTS
WITHOUT A REFINANCE

If you determine a refinance doesn't make sense for you—maybe you lack the equity, don't have the money for a cash-in refinance, or your credit score won't qualify for a great rate—you can still get ahead on your mortgage. Simply add extra money to your monthly payment. All you need to do is verify with your loan servicing company that the money is to be applied to paying down your principal. This is in fact my recommended strategy if you have any doubt about your job security, or if you do not want to lock in the responsibility of higher payments on a 15-year loan. By sticking with your existing mortgage and just making optional extra payments you have the flexibility to stop those extra payments if the need arises. A table on page 200 in the class on retirement strategies in your 40s and 50s illustrates the advantages of this very clearly.

TIP: Lenders usually have programs that offer to help you speed up your payment process. But there are often fees charged to enroll in such a program, and in my opinion they are a complete waste of your money. The fact is, you can pay off your mortgage ahead of schedule without incurring any monthly fees, by simply sending in a larger payment than is due each month. Ignore those bank come-ons and use common sense.

LESSON 6. THE DANGERS OF HOME EQUITY LINES OF CREDIT

Those of you who have been following my advice for years know that I have never liked borrowing against the equity in your home, especially for expenses that don't qualify as needs. Given that I have asked you to embrace the concept of living below your means but within your needs, I hope it is patently clear why I think it is frankly dishonest to borrow against your home equity. It is often an indication that you are in fact trying to live above your means.

In the immediate wake of the financial crisis, lenders were reducing or terminating outstanding home equity lines of credit (HELOCs). But I bet those of you with ample equity and good credit have recently started receiving new offers to open a HELOC. With the eye of the storm past, lenders are looking for ways to generate revenue, and homeowners with strong financials are a likely target.

And the timing could not be worse. While I have always advised against HELOCs, there is a looming risk tied to what is going on in our economy that makes HELOCs especially dangerous right now.

The vast majority of HELOCs are variable-rate loans. The rate is tied to a financial benchmark, such as the federal prime rate. The prime rate is typically 3 percentage points higher than the federal funds rate that you hear about so often in news reports. As I write this in late 2011, the federal funds rate is near zero, and thus the prime rate is 3.25%. When the prime rate moves up or down, so too does the interest rate charged on a HELOC. Lenders will charge a premium above the prime rate—called the margin—that can add 0.50 to 1.0 percentage point or more to the prime rate. For example, in the fall of 2011 some lenders were offering borrowers with good credit a HELOC at 3.75% (prime + 0.5%). That 3.75 sounds so enticing. In fact, lenders are quick to point out how smart it is to take out a low-rate HELOC and pay off your high-rate debt, such as credit card debt or a car loan. Or to finance a car purchase with a HELOC.

Here's what the lender might not be so quick to explain to you: **Interest rates are going to rise, and when that happens your HELOC payments will go up.** It will likely not happen in the next few months, but over the next few years we will see short-term interest rates controlled by the Federal Reserve rise. Sooner or later rates must rise off their historic lows. That makes HELOCs risky;

with the future direction of the prime rate up, not down, you will likely encounter higher payments. Consider what happened just a few years ago: In May 2004 the prime rate was 4%; by the end of 2005 it was 5%. A year later it was at 7% and by December 2006 it had shot up to 8.25%. Homeowners who had HELOCs tied to the prime rate saw their rate more than double! Take out—and use—a large HELOC and in a few years you may well find yourself stuck paying the line back at a much higher interest rate.

If you fall behind on a HELOC the lender can foreclose on your house. A HELOC is what is known as a secured loan, meaning it has collateral. And that collateral is your home's equity. If you were to get in so much trouble you could not keep up with your HELOC repayments, the lender could foreclose on your home to use the equity to settle your balance due. That is why it never—and I mean absolutely *never*—makes sense to use a HELOC to pay off credit card debt or to pay for a car. Credit card debt is unsecured; if you can't pay it off no one can come take your house from you. But if you transfer the credit card debt to a HELOC you have put your home at risk if you don't keep up with the payments. I also don't think it ever makes sense to use your home to pay for a car; I'd rather you use a regular car loan. In the event you fall behind on a car loan, you risk losing just the car, not your house.

HOME EQUITY LOANS

I also have to say that I am not a fan of a home equity loan (HEL) either. A HEL typically has a fixed interest rate. That indeed will make it more appealing than a HELOC in a rising-rate environment. But the more pressing issue is why you are tapping into your home equity at all. It is a clear signal, in the majority of instances, that you are trying to live beyond your means. My bottom line is that if you are tempted to use a HELOC or a HEL, take that as a warning signal that perhaps you are not standing in the truth of living below your means but within your needs.

LESSON 7. REVERSE MORTGAGES

In the coming years I expect reverse mortgages to become increasingly popular among retirees who are eager to find extra income. A reverse mortgage is available to anyone who is at least 62 years old and owns a home outright, or has a small mortgage balance remaining. If you are married and both spouses are on the home's title, the youngest spouse must be 62 before you can consider a reverse.

With a reverse the borrower can opt to receive a lump payment, or an ongoing payment for a set period of time, or a line of credit in which the home equity is the collateral for the loan. It is literally a way for retirees to live off their homes.

While I think a reverse can make sense in certain circumstances, it is not nearly the win-win it is often made out to be. There are many costs and risks to doing a reverse that you must fully understand.

REVERSE MORTGAGE BASICS

The vast majority of reverse mortgages are loans that are insured by the Federal Housing Administration. The formal name for these FHA-insured loans is Home Equity Conversion Mortgage (HECM). The maximum home value that can be tapped for an HECM is based on home values in your area. The upper limit in 2012 for people living in high-cost areas is $625,500. But that is just a limit used to calculate the benefit you can receive; in fact, no one can receive a payment anywhere near the full value of their home; typically your original loan amount might be 60% or so of your equity.

The percentage of your equity that you can tap is based on a calculation that factors in your age and current interest rates. Your credit score is not a factor.

The younger you are the less you can borrow. For example, in late 2011 a 62-year-old with a fully paid-off mortgage and a home value of $625,500 in a high-cost area might qualify for a maxi-

mum reverse mortgage of about $360,000. A 72-year-old might
qualify for a $396,000 payment. All reverse mortgage payments
you receive are tax-free.

I realize that sounds like a lot of money—it is a lot of money—
but what you must realize is that once you borrow the money
your account begins to ring up interest charges. You never have
to repay a penny while you live in the home. But when you move,
or you die, the loan must be repaid. (If you move into an assisted
living facility or nursing home for more than twelve months you
are deemed to no longer live in your home, and the reverse loan
must be repaid.) And you, or your heirs, will owe the principal
and the interest. Now one great aspect of a reverse mortgage is
that you will never owe more than the value of your home when
you leave, but every penny of the sale could well indeed go to
the reverse mortgage lender to settle your loan—meaning you
or your heirs may not have any equity left when all is said and
done.

Another consideration is the cost. Traditionally, reverse mortgages have been quite expensive. The up-front fees to open a standard HECM reverse mortgage can add up to 10% of the loan
amount. In late 2010 a new type of reverse, called the HECM
Saver, was introduced. It eliminates many of the up-front fees,
though the amount you can borrow through the program is about
15% or so lower than what is available with a standard reverse
mortgage. In both versions you will pay an ongoing annual "insurance" premium of 1.25% of your loan amount.

I have to say that I think reverse mortgages are a potentially
dangerous step for many retirees. It is far too easy to get blinded
by the prospect of receiving much-needed income today and over-
look some important considerations.

Please understand that after you take out a reverse mortgage
you are still responsible for all costs associated with running your
home—the property tax bill, the insurance bill, the utilities, and all
maintenance costs. If you can't afford the upkeep of your home it
makes no sense to do a reverse mortgage. You will just end up having to sell eventually when you realize you can't afford the home,

and whether you have any equity left after the sale depends on the size of the reverse loan that must be settled.

And as I mentioned, a reverse will also impact the estate you leave for your heirs. When you die, the loan comes due. The lender cannot charge more than the value of the home, but every penny of the sale could in fact go to the lender, leaving your heirs without an inheritance. I also want you to know that if your heirs decide they want to keep the home after you pass, they would in fact owe the lender the full value of the loan, even if it exceeds the sale value of the home. For example, if your reverse mortgage balance is $300,000 when you move or die, and the home sells for $260,000, the lender will receive just the $260,000. You or your heirs would not need to come up with another $40,000 to settle the loan. But if your heirs decided they in fact wanted to keep the house, then they would owe the full $300,000.

My recommendation is that you think of a reverse mortgage as a last-resort emergency fund in retirement, not a primary piece of your retirement plan from day one. If money is so tight at age 62 that you think you need a reverse mortgage, my concern is what happens at age 72 or 82? If you tap all your home equity through a reverse at 62 and then at 72 you realize you can't really afford the home, you will have to sell the home, and you may end up giving most or all of the sale price back to the lender to settle up. What will you live on then? I would much rather you base your retirement on other income sources—your savings, Social Security, and a pension. If later on in retirement you need extra income, then you can consider a reverse mortgage, but go in with your eyes open.

You can learn more about reverse mortgages online at www.hud .gov/offices/hsg/sfh/hecm/hecmabou.cfm. You can calculate an estimate of what you might be able to receive from a reverse mortgage at www.reversemortgage.org.

LESSON 8. INVESTING IN REAL ESTATE

Whether you are considering buying investment property today or are wondering what to do with an investment that is now underwater, it is important to understand how very different the rules and regulations are for income property compared to a home you live in as your primary residence.

WHAT YOU NEED TO KNOW BEFORE YOU BUY INVESTMENT PROPERTY

With home values down 30 to 50%—or more—I know that many of you think now is a great time to invest in real estate. I have to say, my experience is that the people who are so quick to see the upside often don't properly prepare for the potential downside. Owning investment property is a risky investment. There is no guarantee the property will rise in value—or rise in time for you to flip or refinance as you had hoped—nor is there any guarantee you will always have responsible tenants. Please do not consider buying unless you have carefully prepared for all the what-ifs:

You must have an eight-month personal emergency fund *plus* a one-year fund to cover the carrying costs on your rental property. If you are going to invest in a rental property your personal emergency fund is not to be a part of your plan. You must have a separate fund that can cover up to one year's worth of mortgage, tax, insurance, and maintenance costs for your property. The biggest mistake I see people make is that they wrongly assume they will always be able to rent out the property, that rental rates will always rise, and that their tenants will treat the property with great care. That is what I would call wishful thinking—and it could lead you down the road of ruin. You must have an ample investment property emergency fund to fall back on.

Real estate must be part of a diversified investment portfolio. I have had too many conversations with people who told me they lost everything in real estate when the bubble burst. They insist they were well diversified because they owned several properties in different neighborhoods. That is not my idea of diversification.

That is owning a lot of the same type of asset. Investing in real estate must be done after you have taken care of your other investment goals. If you are not contributing to your retirement funds you have no business investing in real estate. And if you do own investment property, that is never a reason to stop or slow down your retirement savings.

Understand that you will pay more for financing. If you want to take out a mortgage to invest in real estate, be prepared for an entirely different set of lending rules compared to buying a home for your personal use. Lenders will often insist that your down payment for a real estate income property be at least 30% of the purchase price, and the mortgage rate will also be higher than the rates charged for a home you live in.

There's little help if you fall into financial trouble. All the various federal programs we have in place today to help are only for mortgages used for a primary residence. Investment properties are not eligible for any assistance. That makes perfect sense. Aid should be to help families stay in their homes, not to come to the rescue of investors and speculators.

WHAT TO DO WITH AN INVESTMENT PROPERTY THAT IS UNDERWATER

For those of you who already own an investment property that is currently worth less than your outstanding balance, I want you to carefully consider your options.

If you are just 10% or so underwater and the rental income is still enough to cover your carrying costs, then I would not advise you to sell right now even if your lender agrees to forgive any unpaid mortgage balance. It is important to understand that the IRS will not forgive that shortfall. The valuable tax break that is in place through 2012 that exempts homeowners from owing income tax on the difference between their mortgage balance and their sale price does not apply to income properties. If you sell an income property at a loss you will still be handed a 1099 tax form that reports the difference between the mortgage balance and the sale price as "income" that was paid to you. So let's say you have a

$250,000 mortgage and your property sells for $175,000. Even if the lender agrees to not come after you for the $75,000, that $75,000 will be reported as taxable income to the IRS.

And let's not forget that as a seller you will have to pay the agents' fee—typically 6% of the sale price—and other closing costs. That just adds to your loss at this point.

If you are more deeply underwater, or the gap between the current rent the property can generate and your mortgage is too big a monthly cost, then I ask you to read my advice from earlier in the chapter on how to navigate your way through a short sale or foreclosure.

LESSON RECAP

- Recognize that a home is not a liquid investment.
- Base your housing decisions on the expectation that long-term price appreciation will likely match—or slightly exceed—the inflation rate.
- Consider a rental if you are not sure of your long-term plans.
- If you are considering a mortgage modification, understand the many risks.
- If you are 10% to 20% underwater and can afford your mortgage, stay put or agree to cover the entire mortgage if you want to sell.
- If you want to sell, stand in the truth that you should pay the difference between the mortgage cost and your sale price.
- If you are 40% to 50% underwater, walking away may indeed be the best move—but understand the liabilities if you go this route.

CLASS

5

CAREER

THE TRUTH OF THE MATTER

The American workplace has been undergoing some dramatic changes—general trends that have been playing out over decades and painful contractions brought on by the recession that took hold in 2008. If you are among the nearly 14 million Americans out of work or the more than 8 million getting by with a part-time job as of late 2011, you are feeling the pain of these changes most acutely. But even those of you lucky to have work—and work you love, I hope—must recognize that changes in our economy will present new challenges over the course of your career as well.

The American Dream of the last century seemed to promise jobs for everyone willing to work, a paycheck every Friday. That particular American snapshot, from where we stand today, indeed seems like it comes from a bygone era. In the simplest of terms, we have a far greater supply of workers than we have jobs, and this will not change for a long time. While I believe we have turned the corner in terms of job losses, it could be years before the massive backlog of

people looking for work will find employment. Throughout the first
eight months of 2011 it was a rare month when job growth exceeded 100,000 jobs. That is far less than we typically have during
an economic recovery. But here's what you need to understand: If
new job growth were to stay at that monthly pace it would take
more than a decade for everyone looking for work to find work.
Even if we saw the pace of job growth rise to 250,000 a month the
backlog would still take five years to work down.

Here is the harsh reality: I do not believe we will see a dramatic
acceleration in new job creation. In the private sector, employers
are focused on getting more out of their current workforce—
through technology and longer hours—to meet any pickup in their
business. This is what is known as productivity. You better believe
companies are more interested in boosting productivity before they
begin to hire aggressively, and I expect this trend to continue in the
coming years. And when employers do decide to hire, the reality is
that many will be looking to fill holes with "temporary" contract
workers who work full-time jobs, but without benefits.

The situation in the public sector is even more dire. Given the
political climate in Washington, it's hard to envision any substantial expansion in the federal payroll in the coming years. And the
severe budget deficits and reduced revenues that state and local
governments are experiencing makes it unlikely they will be able to
go on a hiring binge anytime soon. In fact, in 2011 we began to see
sharp layoffs in all public-sector employment.

Adding to this job shortage is the fact that the workforce is
growing older and people are staying in their jobs longer, so there
is less turnover. The Bureau of Labor Statistics reports that the percentage of Americans age 55 and older still working increased
from 29% in 1993 to a record 40% in 2011. And the BLS fore-
casts that trend will continue; it estimates 43.5% of the 55-plus
contingent in 2018 will still be working. Many older workers are
deciding they want—or need—to stay in their jobs past traditional
retirement age—a move I endorse—in order to save more for retirement. That has the potential for creating a traffic jam on the career ladder; it's harder to move up—and make more money—if the
rung above you is still occupied.

Will we see new jobs created in the coming months and years? Of course. Though we will no doubt face ongoing bouts of volatility in the markets, I do believe the worst of the economic slide is behind us. But all that means is that the patient—our economy—is out of the ICU but still has a long slow road of recovery ahead. When it comes to finding work and reaping the rewards of gainful employment in this current economy, I don't think anyone would assert that the American Dream is alive and well. However, I am a firm believer that ingenuity and invention often spring from adversity. And I can tell, even from the calls and letters that come in to my CNBC show, that many of you are figuring out ways to bring about change for yourself. Small businesses are springing up; locally produced food and goods are in demand; people are heading back to school to acquire new skills or to bring more to the job they're in. The American entrepreneurial impulse is strong—stronger now than it's been in years.

I felt it was important to account for work as we try to define the various aspects of the New American Dream because it was built into the American promise of opportunity: Hard work and dedication bring rewards. But there is, of course, no one-size-fits-all advice to be had in this category. You may be rising in your career but find that your job promotion came with more work and no increase in salary; or maybe you are frustrated that despite your strong performance, you haven't gotten a raise in four years and instead are told you should feel lucky just to have a job in this economy; or maybe you are just plain exhausted from having to work two jobs to make ends meet. All of these various states of employment are affected in one way or another by our sluggish economy. It's hard to think of an industry that has been untouched by the recession. And so no matter what your status, this is an opportune time to take stock of your working life.

I've organized the Career Class into three lessons that cover the gamut, in broad strokes:

- Advice for the Employed
- Advice for the Unemployed
- Starting (and Running) Your Own Business

LESSON 1. ADVICE FOR THE EMPLOYED

"Hope for the best; plan for the worst." I put my faith in that credo. You might have heard me repeat it in the context of discussing the need for life insurance, but it is also an excellent guide for how to manage your career in this era of slow economic growth. If you are being honest with yourself you would look at the continuing fallout from the financial crisis—nearly one in five Americans is either unemployed or underemployed as of late 2010—and consider for a moment what if it were you. In fact, that may be the best career strategy for these times: Behave as if a layoff or furlough will happen to you. Hope that it never happens, but if you plan as if it will, you and your family will be well prepared to weather any setback and get back to work as fast as possible.

BUILD YOUR PLAN-FOR-THE-WORST FUND

Yes, I am talking about having an emergency savings fund that can cover up to eight months of your living expenses. Back in 2008, when I began to insist that everyone increase their savings fund to an eight-month cushion, I took a lot of heat. *Why do I have to save so much when everyone else says three months is enough?* you asked me. When I appeared on *The Oprah Winfrey Show* in January 2009 I suggested that families in which both adults were working should experiment and see if they could handle their expenses if they lived off just one income; for individuals my recommendation was to pretend you had a 50% pay cut and see if you could still cover your bills. I knew it would be a stretch, but I wanted everyone to understand what could happen if they faced a layoff. Besides, by making do with just 50% of your current pay you would be able to shovel more—faster—into an emergency fund. Oh, the pushback I got from so many of you! You told me I was being too pessimistic and dramatic. You told me that it was impossible, that you could never live on less than you are living on now. You told me that you had worked for 20 years for your company and there was no way you would lose your job. And then the unthinkable happened. I'm sorry to say, I was right. As of fall 2011, more than 40% of unemployed Americans have been out of work for more than six months, and nearly one-third have been unemployed for more than a year.

That is why I asked you then and I am asking you now to build an emergency fund that could pay your family's bills for at least eight months. Yes, I realize you may collect unemployment benefits, but typically these payouts cover just a fraction of your prior salary. Do not skimp on your savings because you think unemployment insurance will be all you need.

I understand it will take time for you to build up eight months' worth of expenses in your savings account. But don't get overwhelmed and give up before you start: The immediate goal before you is to focus on how you can trim your spending so there is more left over each month to dedicate to your "plan for the worst" fund.

LIVE BELOW TODAY'S MEANS

I hope each and every one of you has uninterrupted career success that brings you a steady stream of raises and promotions. But I never want you to base your current lifestyle on the notion of what you think you might be making years from now. There is no guarantee your salary five years from now will be appreciably higher than it is today. Maybe yes, maybe no. I want you to make financial choices today that are affordable based on what your household income is today, not what you hope it will be in the future.

As an example, let's all remember what was happening with real estate in 2005 and 2006. Buyers were guided into negative-amortization loans or option ARM loans that offered super-low initial rates that wouldn't move higher for three or more years. The standard advice back then—advice I warned people not to heed, by the way—was that it was smart to get one of these loans because you would surely just refinance into a different mortgage before it came time for your mortgage to adjust to a higher rate, or you would be able to sell the house at a nice profit and walk away with money in your pocket. Except it never was a sure thing. And much of the housing crisis we are still dealing with—and will likely be dealing with for years—is a result of the fact that so many people who took out those mortgages and bet they would be able to flip or refinance before the adjustment lost the bet, big-time.

Don't make the same financial bets with your career by living beyond your means today based on the risky assumption that you will be making a lot more in the future. I hope you will be making more. A lot more! And if that is what occurs, then you can revisit your spending when you in fact have that money. But please do not borrow more today than you can honestly afford today. I'd much rather you rent or buy a smaller, less expensive home, or purchase a less expensive car today, than stretch to buy something that you know deep down is an act of living beyond your means.

VACATION STRATEGY

I also want you to think through your vacation strategy. In these very challenging times, when you are being asked to do more than ever before at your job, there is no question that you need a break. My advice is to take every vacation day you are entitled to! Particularly if your employer is unable to give meaningful raises, then time off becomes a valuable currency. Time away from the job is important for your health and important for your family. But I am not giving you permission to spend whatever you want. Your vacation must be an affordable vacation. The cost is not "just" $1,000 or $2,000 or $3,000. That is $1,000 or $2,000 or $3,000 that isn't going into your Roth IRA, your child's 529 college plan, or your emergency fund. And don't you dare take any vacation that you cannot at least pay for up front in cash. There is absolutely no excuse for planning an expensive vacation that you "pay" for by putting it on a credit card because you're not able to pay for it immediately. I don't care if that card charges you just 5% or 10% interest—though let's stand in the truth and admit it, more likely you're paying 15% or higher. Taking on debt for a vacation is an act of financial dishonesty: no ifs, ands, or buts. You are denied! Do you hear me?

I am asking you to balance your vacation dreams against your other financial dreams. How about a less expensive vacation so you still have more to put toward your longer-term goals? I also want to recommend you think about a stay-at-home vacation. Pry yourself free of the BlackBerry or iPhone and make it clear to everyone you work with that you are indeed on vacation and are to be contacted only if there is a true emergency. Then plan every day just as you would a getaway. Yes, you are absolutely allowed to go to the movies and enjoy some meals out; it's okay to spend some money. The goal is simply to spend a whole lot less than you would on a vacation that includes airfare, a hotel, and three meals out every day. If you happen to live in a big city, why not plan a few days doing all the things tourists do but you never seem to have the time for? Some of my most memorable time off is playing tourist when I am at home.

GRAB YOUR FULL RETIREMENT BONUS

Look, you and I both know, big bonuses have become rare in recent years. So tell me this: Why are so many of you turning down a *guaranteed* bonus every year because you aren't being smart with your 401(k)? As I explain on page 169, if your employer offers a 401(k) matching contribution, be sure you are contributing enough to get the maximum match. Do you see my point? That match is a bonus. Many plans offer a 50-cent match for every dollar you contribute, up to a set maximum. For example, if you make $50,000 and your employer offers a 50-cent match on every dollar you contribute up to the first 6% of your salary, that's $1,500 a year in a matching bonus you could be collecting ($50,000 x 6% = $3,000; 50% of $3,000 is $1,500). Yet about 20% of workers eligible for a match do not contribute enough to earn the maximum match. It never makes sense to turn down free money; and in a world where raises and bonuses may be meager, making sure you grab the full matching contribution is crucial. Who knows, at your next job you might not have a 401(k) or maybe your employer will not offer a match. Take advantage of this great deal while you can.

MAKE YOUR CASE FOR A RAISE AND PROMOTION THROUGH YOUR WORK

I ask that you take a clear-eyed look at your attitude toward work and pay. Are you expecting to be paid more because of a sense of entitlement, because you've hung in there year after year, or because you are doing spectacular work?

When I was a financial advisor I often had clients who came to me upset when they didn't receive the raise or promotion they expected. When I asked them why they thought they deserved the raise they often said to me, "Because it's been a year and I am working so hard." Mind you, this was in the early 1980s when we were coming out of a recession. Though the situation was different back then—we were grappling with high inflation—there are some striking similarities between that moment in time and where we are, economically, today. One such similarity: Employers were cautious and conservative in how they spent money, just as they are today.

It wasn't always an easy conversation with my clients, but what I told them back then is the truth I ask you to stand in today: No private-sector employer has to give you a raise. No one is obligated to dole out a bonus. As valued as you are by your employer, the reality is that there are a lot of very talented people who could replace you among the unemployed and underemployed. Please do not think the reason they are out of work is that they aren't as good at their job as you. There are literally millions of extremely talented people who are out of work. The financial crisis and recession didn't merely clean out the deadwood; it took a lot of hardworking, competent, professional workers with it too.

I hope this doesn't cause you to become paranoid and make you afraid of ever asking for a raise or bonus. Here's what I used to tell my clients:

Make those you depend on for a paycheck dependent on you. What you want to do is make yourself so valuable, so close to irreplaceable that your employer is doubly motivated to make sure you are happy in your work, and your pay. When you overdeliver on every part of your job and exceed expectations, you are making your case loud and clear to be compensated for your work. When I wrote *The Money Book for the Young, Fabulous and Broke* in 2005 my advice for 20-somethings was to just put their heads down, work super hard, and not sweat the pay. Build a reputation, make your mark, put in the effort, and you will be on solid ground. That advice applies to all ages today. You must double down on making yourself an absolutely essential piece of your firm's success. That should be your goal at any time, but in these times of economic stress it is imperative. It is how you keep moving forward in a very competitive job market.

I am not suggesting it will protect you from ever being laid off. But I can guarantee you that if you are laid off because your firm is struggling, your reputation will precede you and your manager will likely help your efforts to find a new job by providing a glowing reference. It will also likely put you at the top of the list for being rehired when the company rebounds.

Now that said, I realize at a certain point you may in fact feel your nose has been to the grindstone plenty long enough and you know you have put in the work to merit a raise. Okay, be smart here. Do not request a meeting with your boss, stomp in, and simply state, "I deserve a raise" or "Can I have a raise?"

I want you to be more tactical and frame the conversation by making your expectations clear.

HOW TO ASK FOR A RAISE

Start by preparing a one-page presentation that documents all your accomplishments—exactly how you contributed and continue to contribute to moving your employer's business forward, and how you have delivered specifically for your manager. Make sure your manager has that document at least forty-eight hours before the meeting. Next you need to decide how much of a raise you want. Let's say you want a 5% raise. When you are sitting with your boss, start the conversation by saying, "Given my accomplishments and ongoing contribution to our business model, I would like you to consider a raise of 5 or 10 percent." You make the amount you want the lower of the two choices. In any case, make them no more than five percentage points apart. Now, why do I want you to do this?

This goes back to a lesson I learned when I started out as a commission-based stockbroker in the early 1980s. I was trained to be a professional salesperson to call up clients, and after sharing an investing idea with them, I would ask, "Would you like me to buy five hundred shares or one thousand shares?" The rule was never ask a yes-or-no question, because if they said no there was nothing else I could say. I want you to do the same when discussing your salary with your boss. When you walk in and say you want a raise of 5 or 10%, you have just shifted the conversation about whether you deserve a raise to how big a raise you deserve.

Save Your Raise

If you are living below your means but within your needs, you will not need to use any part of a raise to cover your existing expenses. But you and I both know that if you aren't careful you will soon find your expenses rising to meet your new, higher paycheck. Please don't squander your raise. If you have yet to amass an eight-month emergency fund, I want you to aim to save 100% of your raise. If you already have the eight-month emergency fund taken care of, I want you to aim to still put at least 75% of your raise toward any of your other saving and investing goals or paying off your credit card debt. The balance you can use as needed. So let's say you get a 4% raise. That means that at least 3% must be earmarked for your savings goals. The other 1% is yours to spend. Remember: You are standing in your truth when the pleasure of saving is equal to the pleasure of spending. My suggestion that you save the majority of a raise is not to be taken as a punishment. I am showing you how to realize your dreams.

CHANGE YOUR ATTITUDE BEFORE YOU
CHANGE YOUR JOB

In the first class of this book, I explained that there is rarely a bad situation that can't be improved by a change of perspective. It's not that you can't afford a house; you can afford a less expensive house. The problem isn't that you were turned down for a car loan, but that you were shopping for a car that was too expensive. Change your perspective—and budget—and you can reach your goal. I think that idea is especially timely in how you manage your career.

As we all know, finding a new job is not exactly a snap these days. As I write, there are five job seekers for every job opening. If you are unhappy in your current job, my advice is to take a step back and see how you might be able to make it work for you, so to speak. The truth you must stand in is that in this lousy job market, the job you have is a great job, for it is a job. And I want to be very clear: You cannot afford to walk away from any job today without having another job lined up. I don't care how talented and well connected you are, that is just crazy in this environment. It is infinitely easier to get a new job if you still have an old one. Ignore this advice and down the line you are going to end up saying, "I wish I hadn't." Please don't make that mistake.

That puts it on you to figure out how to turn around a frustrating job situation. If you can't stand your boss, get strategic about transferring to another division. Wish you had more responsibility? Well, come up with ideas for how you can expand your work. Right now your manager is probably overloaded and worried about her career. Ideally she'd be looking out for you, but this isn't exactly an ideal time. So be proactive. Don't just complain that you're unhappy; offer up ideas on new challenges you could take on that would make you happy. And don't tie it to a pay raise. Do the work first, and the pay will follow. That's just the way it has to be in these economic times.

I also want you to think of how you can change your life away from work, to make the work less frustrating. Hobbies. Working out more. Leaving the office a half hour earlier so you have a little more family time before the fire drill of dinner-homework-bedtime. You can fix a lousy job by reducing its impact on your waking hours. Change your attitude, or your perspective, or your priorities, and watch how things fall into place.

What You Must Have Lined Up Before You Voluntarily Leave a Job

- **Another job.** (If you are thinking about starting your own business, please carefully read my advice that begins on page 141.)
- **A 16-month emergency fund.** You read that right: If you don't have a new job lined up before you quit your old job, then you should have a 16-month emergency fund saved up. Why 16 months? Because it can take you that long to find your next job. It's as simple as that.
- **Health insurance.** If you leave a job voluntarily and your next job doesn't provide coverage, or you decide to start your own business, you must make sure you can get coverage elsewhere. If you won't be able to switch over to a spouse's plan, shop for new coverage before you give notice. The cost of insuring a family of four can be $1,000 or more a month. And you want to make sure you have coverage in place before you give notice. You can search for individual policies at ehealthinsurance.com.

LESSON 2. ADVICE FOR THE UNEMPLOYED

Anyone who is out of work must stand in the truth I presented at the beginning of this class. Our slow economic recovery means job growth will remain sluggish and that in turn means we could be facing years during which the number of people looking for work will far exceed the number of job openings. I wish I could tell you that if you can just hold on a bit longer everything will make a big turn for the better and there will be plenty of new opportunities. But, sadly, that is not the truth.

Here are my recommendations for adjusting your career dreams to today's realities:

CUT YOUR SPENDING IMMEDIATELY
ONCE YOU LOSE A JOB

There is a dangerous tendency to just stick with the status quo right after you are laid off. Between your severance, unemployment benefits, and your emergency savings you think you are going to be fine for a while, so you don't feel the need to cut back. But I want to repeat a startling statistic from earlier: Nearly one-third of the unemployed in late 2011 had been out of work for at least one year. That's likely a lot longer than your severance, and even if your state has expanded the amount of time you can receive unemployment benefits during this slow recovery, the payments, as noted earlier, typically will cover just a fraction of your prior salary.

That makes your emergency fund all the more important. In fact, my advice is that every family that is dealing with a layoff should take measures to make their emergency fund last as long as possible. I realize it may be harder to add to your emergency fund when your income is reduced; that's not what I'm suggesting. The goal is to cut your expenses as much as possible, as quickly as possible. Review every expenditure. Spending that you could afford when you had a job is not necessarily spending you can still afford.

How much to cut? Stand in the truth of the job market in your area, and your field. If you know it may take time to find a job—any job—you must be very aggressive in scaling back your expenses right now. Challenge yourself to reduce your expenses so your eight-month emergency fund could last twelve months. If that means getting rid of one of the cars, or scaling back the kids' after-school programs, so be it.

DO NOT DIP INTO YOUR RETIREMENT SAVINGS

As we discussed in "Stand in Your Truth," one of the biggest challenges is to weigh the long-term impact of any financial decision.

Yet often we get so caught up in the moment that we don't stop to think through the impact that decision will have on our long-term financial stability.

This is especially tricky when you have lost a job. You become so focused on just getting by today that you think it is okay to borrow from your future. So instead of leaving your 401(k) growing for your future retirement, you cash it out the minute you are laid off or you chip away at it. You tell yourself you will worry about retirement later; you need to pay the bills today.

I want you to know how very sympathetic I am to the stress of paying the bills when you have been laid off. But I do not want you to touch your retirement savings. As I explain in all three of the Retirement Classes, the truth you must stand in is that your personal savings are going to play a pivotal role in whether you in fact can live the life you want and deserve in retirement. And the only way that will happen is if you leave your retirement savings alone.

MAKE SURE YOUR CREDIT PROFILE REMAINS STRONG

As a job hunter it is your job to impress potential employers, right? You need a résumé that grabs their attention, you need to make an impression during the interview process, and you'll be relying on your references to sing your praises. You also may need your credit report. If you are applying for a job that requires you to handle money in any way, a potential employer will want to make sure you don't have any red flags that might make you a high risk around the cash register or dealing with the company's finances. And even if you aren't applying for a finance-related position your credit report can still be an important factor in whether you get hired. The credit report has become a data point employers like to consider as an insight into your sense of responsibility and stability. If they find a financial mess, it could give them a reason to reconsider hiring you. In today's world, where you are competing against so many other applicants, don't let a shaky credit report keep you from your next job. That means making sure you stay current with all your bill payments.

If you already have some dings on your report and a potential employer asks for permission to have a look, take control of the situation. Give them permission, but tell them the truth behind your credit report. Acknowledge the problems; don't hide from them. I can't guarantee that standing in your truth will get you hired, but I can guarantee you that hiding from the truth and letting a hiring manager find out on his own will likely work against you.

DO NOT GO BACK TO SCHOOL TO AVOID A HARD JOB MARKET

I am all for learning new skills that will help you land a new job. That's a great use of your local community college. But I do not condone going back to school full-time just because you can't find a job. You have to have a better reason for going back to school. My litmus test is pretty simple: If the first time you thought about going back to school was about three weeks after your severance ran out, you are using school as an escape hatch. Here are the questions you need to carefully ask yourself—and answer truthfully—if you are considering returning to school:

• **Am I looking for an excuse to stop looking for a job?** I am not minimizing how difficult—and even depressing—it can be to remain optimistic and positive in your search for work. But I would recommend you adjust your job criteria instead of giving up. As I explain below, one of the realities all job seekers need to accept is that a job that pays less than a former job is better than no job at all.

• **Do I need this degree or certification?** Read that carefully; the emphasis is on "need." If you haven't been told outright by those in a position to hire you that you in fact lack a key skill, then why are you so intent on going back to school? Is it because you know for a fact it will make you a better job candidate in the future, or because you think it's smart to bide your time in school until the job market improves? As I have explained earlier in this class, I think that could be years, not months.

- **Can I afford to go back to school?** You are not to tap your emergency savings if it reduces your cushion to less than eight months of living expenses. And as I just explained, you are not allowed to touch your retirement savings. If you are considering taking out a loan to finance a return to school, please make sure you read the college loan lesson in the Family Class. The advice holds whether you are 18 or 38 or 58: Never take on debt that you will have trouble repaying. And when you are older you need to consider the impact more debt will have on your other financial goals. I do not want you to borrow for school if it means that once you have to start repaying the loan you will stop saving for retirement or delay paying down your mortgage.

GET TO WORK AS FAST AS POSSIBLE, RATHER THAN HOLDING OUT FOR A BETTER OFFER

The longer you are out of work, the harder it becomes to find work. Potential employers worry that your skills may no longer be as up-to-date as those of another candidate who is currently employed.

I know you have no intention of becoming chronically unemployed, but what you may not realize is how your mindset could be keeping you from getting back to work faster:

- **Do not hold out for the same job, and the same pay.** An important lesson in the "Stand in Your Truth" chapter was the importance of dealing with what is real for you today, rather than staying stuck on what you had in the past. That is very relevant in your job search. What you made at your last job, what your responsibilities were at your last job, is irrelevant. To get back to work you must focus on what is real today. A potential employer with so many qualified candidates to choose from does not really need to worry too much about matching your pay and benefits from your last job; all that matters is what the current market rate is for your job. The faster you accept this cold fact the faster you will get back to work. If your friends and colleagues can't give you a sense of what is reasonable pay for the jobs you are seeking, web-sites such as payscale.com and salary.com are a good reference.

If your issue is that you can't find any job opportunities that match your skills or salary range, the solution is to not sit back and wait for those jobs to surface. Remember, the focus must be on getting back to work as fast as possible. If that means taking a job that is "less than" your last job and that pays less, I am telling you to take that job! Please listen to me here: In this job market you simply cannot afford to be patient. You think you'll just give it two more months, then that becomes five months, then a year. And now you have been out of work so long you lose your competitive edge compared to other job seekers who are still working. Having a job today—any job—is far better than continuing to look for a job.

HOW TO DEAL WITH A STEEP PAY CUT

Over the past few years I have been told by many unemployed people that they can't afford to take a lower-paying job because it won't cover all their living expenses. My answer to them is that they are not standing in their truth. I am going to keep saying this: The reality of today's economy is that making something is far better than making nothing. If your last job paid $150,000 and right now you can only find a job that pays $80,000 you must take the $80,000 job. And be happy you have work. If that means your family must reduce its spending drastically, that is your family's truth to stand in. Obviously when you are taking a severe pay cut, trimming the cable bill and eating out less isn't going to solve your shortfall. You may need to move to a less expensive home, in a less expensive part of town. You may need to consider public schools over private schools.

A special note for stay-at-home moms: You and I know that what you do is indeed work, and it is in fact the most important "job" in your family. It is so very important that you understand that what I am about to say to you comes from a place of deep respect: Can your family really afford for you to remain a stay-at-home parent? I know that is what you want. And let me be clear: I know the incredible value and gift you are providing for your family. But I am asking you to open your heart for a few minutes and consider that what your family may need from you right now is income. I am not suggesting you take on a 50-hour-a-week office job. How about something part-time? Maybe something that allows you to work from home? Nor am I suggesting that this be a permanent change, only that extra income might be just what your family needs from you right now. That might be the truth you need to stand in—it might just be the best way you can take care of your family today, given their financial needs.

LESSON 3. **STARTING (AND RUNNING) YOUR OWN BUSINESS**

Being your own boss has long been a dream of many, and I understand how alluring it can be right now. For those of you unable to get hired, launching your own business seems like a great way to get back to work. And I know many of you are tired of the long hours and lack of advancement at your current job; the dream is to put all that time and effort into something that you own for yourself.

MAKING IT WORK

Being your own boss can indeed be a smart, proactive twenty-first-century strategy, given how many of the old advantages of employment have disappeared. If you're not going to receive a pension or retiree health benefits, and if even the hardest working, most valued workers have little job security, working for a corporation doesn't exactly have the same allure as it did in past generations.

However, at the same time I am concerned that many of you may be considering starting your own business as a solution for the fact that you can't find a job, or because you are simply sick of working for someone else. Neither of those is a sufficiently good reason, in my opinion. Starting your own business is not a Plan B.

You do not decide you want to run your own business just because you have run out of patience looking for a job or working for someone else. You better have a passion, an entrepreneurial talent, and a seriously careful financial plan. In my opinion, the best dreamers are, at their core, deeply, deeply pragmatic.

LAUNCHING A BUSINESS: CAN YOU AFFORD IT?

Before you make a move, I would ask you to make a clear-eyed personal assessment and then come up with a business plan.

The Personal Checklist

I am going to assume you have a fabulous business idea and the expertise to pull it off. Passion? Check. But that's not enough to get my approval. You must also show me that you:

- Have an eight-month emergency savings fund.
- Do not have any credit card debt.
- Have a FICO credit score of 700 or higher.

The Business Checklist

If you pass those first three tests, great. Now let's focus on how you will finance the business:

- You have savings (not your personal emergency fund) that can cover up to one year of operating expenses for your business.
- You will not tap your retirement savings, home equity, a college fund, or any asset to pay for your start-up costs.
- You will not use your home as collateral for any personal or business loan.

I know those are some tough restrictions to meet. But listen closely: I have seen so many enthusiastic entrepreneurs not only lose their business, but do horrible damage to their family's financial security when they pour everything into an idea that does not make it. I am a huge cheerleader for anyone who has the dream to be their own boss, but only if the pursuit of that dream does not undermine any of your other dreams.

IT'S NOT A NO . . . IT'S A NOT YET

If you have credit card debt or you don't have enough excess savings to cover twelve months of operating capital for your business, I am not telling you to stop dreaming. I am asking you to move slowly. Keep working at the job you have, or get any part-time work you can so you can get your finances in great shape before you launch your business. Think of this as a high-level athletic competition. If you walk out onto the field in poor financial shape, the odds are you will lose. Spend some time in the start-up gym, doing some financial training, so to speak, and walk onto the field in amazing shape and you will have the stamina to stay in the game much longer, thereby increasing your odds of coming out a winner.

I also recommend that before you move forward on any start-up you become expert in the basic bookkeeping and balance-sheet management that is the key to running a business. I recently stepped in to help a family that was not only deep in debt, but the husband's paycheck was being garnished by the IRS because his wife, who had started a successful home-based business, had not been sending in her required quarterly federal self-employment tax payments. Nor was she making state tax payments. This tends to trip up so many first-time entrepreneurs. Even if you are running a home-based business with no employees, you must pay tax, every quarter. You can hire a small business accountant to help you set up all your tax and payment systems. (Or, if you are a sole proprietor and will simply report your business on Schedule C of your federal 1040 tax return, you can use online tax preparation software such as TurboTax designed for small business tax filing. It will compute your estimated tax payments for the coming year, and print out the forms you will need to file.)

LET'S TALK CASH

I want to take a minute to address those of you who may be thinking of starting a business in which you may often be paid with cash, such as working as a massage therapist or gardener. I hope you are responsible enough to stand in this very important truth: Cash is income, and our country relies on all of us paying our share of income tax to support our public services. To not report cash income and not pay the tax that is owed is dishonest. I am not just talking about breaking the law—that should be enough to stop you right in your tracks—but something that runs even deeper into your values. If you have children, please think about the lesson you are imparting; you are basically letting your children know that you think it's okay to abandon your responsibility as a citizen of this country.

PROFIT AND LOSS

Now, in addition to understanding your tax liabilities, you also need to be able to know your way around a basic profit-and-loss (P&L) financial statement. No idea what that's about? That's the first sign you're not ready to launch a business. There are many books and software programs such as QuickBooks on the market to help you get a grip on the financial and business requirements for a successful start-up. I would also encourage you to check in with your local community college to see what courses might be available. And as I explain later in this class, if you live near a Small Business Development Center (SBDC), check in and see what materials and classes are available to help you learn the basics of being your own boss.

WHERE TO GET THE MONEY TO START YOUR BUSINESS

Ideally you would not need to borrow any money to get going. But I know that may not be feasible. The biggest mistake I see entrepreneurs make is that they get so caught up in their passion that they make a mess of their financial life. Here's what you need to consider before you borrow money:

• **Your personal credit card.** Be very careful about tapping your credit card to cover start-up costs. If you suddenly have a lot more in unpaid credit card bills and it sends your overall debt-to-credit limit higher, your FICO credit score will fall. That could make your credit card issuer nervous enough that it cuts your credit limit, sending your FICO score down even more, and could cause the interest rate on new charges to jump higher. All of that can have all sorts of repercussions throughout your family's financial life; you'll pay more for a car loan, and it could impact your insurance rates. It would also hurt your ability to get a business loan; what lender wouldn't look at your personal finances to gauge your creditworthiness as a business owner?

Let's face up to what could happen if your business doesn't make it and you want to get a job working for someone else. If your spending on your business caused you to fall behind on your credit card payments, that could show up as a ding on your credit report; as I explained earlier in this class, potential employers often will check your credit report when considering your job application. You can't afford for them to see any reason not to hire you.

The best way to keep your FICO credit score strong is to make sure that your total monthly balances are just a small fraction of your overall credit lines. There's no magic formula to what FICO deems ideal, just that a 10% debt-to-credit-limit ratio is better than 20% and 20% is better than 30%, etc. I understand you may want to tap your credit lines in the early months of getting your business rolling, but you are to never let your balances exceed 30% of your overall available credit lines. Any higher and you could run into trouble being able to pay it back promptly; it may also set off alarms at the credit card companies.

• **A business credit card.** Please be extra careful here. Credit card issuers have actually stepped up their offers for "professional" cards of late. Not because they are committed to supporting small business, but because these cards are not covered by the 2009 credit card reform legislation. So all the important protections you now have with a personal credit card are not covered when you use a business card.

You also need to understand that if you were to fall behind on your business card payments, or default on them, it can be reported to the credit bureaus and will impact your personal credit report and credit score. Do not for one minute think that business is business and personal is personal.

If you decide that a business card is a good deal, I want you to treat it as if it were part of your "personal" credit. My advice that your monthly balances not exceed 30% of your overall credit limits includes your business card. Do not look at your business card debt as "separate" from your family's credit situation. Treat it all as one pot, so you will not allow yourself to become overextended. Let's be real here: If you go crazy with spending on a business card it will ultimately cause plenty of financial pain for your family.

• **Family and friends.** In the Family Class, I address myself to those who are asked to help a family member in need, but in this case, I would recommend you read those passages (see page 66) in order to understand the dynamic and what you are really asking of relatives and friends when you ask them to loan you money or invest in your start-up. It is dishonest and manipulative to ask someone who cares about you to give you money if you know they truly cannot afford it. And you should never—and I do mean never—ask anyone to cosign a loan that would put their home or any other assets at risk. Chasing a dream that could ruin a loved one is in no way a dream I can endorse.

• **A bank or credit union loan.** You should by all means sit down with your local bank or credit union and ask them what their loan programs are for start-up businesses. But what you are likely to hear is that they won't give you a business loan unless you have a year or two of operations under your belt—and you can show you have positive cash flow. You will also likely need a strong credit score and proof that you have money of your own invested in the business, what is known as equity. You will also need collateral for the loan. You are never to use your home as collateral. Absolutely never—do you hear me? It is one thing to lose your business, but do you really want to lose your home at the same time? For that is what will happen if you can't repay the loan.

• **Start-up grants and microloans.** Okay, now finally some upbeat news: There are indeed resources to help small business start-ups. Locate the economic development divisions of your local and state government and ask for contacts that can help you figure out whether there are any government grants and subsidies to help you launch your business. I also highly recommend you find a regional Small Business Development Center (SBDC) that you can consult with. SBDCs are nonprofit organizations—often they are housed within colleges—that provide training and assistance to small business owners of all sizes. Through an SBDC you can learn about the Small Business Administration's microloan program. The SBA does not make loans directly; rather it offers guarantees to lenders who make the loans. There are many different types of SBA-backed business loans, but most of them require you to have a viable business up and running for a few years. The microloan program is more flexible. In 2011 the maximum loan amount was increased to $50,000.

Go to The Classroom at www.suzeorman.com: There you'll find the link to the SBDC page on the Small Business Administration's website. Or find local SBDCs at win.bplans.com/sbdc.

A FEW WORDS ABOUT MICRO LENDING

Given how picky conventional lenders have been the past few years, I think one of the best opportunities to land financing for a start-up is through a private micro-lending program. Many of these programs are currently run on a local—rather than a national—level. One way to find programs in your region is to do a quick web search; simply type your hometown's name along with the term "small business micro lending" into your search engine. And be sure to ask around—the nearest SBDC is always a good resource for local micro lenders that specialize in connecting lenders and borrowers in your town.

These micro-lending programs can be a fabulous way to secure a small loan for your young business. But please proceed with care. Each organization has its own rules on qualifying for a loan and provides guidance on how to borrow manageable sums. What's great is that loans tend to be short-term (two to five years) and at a fixed interest rate. A fixed-rate loan is much better than using a variable-rate credit card to fund your business. But micro-lending loan rates can still be as high as 15% or so. Top-notch micro lenders will be sure to work closely with you to show you your monthly loan payments; it is always wise to borrow less if that means you will have more confidence you can make the payments.

RUNNING YOUR OWN BUSINESS

Managing your business has never been harder. But there is also great opportunity. If you have an innovative product or idea, or can deliver your service for less than other businesses, potential clients will be interested in listening to your sales pitch. When their business is great they are less inclined to make changes; why fix what's not broken? But in today's economy, with businesses laser focused on wringing out more productivity and searching for every and any competitive edge, you might actually have an easier time getting new clients.

That said, it would be naïve to suggest this is not the hardest of times for many small businesses.

Here is what you need to consider before deciding to expand or close down:

WHEN TO EXPAND YOUR BUSINESS

One of the hardest decisions any business owner must make is when to take the plunge and expand. We've all heard the saying,

"Grow or die." But the stakes are so high right now; overextend yourself in a very challenging economy and you could lose everything. I want to be clear that I am a big believer in growing your dreams. But only if the time is right.

My advice is to always trust your gut. Not your accountant who tells you the numbers look good, or your financial advisor who shows you compelling spreadsheets of what your wealth could potentially be if it all works out.

There really is no such thing as a wrong time to launch or grow a business, as long as you do it responsibly. At the website of *Inc.* magazine is a wonderful slide show of now-iconic U.S. firms such as Walt Disney, UPS, and Domino's Pizza that in fact got their start during a recession, often with nothing more than personal savings or small personal loans to fund the start-up. Yes, they are huge global firms now, but they too got their start as small businesses. Type "Inc 17 recession success stories" into your browser's search box and prepare to be inspired.

IF IT DOESN'T FEEL RIGHT, IT ISN'T RIGHT

Doing something because you think you should—whether it is loaning money to your cousin or expanding your business—is not standing in the truth. You are only to take action when you feel deep down in your bones that it is the right and honest move for you. If the thought of expanding your business makes you queasy, you should be cautious. I am not talking about the butterflies that settle in when you are excited or nervous. But if you are waking up at night with worry, listen to what your body is telling you. If your spouse or partner does not think this is the right move, right now, listen to that as well. There is no business that is more important than respecting the love of your family.

I've probably turned down ten times as many business opportunities as I have accepted. Not because they were bad ideas. In fact, some of my closest friends and family have told me more than a few times that I was crazy to have walked away from deals that would have paid me quite well. But I have always listened to my gut. If I do not literally feel that a decision is right for me, right now, no matter how much money is involved, I simply say no.

I am all for expansion, but one problem that sinks many expansion plans is an assumption that the next store or the next client will automatically pay off. There is a tendency to forget that if you are physically expanding your operations the expansion comes with fixed new costs, and it may take months, if not years, to earn the extra revenue that fully covers the expenses. Moreover, if your expansion includes hiring more employees, you need to think through how many months you may need to pay that salary—and those benefits—before the new business starts seeing positive cash flow that helps you cover your extra payroll expenses.

None of that is meant as a reason to not expand. But I want your expansion to be lasting. Not a three-month or six-month "mistake" that ends up jeopardizing your hard-won success to date.

How do you know if you are financially ready to expand? For starters, you must have at least twelve months' working capital saved up to pay for your expansion. This is in addition to the twelve months' working capital for the expenses of your existing business. In other words, before you expand you must have an extra cushion of working capital to help you pay for the expansion as it gets off its feet.

Given the success of your existing business you will now also have more options to borrow to fund your expansion. Please be very careful. You are never to borrow against your personal assets. So no second mortgages or home equity lines of credit. Losing your business is bad enough; losing your home on top of that would be tragic. Any bank or credit union that will extend you a business loan is indeed going to ask for collateral; likely that will be assets of your existing business. I recommend you sit down with a trusted accountant or financial business advisor and carefully run through all of your financial statements and projections for your expansion. You want to leap only when you feel confident you can land on your feet.

WHEN TO CLOSE YOUR BUSINESS

All business is cyclical. There are ups and downs. Opportunities and setbacks. Yet the down cycle brought on by the financial crisis in 2008 has been especially brutal for many of you, and has not yet fully loosened its grip. When nearly one in five Americans is either out of work or just getting by with a part-time job, any retail business is going to feel the pain. And those of you running a business-to-business operation have seen your bottom line suffer as your clients have scaled back their own operations.

Standing in Your Truth in Business

We are all hoping things get better soon, much better. But hope is not a viable business plan. I can imagine how hard it is to contemplate closing down a business that you started, nurtured, and invested so much hope in. I do not for one minute minimize the frustration and heartache you must feel whenever you stare at the red ink and ponder letting go. But letting go of a business that is no longer able to support itself—and your family—may be the smartest and bravest business decision you ever make. From my vantage point, it takes far more courage and intelligence to walk away than it does to stay. I am asking you to call upon every lesson you learned in the "Stand in Your Truth" class and ask yourself if it is time to let go of a struggling business.

Here are some of my warning signs that you can't afford to keep a business going. If you have taken any of these steps, or are contemplating any of these moves, please stand in your truth that it is time to close down your business.

- **You have begun to use your family's personal emergency fund to cover your business expenses.** What will you live on if after depleting your family's savings the business has still not turned around?
- **You are tapping into your retirement savings.** This is a dangerous and costly mistake.

- **You are tapping a HELOC.** Losing your business is hard enough. Don't put your family's home on the line as well.
- **You are paying only the minimum due on your credit cards, while adding more new purchases to your unpaid balance.** That is a hole that will be hard to dig your way out of, and as I explained earlier in this class it will set off a cascade of costly consequences.
- **You have not paid yourself a dime in six months.** You are essentially working for free while your debt load increases.
- **You are asking a family member to cosign a loan or give you money that jeopardizes their security.** It is entirely dishonest to knowingly weaken another person.

If any of these signs apply to you, I am asking you to wake up to the truth. Please do not keep throwing good money after a bad business that is no longer viable. In retrospect this is a decision that will allow you to say, "I am glad I did," rather than "I wish I hadn't."

Closing Down a Business Responsibly

If you decide the strongest act right now is to close your business, please take care in winding things down.

As soon as possible, let your employees know what you are contemplating. It is an act of respect that will last a lifetime. You cannot control the fact that your business has reached an impossible impasse, but you have absolute control over how you treat your employees during this difficult time. Every extra week or month you give them not just to look for another job but also to beef up their savings and reduce their expenses is time you have given them by sharing your business's truth.

Then turn to the practical steps involved in closing down a business. Depending on your business structure, you may need to notify your state and local governments that you are no longer in operation. If you had employees, the IRS expects you to pay any payroll tax still owed, and you will need to let the IRS know of your plans to stop operation. Your accountant will be able to guide you through the paperwork. At the same time, closing down doesn't absolve you from paying outstanding bills. If you can't see your way to making good on those debts, do not run or hide. Hire a bankruptcy lawyer to help you stand in your truth. I do not bring up the topic of bankruptcy lightly. It is indeed a serious step with serious repercussions. But closing your eyes and hoping no one will "come after" you for unpaid bills or taxes is not standing in the truth.

At the website nolo.com you can find solid basic information on what you will need to take care of to properly close down a business, as well as a "Bankruptcy Center" that is a great starting point for understanding the ins and outs of that process.

And I want you to listen to me: When one door closes, another opens. This business is ending. That does not mean your life is ending. Nor does it mean there cannot be another business dream in the future. You are doing what is right for you—and your family—today. Be proud of your strength. And use that strength to propel you forward into your next career.

LESSON RECAP

FOR THE EMPLOYED

- A large emergency fund has never been a more important career management tool.
- Make sure you grab every dollar offered in a 401(k) match.
- Never leave a job without another job lined up or a significant amount of savings that can sustain you for two years.
- Raises are not an entitlement. Make your case by helping propel the business forward.

FOR THE UNEMPLOYED

- Do not wait for the best job; take the best option that you have today.
- Set your salary demands based on the current marketplace. What you made at your last job is not relevant.

- Accept that to "afford" a lower salary, your family may need to reduce its spending dramatically, including moving to a less expensive home.
- Going back to school must be based on a clear-eyed strategic assessment, not merely the fact that you are tired of looking for work or hope to "wait out" the bad job market by going back to school.

FOR ENTREPRENEURS

- Have large cash reserves before you launch a start-up: an eight-month personal emergency fund and a separate business savings account equal to twelve months of your anticipated operating costs.
- Keep your overall credit card balances (personal and business) below 30% of your outstanding credit limits.
- Carefully consider your expansion plans. Trust your gut on what is the right move for you.
- Stand in the truth if your business is not able to produce the revenue you need to be self-sustaining. Closing down a business is a sign of strength; going deep into debt—especially tapping personal assets such as your home equity—is the worst career move you will ever make.

A Note About the Retirement Classes

The rules of retirement planning—and living in retirement—are so critical and so complicated that I could not limit the information to just one class. Therefore, I have divided the subject into three separate classes aimed broadly at three different stages in life:

- **Retirement Planning in Your 20s and 30s.** This class provides lessons on how to make the most of your most valuable asset: your age!

- **Retirement Planning in Your 40s and 50s.** This class covers all the mid-course fine-tuning you must make at this critical juncture to ensure you will indeed reach your retirement dreams.

- **Living in Retirement.** This class includes steps current retirees can take today to make the most of their money amid current record-low interest rates.

I encourage you to jump right to the Retirement Class that addresses where you are as of today. But I also hope you will circle back and read the other chapters as well. As I shared in the Family Class, the more we start talking to our loved ones about money the stronger we will all be. Reading the other Retirement Classes can be a way to start important conversations. It's also a way of preparing yourself for what lies ahead—and a way to educate yourself about what your children and their children might be up against too.

The Money Navigator
A Special Offer for Readers of The Money Class

Mark Grimaldi is the chief economist and portfolio manager of the highly respected *Navigator Newsletters,* monthly newsletters that offer information on the economy and investment advice for no-load mutual funds, ETFs, and 401(k)s. Mark has an uncanny record: He accurately forecast the bursting of the housing bubble, the economic recession, the great gold rush, and other market milestones. I am an admirer of Mark's work, so I was thrilled by the idea that together we could offer something special for readers of *The Money Class* who are interested in learning more about ways to invest.

In The Classroom at www.suzeorman.com you will find a link and instructions to activate a free one-year subscription to *The Money Navigator* newsletter. Enter "financial freedom 2" as the gift code to activate your free trial subscription. This online newsletter includes Mark's recommendations of no-load mutual funds and ETFs that invest in dividend-paying stocks. It will indicate what advice to follow depending on your age and where you are in your retirement planning—just as I've organized the retirement information in this book—and will help you build the right portfolio for you. To learn how to enter The Classroom, see page xv of this book.

CLASS

6

RETIREMENT PLANNING

GETTING GOING IN YOUR 20S AND 30S

THE TRUTH OF THE MATTER

If you are in the early stages of your working life, the notion of retirement will no doubt seem like a hazy point on some distant horizon. Your ideas about retirement are probably shaped by your grandparents' golden years or maybe even your parents' if they have been lucky enough to reap the benefits of decades of labor and can comfortably transition out of their working lives. I have to tell you, your retirement will likely look very different than that of your parents and your grandparents. The concept of retirement in these days of the New American Dream is most definitely changing, no matter if you're in your 20s or your 60s. But even as I am asking you to let go of assumptions about your postwork life, I need you to understand that there is one absolute, bedrock ground rule that will not change, no matter what is happening in the economic climate: You must begin planning for retirement from your first day on the job. Do not squander precious time because you can't wrap your head around the concept of giving up money now for some theoretical notion of a life of leisure, half a century away. Let me show you why retirement planning needs to be a part of your agenda right here, right now.

The first truth to accept: You and you alone will be responsible for the quality of your life in retirement. If you think that the government, your employer, or any system currently in place is going to take care of you financially, you could not be more wrong if you tried. Let's start with what is going on at work. Thirty years ago, 62% of private companies that provided a retirement benefit did all the heavy lifting by giving employees an old-fashioned pension. Employees didn't have to save any money on their own, or figure out how to invest the money. The corporation did all that work and when you retired you were entitled to your pension. Simple as that.

Today, just 10% of private companies have only a pension as their retirement benefit. Instead, we've become a 401(k) nation: 63% of private-sector corporations that offer a retirement plan only offer a 401(k). Another 27% of employers offer a combo of a pension and 401(k). That means 9 out of 10 firms have shifted some or all responsibility for retirement planning onto your plate.

The story is a bit different in the public sector. Many government and municipal employers do indeed offer an old-fashioned pension. But as if I have to point this out, federal, state, and local entities are struggling to come to terms with some very serious budget shortfalls. And the massive costs of providing old-fashioned pensions is a big expense that is coming under a lot of pressure. While pensions that have been promised to current workers will be honored, what we are already seeing is that new employees are increasingly being directed into a 401(k)-like plan rather than a pension, or are being asked to contribute a portion of their salary into the pension. The bottom line here is that even if you are a public-sector employee, chances are you too will soon be required to take more responsibility for your retirement security.

And it's not exactly a fun or easy task. Even if you appreciate the need to be saving today for your retirement security, I understand the scars that have been left by the financial crisis and bear market. Unlike your parents and grandparents, who have also lived through profitable bull markets, those of you in your 20s and 30s have no muscle memory of what it feels like when markets rise. Being told a secure future depends on staking a lot of money—your money—on a system that you don't have much faith or trust in is a tall order.

And let's talk about Social Security for a moment. There's actually some good news here. I know that many younger adults are convinced they will never see a penny from the system, given all the ominous talk about Social Security "going broke." That's just a lot of fearmongering. Please listen to me very carefully, for I want you to be in possession of the facts: If we don't do anything to "fix" Social Security before 2037, we will run into a situation in which the system cannot pay out 100% of the benefits that are promised today. But that does not mean the system will pay out zero either. The fact is, benefits would basically have to fall by about 25%. In other words, beneficiaries would get about 75% of the benefit they are being promised today. Granted, a 25% or so reduction isn't exactly cause for celebration, but it's a long way from nothing. And if Washington ever decides to get serious about "fixing" the problem, there are some very reasonable options that aren't nearly as dramatic or horrible as the fearmongers would have you think. Social Security is most definitely in need of tweaking, and yes, on some level those tweaks will effectively reduce the benefit you receive, but the benefit is not going to evaporate completely. Social Security will be there for you, though for some of you it may be at a reduced benefit from what is promised today.

But if you want to keep thinking Social Security won't be there for you, I see that as good news too. As much as I want you to understand what's really going on with Social Security, I am sort of glad you are skeptical about others providing for you in retirement. That should motivate you to get started on saving on your own. Let's agree, then, to think of Social Security as what it was always meant to be: a safety net. It will pay out something. For you, it will be a nice income stream to add to your own savings. A side dish, not the main course. Consider that the average benefit for a retiree today is about $1,200 a month. The average benefit when you retire will of course be much higher given the path of inflation, but if you are here in my class we both know that the inflation-adjusted equivalent of $1,200 today in 40 or 50 years will not be the entire solution for your retirement dreams. So go right ahead, you have my full permission to assume Social Security isn't going to exist for you. That should be plenty of motivation to focus on your 401(k) and IRA.

All that said, I understand how easy it is to put retirement planning on the back burner, especially when it is decades away and there are more immediate priorities—like paying this month's bills. I know what you're thinking, because I've heard it before: You tell yourself that you'll just save more down the line when you're making more. If that is the kind of thinking you're indulging in, then you need to accept this truth: As you get older, saving for retirement becomes harder, not easier. This particular law of money is very simple: The more you make, the more you spend.

Just ask your parents, or an older friend or colleague. As you get older you will likely find yourself in the middle of a financial juggling act. Should your money go for the mortgage or the college fund you want to start for your young children? Speaking of college, you probably are still paying your student loans off. What about helping your parents, who have also been lousy at saving? And a vacation—*you need a vacation*—and new clothes! The list goes on and on—trust me, there will always be a long list of needs and wants competing for your dollars as you get older and your life gets more complicated.

Most of us, when we're young (and some of us when we're not so young . . .), opt for the immediate gratification of spending, which knocks retirement saving down the list of our so-called priorities and then we find ourselves in a horrible bind. I've seen this happen time and again: Just as you make the turn into your 50s you suddenly wake up and realize the finish line is fast approaching. That's when the panic sets in. You realize that your years of neglect probably means you won't be able to retire when you want, with the money you need. You desperately try to make up for lost time, but your money is already committed elsewhere and long-held habits are hard to change. I implore you: Learn this lesson before it's too late. Retirement planning takes time and commitment—and it is never, *never* too soon to start. That is more true now than it ever was before.

I happen to think that those of you in your 20s and 30s could be the big winners in the coming decades. You have just lived through some very unsettling times. We all have. But the big advantage you have is that you don't have big losses to make up for or years of mistakes to overcome. And you have a great deal of time to make your dreams into reality. Use your time wisely, stay strong and committed to living in the truth, and I am absolutely confident you can have everything you dream of.

I have organized this Retirement Class into four lessons:

- Time Is Your Greatest Asset
- Retirement Accounts Explained
- How Much You Need to Save for Retirement
- Investing Your Retirement Money

LESSON I. TIME IS YOUR GREATEST ASSET

The single biggest favor you can do for yourself right now is to start saving for retirement. When you are young you can take advantage of the one resource you have in abundance: time. The longer your money has to grow, the more money you will have when you reach retirement. I wasn't surprised to see a recent survey that asked people in their 50s what their biggest regret was when it came to retirement planning. The resounding answer: not starting earlier. Standing in your truth is often an exercise in imagining your life years from now and knowing you will be in a position to look back over your choices and say, "I am glad I did," rather than "I wish I hadn't." Please take the lead from those 50-year-olds who say they wish they hadn't waited so long to get serious about saving for retirement. Right now is when you write the script of your future. Commit to saving. You will be so glad you did. The fact is, the sooner you start, the less of your own hard-earned income you will need to put aside to reach your retirement dreams.

Let's say at age 25 you start saving $416 a month for retirement in a Roth IRA. That works out to $5,000 over the course of a year, which in 2011 was the max annual contribution at your age. And let's assume you keep saving that $416 a month all the way until age 67 and your average annual rate of return is 6%. Why 67? Currently, that is the age at which you will be entitled to full Social Security benefits. If you were to start saving for retirement at age 25 under these terms, at age 67 you would have about $950,000 saved.

Now let's go with your theory that you can afford to wait and you start saving later on. Let's say you delay your retirement savings until age 45. If you invest the same $416 a month and earn the same average annualized 6% rate of return, you will have about $225,000 at age 67. The twenty years of lost time have cost you $725,000!

Another reason I want you to appreciate the value of getting started earlier is entwined with why I have used a 6% average annualized rate of return in the example I just ran through. Years ago, when I was first writing books for your parents, I used a 10% or 12% annualized rate of return, because in those times the economy and our markets were producing gains that strong. In fact, the long-term average annualized rate of return for U.S. stocks going back more than 80 years is right about 10%. But you and I are standing in the truth of what is real going forward, rather than wishing for what we would like to happen. And I think using a 6% annualized rate of return is an honest reflection of what a well-diversified portfolio might return in the coming years, based on the fact that our economy is not likely to grow as fast. So if we plan for lower returns, getting an early start on saving becomes even more important than ever. It's just another way you have to do more of the heavy lifting; when the markets were gaining 10% or 12% a year they did a lot of the "work" for you. At half that pace, your future retirement stash is going to rely more on what you manage to save.

> **Go to The Classroom at www.suzeorman.com:**
> To figure out what your retirement savings could be if
> you get started today and keep saving until you are ready to re-
> tire, use the Compound Interest Forecaster in The Classroom at
> my website. Please stand in the truth and use an expected rate of
> return of no more than 6%.

LESSON 2. RETIREMENT ACCOUNTS EXPLAINED

I want to make sure we are all on the same page about the different types of retirement accounts you can put money into in order
to fulfill your dream of retirement. I have indeed covered these topics in great detail in prior books. If you are already up to speed on
how 401(k)s, 403(b)s, and individual retirement accounts (IRAs)
work, please jump ahead to the next lesson. For everyone else,
here's a quick rundown of what you need to know:

RETIREMENT PLANS OFFERED BY EMPLOYERS

Many of us have access to a retirement plan at work. They have
many different names, but essentially they all work in the same
way. The most common workplace retirement plans are 401(k)s,
403(b)s, 457s, and the Thrift Savings Plan.

A 401(k) is offered by for-profit companies. A 403(b), also
known as a tax-sheltered annuity (TSA), is a retirement plan for
certain public-sector employees such as teachers, as well as some
nonprofit workers. The 457 plans are offered to government employees and can also be used by nonprofits as well. The Thrift Savings Plan (TSP) is offered to federal civilian employees as well as
members of the military.

The basic structure of all of these employer-based plans is similar: You contribute a portion of your salary into a personal retire-

ment account held at your place of work. Some employers add a matching contribution and some do not.

In 2012, the maximum annual amount allowed by federal law that you may contribute to a 401(k) if you are under 50 is $17,000. (This amount is adjusted annually, when necessary, to keep pace with inflation. Check with your plan at the end of October to find out if the limit will be raised for the coming year.) Your employer has the right to set an even lower limit. For example, if your employer allows contributions equal to 10% of your salary, and you make $40,000, your contribution will be limited to $4,000.

Your contributions lower your taxable income. Money you invest in a company-sponsored retirement plan reduces your taxable income for that year. So, for example, if you make $60,000 and you put $10,000 into a 401(k), your taxable income drops to $50,000.

Your money grows tax-deferred while it is invested. You owe no tax as long as your money stays inside your retirement plan. That is, your money grows tax-deferred. There is a big difference between tax-deferred and tax-free, so I want to make sure you understand this completely. Tax-deferred means that you will eventually owe taxes on the money, just not now. Tax-free means you owe no tax. But make no mistake, the tax-deferred benefit is indeed valuable. Allowing your money to grow over decades without having to pay taxes each year is a big deal.

RETIREMENT PLAN WITHDRAWAL RULES

Once your money is invested in a company retirement plan you will want to leave it untouched until you are at least 59½. That's the age when the federal government says it's okay to start making withdrawals. If you want to withdraw money before that age you will have to pay a 10% early withdrawal penalty. (One exception is if you leave the employer where your 401(k) is and you turn 55 or older in the year you left service; in that case you can make withdrawals in any amount you want from that account without owing the 10% penalty. Please note, however, that this exception does not apply to IRAs.)

Any money you withdraw from your traditional 401(k) will, however, be subject to ordinary income tax. Through the 2012 tax year, ordinary income tax rates range from 10% to 35%, based on your income.

Some employers now offer a Roth 401(k), in addition to a traditional 401(k). I explain Roth 401(k)s in greater detail later in this chapter.

NON-WORKPLACE RETIREMENT ACCOUNTS

Whether you work for a company or not, you are eligible to contribute to an individual retirement account (IRA). There are two broad types of IRAs: traditional IRAs and Roth IRAs.

A traditional IRA works much like a 401(k). Based on your income, you may be able to make a tax-deductible contribution, and your IRA money grows tax-deferred while it is invested. When you make withdrawals in retirement you will pay income tax. Again, in most cases if you withdraw money before you reach age 59½ you will owe a 10% penalty in addition to the regular income tax owed on all withdrawals. Please note that all traditional IRAs are eligible to be converted to a Roth.

In 2012 you can contribute up to $5,000 to an IRA if you are younger than 50. Married couples can contribute a total of $10,000, as long as at least one spouse has earned income of at least $10,000.

You can make a contribution to a deductible IRA if:

- You have access to a retirement plan at work and your income is below $68,000 ($112,000 for married couples that file a joint tax return);
- You don't have an employer-based retirement plan (there are no income limits in this case); or
- One spouse has access to a employer-based retirement plan but your joint income is below $183,000.

NONDEDUCTIBLE IRAS

If you do not meet the deductibility rules, you can still contribute to an IRA. The only difference is that your contributions will not be deductible, so you will not get a break on your income tax return for that year. But your investment earnings still get the same advantage of growing tax-deferred until you start making withdrawals in retirement.

ROTH IRAS

If you have been following my advice for years, you are well aware that I think a Roth IRA is the best retirement account you can have.

A Roth IRA does not allow you to claim any tax deduction for your contributions. You invest money that has already been taxed (after-tax income). As a result, in retirement your withdrawals will be 100% tax-free—yes, *tax-free,* not tax-deferred. No income tax, no capital gains tax. As long as you wait until you are 59½ to withdraw earnings on your original contributions and you have had the account for at least five years, there will be no tax on any of it. Your contributions can be withdrawn at any age, any time you want, without a penalty or income tax.

The ability to have tax-free income in retirement is the most compelling aspect of the Roth IRA. In the coming years I expect tax rates to rise. If that comes to pass, having tax-free income will become even more valuable.

Beyond the tax issue, the Roth IRA gives you other valuable benefits. There is no required minimum distribution (RMD) for a Roth IRA. If you do not need the money in a Roth when you're retired, you can leave the account untouched. With a traditional IRA, Uncle Sam insists that you begin to make withdrawals (RMDs, in IRS-speak) after you turn 70½. A Roth can also be a backup emergency fund. Because your contributions are made with after-tax dollars, you are free to withdraw them (though not the earnings on them) at any age without incurring taxes or penalties. I want to be clear: Your goal should always be to leave every penny in your Roth IRA untouched until you retire. Your Roth should not take the place of an emergency fund, but it can serve as a backup in case your primary emergency fund isn't enough to cover your needs in a true emergency.

Roth contribution limits are the same as those of a traditional IRA: In 2012 you can contribute a maximum of $5,000 to a Roth IRA. Married couples can contribute a total of $10,000 (again—as long as at least one spouse has earned income of at least $10,000).

Anyone can invest in a Roth—2010 brought this welcome change in legislation. If you meet the income limits (see below), you can invest directly in a Roth. If your income exceeds the limits, I explain below how you can still benefit from having a Roth.

Income Limits for Direct Investment in a Roth IRA

In 2012, if you are single and your modified adjusted gross income (MAGI) is under $110,000, or if you are married and your joint income is below $173,000, you can invest directly in a Roth IRA up to the full annual limit. (For most of us, our MAGI is the same as our standard adjusted gross income [AGI] on our federal tax return. So what's AGI? It's all the money you made in a year—your income and earnings on taxable investments—minus certain deductions.) Reduced contributions are allowed for individuals with MAGI between $110,000 and $125,000 and married couples with joint MAGI between $173,000 and $183,000. Again, check my website for Roth IRA contribution limits for 2012 and beyond.

If your income is too high for a direct investment in a Roth IRA you can make a contribution to a nondeductible traditional IRA. Fairly simple paperwork is required to then convert that account to a Roth IRA. If this is the only IRA account you have and you make the conversion immediately you will likely owe no tax. However, if you have old IRAs, you may owe tax at the time you convert. I recommend you work with a trusted tax advisor if you have other IRA assets and you are considering a conversion, because the tax rules can be complicated. Your tax advisor can also show you how converting smaller sums over the years can be a smart option.

RETIREMENT PLANS FOR THE SELF-EMPLOYED

If you are self-employed you have a few other options in addition to the traditional IRA and Roth IRA. A SEP-IRA allows you to make a tax-deductible contribution of as much as 25% of your income, up to a maximum of $50,000 in 2012. A solo 401(k) and a SIMPLE IRA are other kinds of retirement plans for the self-employed.

Go to The Classroom at www.suzeorman.com: For those of you who are self-employed, I encourage you to learn more at my website about the special retirement accounts you can invest in.

LESSON 3. HOW MUCH YOU NEED TO SAVE FOR RETIREMENT

Once again, as a first step, I'm going to begin by asking you to commit to living below your means. As I explained at the very beginning of this book, acceptance of this concept—wholly, with your head and your gut—is essential for creating your New American Dream, and it is particularly important when it comes to reaching your retirement goals. The reality is that you must find a way to save as much as possible today for your retirement, no matter how many years away it may be. Finding ways to reduce your expenses today will have a double payoff for you: First, you will free up money that can be redirected into retirement savings. Second, you will have trained yourself to live on less, so you will need less money in retirement to support your (less expensive) lifestyle.

Now that brings us to the two questions I am asked all the time:

- How much do I need to save for retirement?
- Which retirement account is best for me?

THE RETIREMENT FORMULA

The more you save today, the better. If you ask me, there is no such thing as putting away too much money. At a minimum I want you to figure out a way to set aside 15% of your pre-tax salary each and every year, starting as early as possible. If you wait until your 40s and 50s to get serious about saving, you will need to set aside 25% or more of your gross salary. Let's be honest: Playing catch-up at the rate of 25% of your salary is not likely something you will be able to do.

I know, I know. Fifteen percent of your salary today sounds like so much to give up. But it is in fact a solid rule of thumb to make sure the combination of your savings and your Social Security benefit will give you enough retirement income to match about 70% or so of your pre-retirement living expenses. Trust me on this one.

The Best 401(k) and IRA Strategy

Now we're ready to learn how to make the most out of your retirement savings. The goal for most of you will be to have a mix of 401(k) and IRA savings. Here is a step-by-step strategy for how to save for retirement:

STEP 1. Save in a 401(k) plan if your employer offers a matching contribution. Contribute enough to qualify for the maximum company match.

More than 20% of workers don't contribute enough to earn the maximum their company offers to match. I don't care what other financial issues you are dealing with in your life—you must *always* take advantage of a match when it is offered. That match is just like a bonus, and if you turn your back on this bonus it is literally throwing money away.

Every company has its own method for calculating the match. A common formula is that your employer will give you 50 cents for every dollar you put into your 401(k), up to a limit of 6% of your salary. In other words, if you contribute 6%, your employer will kick in another 3%. Let's say your salary is $75,000. If you set aside 6% of your paycheck ($4,500) your employer would then contribute another $2,250. The employer match just boosted your account balance by 50%! That is a seriously great deal. And your 6% plus your employer's 3% gets you to a total retirement savings rate of 9%. That's more than halfway to our goal of 15%.

Please check with your employer to make sure that you are in fact investing enough to qualify for the maximum company match. I have to warn you that an odd quirk in how 401(k) plans are set up for new employees means that many of you may be inadvertently contributing too little to get the full bonus matching contribution you are entitled to.

A few years ago many employers switched to a new system that automatically enrolls all new employees in the 401(k) when they are hired. That is, rather than asking you if you want to join the plan, or waiting for you to sign the paperwork to start your retirement saving, the employer just automatically puts you in the plan. You can always choose to opt out after the fact, but the system is now set up to assume you want to be in the plan from the get-go. That is indeed a fabulous improvement in how our 401(k)s work; it means more people will start saving at a younger age. But there's a kink that needs to be worked out. When most employers automatically enroll a new employee in the 401(k) they set your contribution rate at 3% of your salary. Why so low? Well, the theory is that they don't want to scare you away by setting this "default contribution rate" any higher.

You are being led into a costly mistake. As I just explained, many employers will match your contributions up to the first 6% of your salary, up to a set dollar limit. So if you are only contributing 3% because that's what they set it at when they enrolled you, there's a chance you may not be capturing all of the company match you are entitled to. Give HR a call and make sure you are indeed contributing at a level that guarantees your account will have the maximum employer match added to it.

A word on vesting: The money you contribute to your 401(k) is 100% yours from the moment you make the contribution. But the money your employer contributes to your account typically becomes yours over time. For example, some firms have a three-year vesting formula. After the first year, one-third of the matching contribution becomes yours; after two years another third vests; and at the end of the third year all of the match is 100% yours—that is, you are fully vested. So if you left the company after one year— voluntarily or not—you would be entitled to keep one-third of the match, after two years you would keep two-thirds, and after three years all of the match would be yours.

Opt for a Roth 401(k) if it is offered as part of your plan. A growing number of companies now offer the option of contributing to a traditional or a Roth 401(k). If your plan has a Roth 401(k), it is probably the best choice.

A Roth 401(k) is a cousin to the Roth IRA described earlier in this chapter. The money you use to make your contribution comes out of your paycheck after taxes have been taken out. So there is no up-front tax break on your contributions as there is with a regular 401(k), but once again, the big payoff comes in retirement. Withdrawals from a Roth 401(k) after the age of 59½ are 100% tax-free, whereas withdrawals from your regular 401(k) plan will always be taxed as ordinary income. It's my belief that the ability to have tax-free income in retirement is a smart move, regardless of what happens to tax rates in the future. The Roth 401(k) also gives you a lot more flexibility if you intend to leave money to heirs. Once you reach age 70½ the federal government insists that you start to take money out of a regular 401(k) if you are no longer working; this is what is called a required minimum distribution (RMD). With a Roth 401(k) there is no RMD; you can just let it grow for future generations. And when your beneficiaries inherit your Roth 401(k) they too will be able to withdraw this money tax-free.

STEP 2. Contribute to a Roth IRA.

Once you have contributed enough to your 401(k) to earn the maximum company matching contribution, or if there is no match available, your goal should be to fund your own Roth IRA.

Caveat for those of you with a Roth 401(k): If you are contributing to a Roth 401(k) you could in fact skip this step on Roth IRAs. You could just keep contributing more to your Roth 401(k), above what you need to invest to get the company match. Remember, in most instances you can invest up to $17,000 in a Roth 401(k) in 2012 if you are under age 50. And indeed, if you want to keep things simple, it's fine to focus all your money and attention on your Roth 401(k). The most important thing here is that you are indeed saving up. But if you want to get an A in this class, I think you should consider opening a Roth IRA even if you have a Roth 401(k). With a Roth IRA you have the freedom to invest in thousands of low-cost investments, including exchange traded funds (ETFs), rather than be limited to the choices offered within your 401(k) plan. And even though I never want you to touch your retirement savings before retirement, the fact that you can take out money that you have contributed to a Roth IRA—though not the earnings—at any time without tax or penalty means it can moonlight as a backup emergency fund. So once you get the maximum match from your employer in a Roth 401(k), my advice is to then focus on a Roth IRA.

ALTERNATIVE STEP 2. Contribute to a traditional nondeductible IRA and convert to a Roth IRA.

As I explained above, if your income disqualifies you for direct investment in a Roth IRA, you have a two-step option: Make a nondeductible contribution to a traditional IRA and then convert that IRA into a Roth IRA. If you have other IRA funds please work with a tax advisor before you make this move; the tax rules are tricky and you don't want to have any ugly surprises.

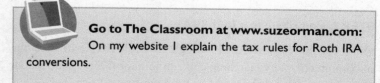

Go to The Classroom at www.suzeorman.com: On my website I explain the tax rules for Roth IRA conversions.

How much to invest in your Roth IRA? Remember what I said earlier: The more you save for retirement today, the better your chances of reaching your retirement dreams. The annual maximum you can contribute in 2012 is $5,000. (At suzeorman.com I will post any changes to these levels beyond 2012.) Make that your goal. What you can afford to save is of course a function of your current salary and your other financial obligations. But please stop here for a moment and seriously stand in your truth. Your future retirement success is rooted in the savings choices you make today. I want you to summon the lesson we discussed in Class 2: You are standing in the truth when the pleasure of saving equals the pleasure of spending. Saving for retirement is your most important savings goal.

Now, if you happen to have a big pile of cash ready to contribute to an IRA, that's great. But what's more likely is that contributing smaller sums throughout the year will be more practical. Here's what you would want to save on a monthly or quarterly basis to reach the maximum annual IRA contribution limit:

IRA PERIODIC INVESTMENT TABLE If you are 49 or younger	
MONTHLY CONTRIBUTION TO MEET ANNUAL MAXIMUM*	QUARTERLY CONTRIBUTION TO MEET ANNUAL MAXIMUM*
$416.65	$1,250

*In 2012 the maximum annual contribution limit is $5,000 for individuals below age 50.

The best way to do this is to set up an automatic investment system that pulls money out of your checking account each month and invests it in your Roth IRA. Do not leave this to your own best intentions; even if you vow you will make monthly contributions it can be hard to stick with a plan, especially when unexpected expenses pop up. It's best to make this an automatic system that takes you out of the equation. The discount brokerage or fund firm you choose for your IRA will have an easy form for you to fill out that authorizes a monthly (or quarterly) transfer from a bank account to your IRA.

Where to Open an IRA Account

I recommend you use a reputable discount brokerage firm such as TD Ameritrade, Fidelity, Schwab, ING, Muriel Siebert, Scott-trade, or Vanguard. I prefer discount brokerages or no-load mutual fund companies because of their low (or no) trading costs, low account fees, and low-expense mutual funds and ETFs. Banks and insurance companies that offer IRA accounts typically charge higher fees. I'd prefer you keep every penny you can invested for retirement, rather than allow any to go toward paying fees. For that reason, discount brokerages or the mutual fund company itself are your best options. Under no circumstances would I open a Roth at a bank, credit union, or insurance company.

STEP 3. Increase your 401(k) contributions.

If you max out on your Roth IRA contribution and you still aren't at your 15% savings goal, then you are to increase your 401(k) contribution (match or not) to get you to 15%.

STEP 4. Save in a taxable account.

If you don't have a 401(k) and you have maxed out on your IRA for the year, you can keep saving more in a regular taxable account. A great strategy is to create a portfolio of a few ETFs. Unlike mutual funds, there typically is no annual tax bill with ETFs; the only time taxes are owed is when you sell your shares at a gain. That's a great way to invest for your long-term retirement goals.

That's it—four steps.

LESSON 4. INVESTING YOUR RETIREMENT MONEY

Making the commitment to contribute to a 401(k) and an IRA is just half the job. You must also take responsibility for choosing the investments you own inside these accounts—yet another task prior generations didn't have to stress over.

Based on the countless questions I get about this subject, it's clear to me that many of you are totally confused about how to allocate the funds in your accounts. When I ask you how your retirement money is invested you typically tell me you have a 401(k) or an IRA. I then ask again, "Yes, but how is your retirement money *invested*?" and you look at me like I am nuts because you just told me you had a 401(k) or an IRA.

Please understand that a 401(k) and an IRA are simply retirement accounts that hold your investments. You must choose what investments to put inside your accounts. If you don't make that choice, your 401(k) or the brokerage firm that handles your 401(k) will often just leave your money in a cash account. Another common scenario I see is that you try to invest the money in your accounts but you get overwhelmed and panic and you decide that cash is the best option.

And I know that some of you aren't investing because you have no faith that investing is the way to go, period. You were spooked by the volatility of the stock market in 2008. The investing community is well aware of exactly how you feel. The CEO of one of the largest mutual fund companies has publicly laid it out that the financial services industry is on the verge of losing an entire generation of investors—young adults like you—who have experienced a whole lot of bear market pain without any offsetting bull market upside to temper your nerves and perspective. In a recent survey of investor attitude toward risk, the biggest drop in a willingness to take investment risk was among the youngest investors—those below the age of 35.

That makes complete sense. No one, not even financial industry honchos, would fault you for feeling that way given what you have lived through. But I am going to ask you to summon all your stand-in-the-truth strength and fight through those feelings. I am not asking you to forget those feelings, nor am I suggesting you are wrong for feeling hesitant to invest in stocks.

But here's where we need to think through what your dream is: retirement. You are not retiring next year, or next decade. It's a dream that is 30, 40, maybe even 50 years off. Yes, I am going to hit you with another riff on the power of time.

The first time-sensitive issue I need you to grasp is that by playing it safe today and keeping all your money in bonds and cash you will miss out on the opportunity to earn returns that exceed the inflation rate. And make no mistake, you must focus on earning inflation-beating gains. It's simple: If your savings do not increase enough to counteract inflation you will not be able to maintain your standard of living in retirement. So I am here to tell you that you must consider investing a portion of your portfolio in stocks.

Just as a guidepost, keep in mind that the long-term average rate of inflation is about 3.5%. So at a minimum you want your investments to be earning at least that much, preferably more. If you are invested in the most conservative option in your company 401(k)—it can be a money market fund or a stable-value fund—you are not earning more than 1%, if that, right now. Yes, a money market or stable-value fund is "safe" in that its value will not go down, but when you are investing for a goal that is decades away you must also think about the risk of your money's purchasing power not keeping up with inflation.

UNDERSTANDING THE UPS AND DOWNS
OF THE STOCK MARKET

The truth is, right now is an absolutely fabulous time to be investing if you won't need that money for decades. None of us can predict with 100% accuracy what is going to happen in the stock market over the next few years, or even the next few months. But when you are investing in a retirement account that you will not use for decades, you shouldn't be focused on what happens right now. To be totally honest, you should look at any market drop as a good investing opportunity.

Now why do I say that? Because when the market goes down you can buy stocks on sale. If you needed that money in a few months or a few years there would be the risk that the price might be even lower. But that's not what we are dealing with here. You have two, three, or four decades until you retire and then you could live another 25 years in retirement. So you shouldn't really care what happens to the stock over the next few years. What you want to stay focused on is the long term and the long-term trend is that stock values rise. Therefore you absolutely want to have some of your portfolio invested in stocks.

And the next time the market starts to slide and your nerves start to justifiably rattle, come back to this truth: When you are young the ability to buy more shares at a lower price is an advantage, not a disadvantage. Look, I am not asking you to break into a celebratory jig every time the market falls. But don't run the other way in panic either. Do not bail. The downdrafts are in fact a great opportunity to build retirement security. That brings us to the importance of dollar cost averaging.

TAKE ADVANTAGE OF DOLLAR COST AVERAGING

One of the great aspects of making periodic investments in your 401(k) and IRA is that it helps you take advantage of an investing strategy known as dollar cost averaging (DCA). By consistently investing sums every paycheck into your 401(k), or making monthly transfers from your checking account into your IRA, you will sometimes purchase stock when prices are high and sometimes when they are low. But the average over the entire time you are investing is far better than trying to invest one big lump sum—assuming you have it. When you use DCA you smooth out your average purchase price. And if you have decades until you will even begin to need the money, the likelihood is that those shares will have grown in value over that time. Moreover, committing to a steady and automatic savings plan—that's what dollar cost averaging is at its heart—ensures you will stick to your periodic investing. And that's the most important step in realizing your retirement dreams.

Buying stocks for your retirement accounts when values are lower is actually what you want. Yes, you read that right: I said you want stock prices to be lower, not higher. Let's say you have $100 to invest and a stock trades at $12 per share. Your $100 will buy about 8 shares. But if the stock price is $10 you get 10 shares. Now let's jump ahead to some future date when the stock is at $15 per share. If you own 8 shares your account is worth $120. If you have 10 shares, your account is worth $150. See what I mean? When you are young and have decades until you will need your retirement money, the ability to buy more shares when prices go down is what you should be rooting for. The ability to save for retirement when prices are lower is a big advantage.

HOW MUCH TO INVEST IN STOCKS

The reality is that each of you must decide for yourself how much of your money to invest in stocks. If you were among those who've developed a fear of the market, I hope I have convinced you to rethink your position. Now, that said, I am not telling you to back up the truck and pile everything into stocks. No, no, no. Do that and you can't help but panic when there is a big market drop. Besides, historically, having at least 20% or so of your account in less volatile investments—such as bonds—has generated almost as strong gains as a 100% stock portfolio, but with less dramatic price swings when the markets go down.

What you want to do is create a mix of stocks as well as bonds and cash. A general rule of thumb worth considering is to subtract your age from 100. So if you are 35, consider a portfolio that has 65% or so in stocks. And just to make sure we're all agreed on why you can't afford to be 100% in bonds and cash: because your money will likely not grow at a rate that can keep pace with inflation.

The bottom line is that you do not want to be an either/or investor. You want both. Some stocks, some bonds. Your 401(k) plan or the discount brokerage where you invest your IRA likely has a free calculator to help you determine an age-appropriate mix of stocks and bonds that is in line with your appetite for risk. Or anyone can use the asset allocation calculators at vanguard.com and troweprice.com.

I think I have been quite clear that the absolute best move for you is to invest a significant portion of your money in stocks when you still have decades to go until retirement, let alone the two or three decades you could live in retirement. That is indeed my best advice. But if you remain unconvinced, and your truth is that you never want to have much or any of your money invested in the stock market, that's your truth to stand in.

But you must also accept the truth of the trade-off you are making: If you do not invest in stocks you will have no opportunity to generate inflation-beating gains. Therefore you will have to commit in a serious way to two important adjustments:

- **Save more.** This is simple math: If your portfolio will be invested in only lower-risk investments that might average 3–4% or so, you need to save more than if you were invested in a mix of investments that might produce returns of, say, 6% or so. Let's say you are investing $500 a month for retirement. If that account earns an average annualized 6% a year for 40 years it would be worth about $995,000. If it earns an average annualized 4.5%, it would be worth $670,000. If you want to end up with the same $995,000 you would need to increase your monthly savings to about $740 a month.

- **Plan on living on less in retirement.** If you make less on your retirement investments, then you will have less to support you in retirement. That isn't necessarily a problem if you create a lifestyle where you are in fact living below your means and can continue that way in retirement. But there's no way in your 20s and 30s to anticipate what your expenses will be 40 and 50 years from now. It's hard to know what they will be 2 years from now! However, I can tell you that if you live honestly today—below your means, but within your needs—you will not only be able to save for retirement, you will have a less expensive lifestyle to maintain in retirement. But if you are saving less today and not investing for growth, and you are not living below your means, well, there is not any sort of truth in there.

CHOOSING THE BEST OPTIONS WITHIN YOUR 401(K)

In most 401(k) plans your employer will offer you investment options that are usually made up of 12 or so mutual funds and possibly their company stock. And then it's up to you to figure out how to invest among all those options.

Many 401(k) plans also offer a simpler approach: a target-date retirement fund that makes all those allocation decisions for you, so rather than have to figure out the right mix of different types of stock and bond funds you can invest in the target fund tied to your expected retirement date—the year will be listed in the name of the fund—and the fund company will take charge of deciding how to allocate your money within the target fund among different types of investments. The way most target funds work is that they own shares in a bunch of other funds. Through one single investment you are buying smaller shares of a mix of different stock and bond funds.

My strong preference is that you do not use a target-date fund. I recognize they are much easier—you just find the right target date, put all your money in them, and you're all set. My primary concern with target retirement funds is that no matter your age, a portion of your money will be invested in bond funds. I have never liked bond funds. Bonds, yes, but not bond funds, and for one simple reason: Since there is no set maturity date for a bond fund, you are never guaranteed you will get your principal back, as you are with a bond (assuming of course that the bond does not default, which is indeed extremely rare). And right now I think it is very dangerous to have any money in long-term bond funds. As I write this in late 2011, interest rates are at historic lows. They will stay there for a bit, but eventually they will need to rise. And the way bonds work, when rates rise, the price of the bond falls. If you are invested in a bond fund that focuses on long-term bonds, you will suffer big losses. And if you are in a target retirement fund you can't control what your bond portion is invested in. You may be stuck with some of your money in long-term bonds. Therefore I would much prefer that you build your own portfolio of funds from the menu that is offered in your plan. I also encourage you to check out *The Money Navigator* newsletter (see offer for free trial subscription on page 156). The newsletter includes recommendations for popular funds used by many 401(k)s.

HOW TO BUILD THE BEST 401(K) INVESTMENT PORTFOLIO

1. **Decide on your mix of stocks and bonds/cash.** As I mentioned earlier, this is yours to determine, based on your truth. From a purely financial perspective, when you are young the majority of your money should be invested in stocks. Start with the rule of thumb of subtracting your age from 100. So a 30-year-old might aim for 70% in stocks. If you're feeling less or more confident about your ability to sleep well in volatile times, adjust accordingly; I would rather that 30-year-old ratchet down to 60% in stocks so she can feel more confident during rough times, than have her commit to 70% or more and then panic when the market slides and pull out of stocks completely.

2. **Look for the lowest-fee funds offered in your plan.** Every mutual fund offered within your plan charges what is known as an annual expense ratio. The annual expense ratio is deducted from a fund's gross return. For example, if a fund earns 5% and its expense ratio is 1%, the real return you will get is 4%. Some funds have expense ratios above 1.5%. Others, such as index funds, charge just 0.20%. Make it a goal to first find the funds with the lowest expense ratios in your plan. Keep an eye out for any funds that are index funds. This means the fund mimics the investments of a fixed benchmark index, such as the S&P 500, rather than relying on a portfolio manager to decide what to buy and sell. Most index funds have lower expenses than managed funds. Low-cost index funds are a reliable option.

3. **For the stock portion:** Typically 401(k) plans offer funds for large, medium, and small companies. It's a good idea to allocate a portion of your portfolio into each category. Stocks of large established companies can provide steadier returns—and often

dividends—while midsize and smaller companies typically hold the possibility of bigger growth opportunities. Take a look inside your 401(k) plan to see if there is an index fund with the name Total Stock Market. The "total" means it invests in a mix of large, midsize, and smaller companies. That's a great way to own big and small companies. An index fund with the term "500" means it is focused on large-cap stocks that are part of the S&P 500; that, too, is a fine choice, though you might want to put a small portion of your money in other funds within your plan that also invest in midsize and small cap funds.

I recommend that 85% of your money be invested in the Total Stock Market fund or a mix of large/midsize/small funds offered in your plan. If you build a mix of large/mid/small funds you might consider following the lead of how a Total index fund currently invests in the three types of stocks: about 70% large caps (S&P 500), 20% midsize, and 10 percent or so in small caps.

The other 15% of the stock portion of your retirement account should be earmarked for an international fund. A diversified international fund that focuses on both developed markets and faster-growing emerging markets is your best move. Or if your plan offers a choice of different international funds, put 10% in the developed markets fund (it may have the abbreviation *EAFE* in it—that stands for an index of developed countries in Europe, Australasia, and the Far East) and the other 5% in an emerging markets fund.

Just be sure that before you invest in the emerging markets fund, you check to see if the main international fund offered within your plan already invests a portion of its assets in emerging market stocks. Your plan's website may have access to this portfolio information. If not, you can find it at the Morningstar.com website. Just type the five-letter ticker symbol for the fund in the search box at the website, and then click on the Portfolio tab. If that fund already has exposure to emerging markets, you can just stick with that one investment.

A word about company stock: Some public companies allow 401(k) participants to invest in company stock. In fact the matching contribution is often made in company stock. You are never to let your investment in any single stock—regardless of whether it is the stock of your employer—amount to more than 10% of your total invested assets. I found it so sad when I learned that more than one-third of BP's 401(k) assets were in fact invested in BP stock. When that stock fell sharply after the 2010 oil spill, the value of BP employees' 401(k)s took a huge hit. This has played out before, the most extreme case being the collapse of Enron, an energy giant, many of whose employees had all their retirement funds invested in the company stock. This is another stand-in-the-truth challenge: We ultimately can never ever be 100% sure about any single investment. To think you know better, or that it could never happen to you, is a dangerous act of financial dishonesty. The honest step is to limit any single stock investment to no more than 10% of your overall portfolio. Then divide the rest of your stock portfolio according to my 85–15 split between U.S. and international stocks.

4. **For the bond/cash portion:** As noted above, I think bond funds are dangerous, but individual bonds are good. Bond funds, in my opinion, absolutely are not. But within your 401(k) all you have access to is funds. So my advice for the next few years in particular is to steer clear of bond funds completely. If your 401(k) offers a GIC (Guaranteed Investment Contract) fund or a stable-value fund— these are other low-risk investments—I prefer them to bond funds. But if you absolutely, positively want to invest in bond funds within your 401(k), please stick with shorter-term funds with average maturities of five years or less. In the coming years I expect interest rates will begin to rise off their current historic lows, and when rates rise, the underlying prices of bonds fall. Longer-term issues typically suffer bigger price losses than shorter-term bonds. So in this environment, I think it is prudent to stick with shorter-term bond funds if you choose to put money in a bond fund at all. I would keep the bulk of your money in the stable-value or GIC and reserve just 20% or so of this slice of your portfolio for bond funds.

5. **Rebalance your portfolio once a year.** One of the keys to successful long-term investing is to make sure you don't overload on

one hot investment, and by the same token, have too little in an underperforming investment. What's hot today won't be hot forever. What's cold today won't be cold forever. That's why you want to rebalance: By constantly bringing your portfolio back in line with your long-term allocation strategy you are not making any outsize bet for or against any specific part of your portfolio.

Let's say you started the year with 15% of your stock portfolio invested in international stocks and 85% in a U.S. stock fund. But at the end of the year, the international markets did so well, while the U.S. markets lagged, that your mix is now 22% international and 78% U.S. I realize this takes discipline, but you want to shift your money around—you can in fact exchange money from one fund to another within your 401(k) without any tax bill to get back to your target of 85–15. It's also important to rebalance your overall stock and bond/cash mix so they stay in line with your long-term allocation strategy. Now, don't go crazy with this; once a year is fine. Or if you're feeling extra motivated, go ahead and rebalance every six months if your allocations are more than 5% off your targets.

That is my best advice on how to build a smart 401(k) portfolio that mixes the opportunity for inflation-beating gains (stocks) with more soothing lower-risk investments.

But I need you to stand in your truth. If, after reading that, you honestly can't see yourself putting in the work to create that portfolio, well, then that is your truth and I will respect it. And I will tell you that your next best option—though inferior, in my opinion—is to choose the target retirement fund in your plan. I would rather you have your money invested in sync with your investment time frame rather than 100% of it sitting in cash, or company stock, or worst of all, you not participating at all. As I said, a target retirement fund may not be ideal, but if you are uncertain about your ability to choose your allocations and follow up on them once a year, this option might deliver peace of mind. If that is your truth, I can only support you when you choose to stand in it. And the reality is that because you are young, your target fund should have very little committed to bonds; the investment pros at the mutual fund company who are in charge of setting the allocation mix within your target fund know full well that you belong mostly in stocks given all the time you have. However, I will continue to hope that as you age and gain confidence you will take control of the allocation of your 401(k). Once you are in your 40s and 50s a target fund will most definitely invest more in bond funds than when you are in your 20s and 30s. So those later decades are the years when I would ask you to seriously consider stepping up and building your own portfolio so that you do not find yourself stuck in a target fund that is overloaded with bond funds.

THE BEST INVESTMENTS FOR YOUR IRA AND REGULAR TAXABLE ACCOUNTS: ETFS

For retirement assets outside your 401(k), you have the freedom to choose among the thousands of investments offered by the discount brokerage you use. That includes mutual funds, individual stocks, and individual bonds, as well as exchange-traded funds (ETFs). I think ETFs are an ideal way to invest the stock portion of your IRA. An ETF is very much like a mutual fund, except its fees tend to be lower. Another benefit is that unlike funds, an ETF's price changes throughout the day to reflect changes in the value of its underlying holdings. A mutual fund, by comparison, has just one price a day, set at the close of business (4 P.M. Eastern). If you place an order to buy or sell a mutual fund at 11 A.M., your price will be based on the closing price at 4 P.M. If a disaster were to happen at noon that day there would be nothing you could do about it; you still would get what the price was at close of business. With an ETF, if you place your trading order at 11 A.M. it will go through immediately and reflect the current price of the ETF at that moment in time. Granted, your long-term retirement funds shouldn't be actively traded on a daily and hourly basis, but I want you to understand the added flexibility you have with ETFs.

One of the big differences between an ETF and a mutual fund is that an ETF trades like a stock, and that means there is a commission to pay each time you buy and sell ETF shares. That's a disadvantage compared to a no-load mutual fund, which does not charge a commission. But one of the most promising developments is that some major brokerages including Fidelity, Schwab, TD Ameritrade, and Vanguard have decided to eliminate or sharply reduce the commissions charged to buy and sell certain ETFs. For investors who want to invest on a monthly or quarterly basis rather in than one lump sum each year, the prospect of making commission-free trades is great news. Someone who invests monthly and in the past paid a $10 fee for each trade can now save $120 a year through commission-free ETF trades.

The website morningstar.com has a terrific amount of information and data about ETFs. I encourage you to educate yourself before you invest.

Some ETFs I recommend as good choices for building a diversified long-term retirement portfolio:

U.S. Stock ETFs

- Diversified index ETFs that give you broad exposure to hundreds of U.S. firms
- iShares S&P 500 (ticker symbol: IVV)
- iShares S&P SmallCap 600 Index (IJR)
- iShares S&P MidCap 400 Growth Index (IJK)
- Vanguard Total Stock Market (VTI)

Diversified International Stock ETFs

- Vanguard FTSE All World ex-U.S. ETF (VEU)
- iShares MSCI EAFE Index Fund ETF (EFA)

BOND INVESTMENTS

For the bond portion of your IRAs and any taxable accounts, I recommend you invest in individual Treasury bonds. Because these are backed by the U.S. government you do not have to worry about default risk. If you were to invest in corporate bonds you would need to build a diversified portfolio of 10 or more issues, and unless you have $100,000 or more to devote to bonds, the commission you would end up paying would be too expensive.

The discount brokerage where you keep your IRA should offer the ability to buy Treasury securities, or you can invest through TreasuryDirect.gov. Just remember to stick with shorter-term issues—maturities of five years or less.

RETIREMENT PLANNING MISTAKES YOU MUST AVOID

Now that you know the key steps to investing for retirement, I want to make sure you don't make some costly mistakes along the way.

• **Do not use retirement funds to temporarily fix a long-term problem.** There is no more costly mistake than using your retirement savings prematurely, to pay for something other than your retirement. Yet I know that many of you have felt compelled during the past few very rough years to pull money out of your 401(k) or IRA to make up for lost income from a layoff or reduced pay. Many more of you have come to me asking if it is okay to take money out of your retirement accounts so you can keep up with a mortgage payment that is no longer affordable.

My answer: No. It is not okay.

I say that with tremendous heartache for what I know so many of you are going through. But I am here to teach you what is best for your long-term security. And you will not be able to achieve your retirement goals if you spend your retirement savings today.

It is impossible for me to overstate how sensitive I am to the hardships many families are going through because of layoffs and other financial setbacks these days. And I certainly understand the desire to use your retirement funds to help you make ends meet during this difficult time. But I am going to ask you to stand up to a very important truth here: If you withdraw money from your retirement funds today, will you solve a problem for good, or will you just buy yourself a little time? Please answer that question based on what you know for sure today, not what you hope may happen in a month or two or three.

What I see so often is that wonderful, well-intentioned families think they are doing the right thing by taking money out of their retirement funds so they can keep up with a mortgage payment. This helps them for a few months, but then when that money runs out they are once again back at square one: They have a mortgage they can still not afford. Making matters worse, they now also no longer have their retirement savings.

It is important to understand that your retirement funds are protected in the event you ever have to claim bankruptcy. No matter how much you owe, no matter to whom you owe it, no court in this country will ever allow retirement savings held in a 401(k) or IRA to be used to repay your debts. Retirement funds are shielded. And you must understand that if you make an early withdrawal from your 401(k) you will owe income tax and a 10% penalty—if you are younger than 59½—on the amount you withdraw. So that reduces the actual amount of the withdrawal you will have left to use, after paying the tax and penalty. And please understand that if you fail to pay the tax and penalty, the IRS has the right to start taking the money you owe directly out of your paycheck.

• **Steer clear of 401(k) loans.** So many of you are tempted to take a loan against money you have in your 401(k) plan to pay off other debts. For example, you tell me how smart you were to borrow $5,000 from your 401(k) through a loan that charges a low interest rate, to pay off your $5,000 credit card bill that charges you 20% interest. That's not nearly as smart as you think.

Let me tell you about the payback rules: If you are laid off from a job, or if you decide to take another job, you must repay the loan that is still outstanding quickly, typically within a few months. If you can't afford to do that, the entire amount of the unpaid loan will be added to your taxable income for the year, so not only will you owe tax on that amount, but if you are younger than 55 in that year you will also have a 10% early-withdrawal penalty to pay.

Furthermore, you will end up paying taxes twice on the amount you borrowed. There is another tax drawback to a loan. When you originally invest in a traditional 401(k) it is with pre-tax money. If you then "borrow" that money you will eventually repay it with money you have already paid taxes on. Now let's jump ahead to retirement. The money you repaid with after-tax dollars is now part of the account you have never paid taxes on. And so when you go to withdraw that money in retirement, guess what? It will be treated again as ordinary income. So you've essentially volunteered to pay taxes twice.

• **Don't cash out your retirement funds when you leave your job.** Another common mistake I see is when people leave a job and they have just a few thousand dollars in their 401(k), so they decide to cash it out, rather than leave it to grow for retirement. This is one of the weaknesses of the 401(k) system: Once you leave an employer, regardless of your age, you are free to do what you want with your account. You can leave it invested at your old employer as long as you have over $5,000 in the 401(k); you can roll it over into an IRA (and convert it to a Roth IRA); and you also have the option to cash it out.

The cash-out option is a mistake that no one at any age can afford to make. Younger adults in their 20s and 30s are typically the most tempted to cash out when they leave a job. I understand what's at play here: You are struggling to make ends meet and you look at your relatively modest 401(k) balance and see a chance to pay some bills, or maybe take a vacation, or upgrade your wardrobe for your next job. I am very sympathetic to how tempting it is to do the cash-out, but it is such a costly mistake. For starters, the money you cash out will be charged the 10% early-withdrawal penalty. Furthermore, if it was invested in a traditional 401(k) you will also owe income tax on the entire amount of the withdrawal. So right there you are walking away with a lot less money.

But it's not just the tax and penalty that makes this a bad move. What I want you to focus on is how you are throwing away decades of compound growth. For anyone around the age of 30 who is considering pulling money out of their 401(k), I want you to always consider the 8x factor: Take the amount of your existing balance and multiply it by 8. That is what your account could grow to by the time you reach age 67, assuming it grows at a compounded 6% annualized rate.

So let's say you have $5,000 in the 401(k) of a former employer. Leave that money invested for retirement and it could be worth more than $43,000 by age 67. I want you to reframe your thinking here. If you withdraw $5,000 today you will probably end up with less than $4,000 after paying the mandatory 10% early-withdrawal penalty and the income tax that is levied on all withdrawals. Or you could leave the $5,000 invested for retirement and possibly have a retirement fund worth more than $40,000. I hope that makes my point crystal clear: There is a potentially huge cost to cashing in a 401(k) when you are young.

WHAT TO DO WITH YOUR 401(K) WHEN YOU LEAVE A JOB

Instead of cashing out an old 401(k) when you leave a job, I want you to keep the money growing for retirement. If your 401(k) balance is at least $5,000 you typically will have the option of leaving your 401(k) in your former employer's plan. If you know for sure that the 401(k) has great low-cost mutual funds, that can make sense. But I have to say I typically think it is far smarter to do what is known as an IRA rollover. This is a straightforward process where you move your money from the 401(k) into a new IRA account at your discount brokerage or fund company. The advantage of doing this is that, as I explained earlier, you will have the

Go to The Classroom at www.suzeorman.com: There you'll find information on how to move your money from a 401(k) to an IRA using the direct rollover method.

freedom to choose from a wider array of investments once your money is in an IRA, including direct investment in Treasury securities as well as ETFs.

LESSON RECAP

Make the commitment to develop a retirement plan in your early years and you will be on your way to a great retirement. I know we have covered a lot of material here, so I want to leave you with a few big-picture goals to focus on:

- Start as soon as possible.
- Make it a goal to save 15% of your pre-tax salary.
- Always contribute to a 401(k) that offers a matching contribution and make sure you contribute enough to earn the maximum employer match.
- Include stock mutual funds in your retirement portfolio.
- Contribute to a Roth IRA.
- Keep your retirement money growing for retirement. No early withdrawals or loans.

CLASS

7

RETIREMENT PLANNING

FINE-TUNING IT IN YOUR 40S AND 50S

THE TRUTH OF THE MATTER

Your late 40s and your 50s are a critical time for your retirement dreams. Even the most carefully thought out retirement plan likely needs a thorough tune-up as you round the bend of midlife—not only because traditional "retirement age" looms on the horizon, but also because the past few years have thrown a lot of new challenges into our path. Your 401(k) and IRA balances may still be recovering from the recent bear market. The home equity you may have been counting on to fund a large part of your retirement may be well below what you were planning on just five years ago. Or maybe your savings plan was set back due to a job loss in your family.

As unsettling as all of that is, there is still plenty of time to act. The actions and adjustments you make today can have a tremendous impact on the quality of life you will enjoy in retirement. But the reality of this midlife stretch is that it requires an absolutely ruthless truthfulness from you and a resolute determination to be thoroughly candid about your financial situation *today*—not what you had 5 or 10 years ago, but right now. I am asking you to take a deep breath, put your fears and anxiety aside for the moment, make an impeccable personal accounting, and then, with my help, make the smartest choices possible based on your current reality. The biggest mistake you can make at this juncture is to sit tight and not act, hoping, praying that somehow between now and retirement everything will work out for the best. That is not standing in your truth. That's the opposite. I'm sorry to break it to you: It's delusional.

I am here to tell you that the choices you make in this decade will have a tremendous impact on whether you will be able to retire with the money and security you desire. It is your willingness to face those decisions today—and adjust your retirement plan as needed—that will allow you a decade from now to look back and say with pride, "I am glad I did," rather than be filled with the regret of "I wish I hadn't." I realize it is easy to be paralyzed by what you think is an insurmountable task, but please listen to me: You are still plenty young and in a position to make sure your retirement dreams can be realized.

Every year the Employee Benefits Research Institute (EBRI) publishes its retirement readiness report; it's a detailed statistical look at how many of us are on pace to have enough money in retirement to meet our basic living needs. What grabs the headlines is that nearly one-half of us are currently at risk of not having enough in retirement to pay the basic bills such as housing, food, and utility costs, as well as paying for out-of-pocket healthcare expenses not covered by Medicare and private insurance. But here's what was deeper down in the study: The majority of that group who are at risk are within 20% of having what they need to be okay in retirement. That is, right now they have 80% of the savings and access to retirement income (pensions, Social Security, etc.) that EBRI estimates they will need to support themselves in retirement. Yes, that's a shortfall, but it's not nearly as dire as the headlines would suggest. Stand in your truth at this stage in your life and you can surely close a gap of that size.

For those of you who are more than 20% away, now is not the

time to give up. I learned a saying from a teacher many years ago that I have often recalled to help me get through tough times in my life, and it goes like this: Be a warrior and don't turn your back on the battlefield.

Obviously the ability to save more at this juncture is a huge part of the puzzle we need to put together between now and retirement. But it's far from the only piece on the table. Reducing your expenses before you reach retirement is a very important strategic move that is often overlooked. We think we have to save, and save, and then save even more so we can "afford" to retire, yet we don't realize that what we need to save is a function of what we expect our expenses to be in retirement. If you can arrange your financial life so you will have lower expenses in retirement, then you don't need to save as much.

Of course, it is impossible to sit down and do a line-item run-through of what you think your living costs might be 20 or 30 years from now. But there are in fact some obvious big-ticket items we can move off your balance sheet. Pay off your mortgage before you retire and you have just wiped out what for most of us is our largest monthly expense. Another big expense center in your 40s and 50s is college costs. For years I have implored parents not to put paying for college ahead of retirement savings. That's become even more important today. I am not just talking about redirecting money you wanted to put into a college 529 plan into your own retirement accounts. Parents must also not overburden themselves with loans to pay for their children's college costs if it means they will still be paying off those loans in retirement. (In the Family Class, I explain a college tuition strategy for parents and children ready to stand in the truth of their New American Dream.)

We also need to embrace the changing nature of what it means to be retired. The classic notion of retirement is that you walked away from your job sometime around age 62–65, never worked another day, and lived for another 10 years or so. But if you retire in your early 60s today, the odds are you will live a lot longer than your grandparents did at the same age. Consider that in 1940 the average life expectancy for a 65-year-old man was just 12 years, meaning that just half of the 65-year-old men in 1940 would still be alive at age 77. Today a 65-year-old man has a life expectancy of 16.7 years. That's four more years of needing to support yourself in retirement. Women's life expectancy has increased from 13.4 years to 19 years over the same stretch. Half of today's 65-year-old women will still be alive into their mid-80s! And I want to make sure you grasp the fact that this means 50% will still be living *past* their mid-80s. In fact, among women who are 85 today, their average life expectancy stretches into their 90s!

In terms of how we view our retirement years, the impact of these numbers is really significant. Because our life expectancy has expanded, we must consider stretching our work years beyond the traditional 62–65 time frame. Unlike past generations of retirees, many of whom could rely on a lifetime pension annuity from their job, most of us retiring in the coming decades will be relying on our own 401(k) and IRA savings. So it's on us to make the money last longer given the likelihood of our longer life spans.

As I will explain in greater detail in this class, devising a strategy for extending your income-earning years through your 60s will help to ensure that your retirement savings can support you throughout your longer life. Don't worry, the advice is not that you must keep working 40-plus hours a week at a high-powered job. The goal will be to find some part-time work that can generate enough current income that it enables you to delay when you start drawing money from Social Security and your own retirement savings, or at the very least reduces what you need to spend of your own savings in your early 60s.

Here are some of the actions to take in your 40s and 50s that we'll cover in great depth in this class:

- Deciding When It Makes Sense to Pay Off Your Mortgage
- Have a Realistic Plan for Working Until Age 66–67
- Delay Your Social Security Benefit
- Estimate Your Retirement Income: How Are You Doing?
- Saving More, and Investing Strategies in Your 50s
- Plan for Long-Term Care Costs

LESSON 1. DECIDING WHEN IT MAKES SENSE TO PAY OFF YOUR MORTGAGE

Are you surprised that the first lesson is about paying off your mortgage? You probably expected me to jump into a lecture of how you need to really get serious about saving much more in your 401(k) and IRA. There is no question that continuing to build your retirement savings is important—you will surely need that money to support you in retirement. But at the same time thinking about the savings side of the retirement challenge is only half the picture. What about reducing your expenses? If you have lower living expenses in retirement you will need less savings to cover your needs, right?

In terms of your ongoing monthly expenses, your mortgage is probably your biggest bill. A troubling trend is that more people are still paying off their mortgage in their 60s. To be sure, the vast majority of older homeowners in fact are mortgage-free, but between 1999 and 2007 (the latest year data is available) the percentage of people age 65 and older with a mortgage rose from 24% to 32%. And I am concerned that many of you in your 50s today will still be carrying a mortgage into retirement.

Many of you, over the past few years, wanted to take advantage of low interest rates and refinanced from rates above 6.5% to rates around 5% or lower. While that move made sense financially, for many it also reset the clock on your 30-year mortgage, extending your total payback time. Or maybe you traded up during the housing bubble—complete with a new 30-year mortgage. Or perhaps you decided the time was right to take advantage of some of the bargains to be had out there and you became a homeowner for the first time. All these scenarios point up the fact that we now have a generation of 50-somethings who will still be paying off a mortgage well into their 70s or possibly their 80s, if they stick to their current payment schedule. That could create tremendous financial stress if you are living on a fixed income. You may well find yourself struggling to cover your other costs, to say nothing of having the ability to spend money on the things you dreamed your retirement would hold, such as travel and spending time with—and money on—your grandchildren.

Continuing to carry a mortgage once you stop working puts your retirement dream at risk. That is why I am starting this Money Class with a lesson on how to get your mortgage paid off before retirement.

Now, I want to be clear, this strategy only makes sense if you can answer yes to these two essential questions:

- **Do you absolutely intend to stay in this house forever?** If you have any doubts about whether you will continue to live in your house after you retire, I wouldn't rush to pay off the mortgage.

- **Can you afford to stay in the house?** Please stand in the truth here: Even if you pay off the mortgage, will your retirement income be enough to cover property tax, insurance, and maintenance costs? I know it is hard to contemplate moving from a home you love and have put so much into, but what would be even more heartbreaking would be to realize at age 75 or 80 that you really can't afford the upkeep of your home and then be forced to uproot yourself at a time when moving may be more trying, both physically and emotionally. If your taxes and maintenance costs are eating up a significant portion of your income today, you have to question how you will be able to handle the payments when you retire; unless you have a big inheritance or have been squirreling away tons of money, it's likely you will have less income in retirement, not more. If that is your truth, please stand tall and be realistic. Rather than worrying about your mortgage in retirement, you should think about downsizing to a less expensive home sooner rather than later. The faster you get into a less expensive living situation, the more time you give yourself to save more because of your reduced expenses.

THE BENEFITS OF PAYING OFF YOUR MORTGAGE

If you answered an emphatic *yes* to both of the questions above, then I have to tell you that paying off your mortgage is an especially smart move in today's investing environment. Right now safe bank and credit union accounts such as certificates of deposit aren't paying more than 1% or so. If you were to use savings to pay off a mortgage that is costing you 5% or 6% (the mortgage interest rate) you would have just earned a higher return on your money: You wiped out owing that 5% or 6% with money that was sitting around earning just 1%. Now, of course you could also use your bank CD for other investments that you think could earn you 5%, or 6% or even more. But let's stand in the truth here: There is no investment in today's market that can give you a risk-free guaranteed 5–6% return. A dividend-paying stock or ETF might earn that much might, but it could also fall in value too, right? There's no such risk when you pay off your mortgage.

I also need you to tune out any naysayers who tell you it never makes sense to pay off a mortgage ahead of schedule because you will lose the valuable mortgage interest tax deduction. Be smart here: In the early years of a mortgage it is true that the bulk of your monthly mortgage payments go toward paying the interest on your loan, and those interest payments are what is tax-deductible. But as the years go by your payments pay off more principal than interest, so the value of that deduction gets smaller and smaller.

For example, let's say you are 50 years old and you just bought a home or refinanced with a $200,000 mortgage. Let's say your interest rate is 4.5% on a 30-year fixed-rate mortgage. That means your monthly payment is $1,013, or $12,156 a year.

If you just keep up with the monthly payment for 20 years, you will reach age 70 still having 10 years of payments left to make. And even though you are two-thirds of the way into paying off the mortgage, your remaining balance is still nearly $100,000, because your payments in the early years mostly went toward paying interest, not principal.

So here you are at age 70, ready to retire. Your plan is that you will just make annual withdrawals from your 401(k) to cover the mortgage. To generate the $12,156 you will need each year requires that you start with a 401(k) balance of at least $500,000. That in itself is a tall order.

As I will explain later in this class, a solid rule of thumb is to aim to withdraw no more than 4 percent of your retirement assets in your first year of retirement. (You then adjust that for inflation in subsequent years.) So 4 percent of $500,000 is $20,000. But remember, there will be federal income tax, and possible state tax as well, if the money is withdrawn from a traditional 401(k). I am going to assume you will have no more than $15,000 left after paying the tax. Granted that's more than your annual mortgage cost, but please realize that the $15,000 or so is probably going to need to cover not just your mortgage but also your other housing-related costs, such as property tax and insurance on the home. At the end of the day, that could be a tight squeeze—and that's making the assumption at the outset that you have a sizable retirement fund to work with. And bear in mind that these are just costs associated with the home. We haven't yet accounted for other living expenses, such as food, electricity, clothing, healthcare, entertainment, etc. And if you were to use most of your 401(k) to cover the mortgage, are you confident your other income sources—such as Social Security—would be enough to allow you to live comfortably in retirement?

The truth is, I know that many of you will not have ample savings in your retirement funds to cover your mortgage and other living costs, no matter how much you can manage to save between now and retirement. So that is why my advice is—if you answered an unequivocal yes to both of those major questions above—that you make it your goal to get the remainder of your mortgage paid off now. Going back to my example, I think it is more sensible to set as a goal paying off the $100,000 or so left on your mortgage before retirement, rather than hoping you will have enough income in retirement to cover the mortgage *and* your other living costs in retirement.

HOW TO PAY OFF YOUR MORTGAGE AHEAD OF SCHEDULE

Get a New Amortization Schedule

At what age do you think you will retire and by when would you like to pay off your home? Later in this class I will make a case that you consider working at least until age 66 or 67 in order to maximize your other retirement benefits, including Social Security. I recommend you use that as a general target. But if you think you may need or want to retire earlier, or you know enough about your industry that it is unlikely you will be able to stay at your current job—and your current salary—all the way until 67, then please stand in the truth and aim to have your mortgage paid off even earlier.

The next step is to call your mortgage company and ask them to send you a new schedule of your payments—called the amortization schedule—that would allow you to have the loan paid off by the date you choose. This will tell you what you need to send in each month to get the loan paid off by that target date.

You can get an idea of what your payments would need to be to accelerate paying off your mortgage by using the mortgage payoff calculator at www.bankrate.com.

Let's say you are 55 years old and have 25 years left on a $200,000 30-year, fixed-rate mortgage that you took out with a 6.0% interest rate. I realize interest rates as of this writing are considerably lower, but I also know that many of you who took out mortgages during the last gasp of the real estate bubble may have been unable to refinance because of lost equity or a lost job, or maybe the new tighter lending standards banks are currently imposing meant you were turned down.

EXTRA PRINCIPAL PAYMENT ADDED TO $1,200 BASE PAYMENT	AGE WHEN MORTGAGE IS PAID OFF	TOTAL SAVINGS (INTEREST PAYMENTS YOU AVOID)
$0 a month	80	$0
$200 a month	71	$79,800
$300 a month	69	$101,100
$500 a month	65	$129,150

If you don't add extra payments you will have the mortgage paid off when you are 80 years old. So the question you should be asking yourself is whether you will be able to keep making that payment through your 60s and 70s, or would it make more sense to find $500 a month today while you still have a paycheck coming in, so you could be mortgage-free by age 65? Let's really think about that: Find $500 more a month today, or else put yourself in the pressure-packed situation of needing to keep paying $1,200 a month from the age of 65 to 80—years when we both know you will not be working at all, or just working part-time—before the mortgage is fully paid off. Stand in your truth: Of course it makes sense to try to pay off the mortgage sooner rather than later. And an added benefit to keep in mind: By accelerating your payments you will avoid owing more than $100,000 in interest payments. That's a huge savings. But the real savings here in my opinion is the money (and stress!) you won't need between the ages of 65 and 80 to keep paying off the mortgage.

How to Come Up with the Extra Money

Accelerating your mortgage payments is something to be considered only if you are in good financial shape. That means:

- You have an eight-month emergency savings fund.
- You do not have any credit card debt.
- You own your car outright, and you are saving for when you will need to purchase another car.

I realize there may be other pressing financial needs for your dollars today, such as lending a hand to adult children who could use help paying their own mortgage as they grapple with a layoff, or assisting parents who are struggling to make ends meet when the income they can earn in this low-rate environment has been reduced so drastically from a few years ago. I am not going to tell you what takes precedence; this is your truth to work through. Instead I would suggest that you spend time in the Family Class, where I discuss how to work through the how and when of offering assistance to your loved ones.

For those of you who are able to take on the goal of paying off your mortgage ahead of schedule, here's your game plan:

• **If you have more than eight months in your emergency fund:** You may use that excess amount to pay down the mortgage. Your emergency savings are likely earning just 1% or 2% these days. Using that money to retire a 5% or 6% mortgage is a great use of your money. But you must never reduce your emergency savings below eight months. You must always have eight months of liquid cash available to cover life's surprises.

• **Reduce your monthly expenses so you can add more to your mortgage payment.** If you are ready to stand in the truth that paying off your mortgage before retirement is the best way to ensure a secure retirement, then you must also stand in the truth that having more income available at the end of the month to add to your mortgage payment is how you make this particular dream come true.

After taking those steps, if you are still looking for more money to use to pay off your mortgage, you can carefully consider scaling back contributions to your retirement funds. Here is a game plan:

• **If you contribute to a 401(k) up to the point of the match:** Keep contributing enough to continue to get the match. But if you have been contributing more than that to your 401(k), redirect anything beyond what's needed to get the match toward paying off your mortgage.

• **If you have less than $100,000 in your traditional IRA:** Keep investing in your IRA, but once you get within 10 years of retirement, consider reducing your IRA contribution by 50% and use that money to pay down your mortgage. For example, let's say you are contributing $500 a month to your IRA. My advice is to reduce that to $250 a month and then put the remaining $250 into accelerating your mortgage payments.

• **If you have less than $100,000 in a Roth IRA:** Same advice as with the traditional IRA, above.

- **If you have more than $100,000 in a Roth IRA:** Figure out how much you need to accelerate your mortgage payments to get it paid off by your expected retirement date. If that monthly sum is more than your current monthly Roth IRA contributions (or the annual equivalent), stop the Roth contributions and use the money to pay down the mortgage. If the amount you want to use for your accelerated mortgage payment is less than your current Roth contributions, great. You can put more money into paying off the mortgage and still continue to make smaller Roth contributions. Let me illustrate that with an example: If all you need is $300 more a month to pay off your mortgage by the time you retire, and you are depositing $500 a month into your Roth, continue to deposit $200 a month into your Roth and add $300 to your mortgage payments. However, if you need all $500 to pay off your mortgage before retirement, stop the contributions altogether and put all that money toward paying down your mortgage.

- **Use money from a Roth IRA.** Money you invested in a Roth IRA—your contributions—can always be withdrawn in any amount at any time without a penalty or tax. And your earnings on those contributions can be withdrawn tax- and penalty-free once you are at least 59½ and have had the account for at least 5 years. If you converted a traditional IRA to a Roth IRA and paid the tax, you need to leave the amount you originally converted inside the account for at least 5 years or until you turn 59½— whichever occurs first—to avoid all tax and penalty. The earnings on your converted money must stay untouched until you are 59½ to avoid tax and penalty.

In any case, I strongly recommend that you do not touch any retirement savings before age 59½. You want that money to grow as long as possible. It is better to aim to get your mortgage paid off by using other income sources while you are working. Once you are within a few years of retirement, tapping your Roth is fine. But please think carefully about how much you can truly afford to withdraw. If you will need income from your Roth to help pay your ongoing expenses in retirement, then it makes no sense to deplete the account. This goes back to my stand-in-the-truth challenge: You are only to pay off the mortgage if you can truly afford to stay in the home.

Later on in this class I am going to ask you to work through an exercise that will give you an estimate of what your monthly retirement income sources may be—from Social Security, from a responsible rate of withdrawal from your 401(k)s and IRAs, and perhaps from a pension. When you go through that exercise, I want you to run the estimates based on a few different scenarios for your Roth IRA: if you don't touch it at all right now, if you were to use 20% of it to pay off your mortgage, if you were to use 40%, etc. The challenge here is to not use so much of your Roth IRA today that it reduces your potential income in retirement to a level that makes you nervous. It's a balancing act. If you have a big pension or you are confident that your Social Security and 401(k) assets will provide plenty of retirement income, then you can afford to tap more of your Roth IRA today.

• **Under no circumstances are you to take an early withdrawal from a traditional 401(k) or IRA.** It makes no sense to withdraw money if you will have to pay the 10% early-withdrawal penalty. Moreover, remember that withdrawals from these traditional accounts count as income in the year you make the withdrawal. A large lump sum withdrawal could put you in a higher income tax bracket for the year. That is not a wise move. Even once you turn 59½ I do not recommend you make large lump sum withdrawals simply to pay off your mortgage. The tax hit will invariably bump you into a higher tax bracket. My advice is to start today with the intention of finding extra monthly income or focus on reducing your expenses so the income you do have can be put toward accelerating your mortgage payment so the mortgage will be paid off before you retire.

STAND IN THE TRUTH

Paying off your mortgage before you retire has an undeniable allure. What greater security is there than knowing no one can take your home from you? And if, later in retirement, you find you need more income, you will be able to take out a reverse mortgage. (See the Home Class for a lesson on reverse mortgages.) So if you are in the home you intend to retire in and your financial truth makes it possible to accelerate your mortgage payments, I think this is a great step to take, beginning in your 50s.

But please promise me that if you reach this conclusion, you have made the decision while standing in a very real and responsible truth. I know you love your home. I appreciate that the idea of having a family home for your children and grandchildren to return to is a classic part of the American Dream. The allure of this image is incredibly powerful. So I recognize that it will take a great amount of fortitude to face up to the reality of your situation as a homeowner. And if you have to rewrite this part of the American Dream for yourself, it will no doubt be a painful and disappointing reckoning. It may be the most difficult kind of letting go to relinquish the dream of a family home and replace it with a more modest living arrangement. The consolation I can offer you in return, however, is security and peace of mind, in knowing that you have made a difficult but correct decision that is in accordance with your truth. You will know you did what was right, not what was easy.

LESSON 2. HAVE A REALISTIC PLAN FOR WORKING UNTIL AGE 66–67

If there has been one singular shift in America's retirement dream since the onset of the financial crisis, it is that many of us must plan on working longer to make up for the money lost in the market crash, for the loss in home equity, or to make up for years when we may not have been saving as much as we needed.

For those of you who fit any of these descriptions, I want to make sure you have a realistic game plan for how you will leverage working longer into a secure retirement. I realize that many of you may in fact *want* to work longer, for reasons that have nothing to do with finances; you want to stay engaged in work for the sense of satisfaction and vitality it provides. I think that's great. But my lesson on delaying retirement and working longer is focused on those of you who *need* to work longer.

Frankly, I am concerned that many of you may be heading for big trouble by overestimating your ability to work longer. As much as I believe that we should all plan to work longer, we also must keep saving, and saving aggressively, today in case we cannot continue to work as long as we might like.

According to the nonpartisan Employee Benefit Research Institute, more than 40% of workers today say they expect to work past age 66—nearly double the percentage that said the same in 2000. But the reality is that 40% of people end up retiring before they expect to; the most common reasons are poor health or being laid off. It's also interesting to see that while 70% of workers near retirement today say they intend to work in some capacity after they retire, the data shows that in fact just 23% of current retirees continue to work. I mention all of that because it is important to recognize that even if your intention is that you will work longer, you must also plan for the possibility that you may not be able to.

DOWNSIZING TO A LOWER-PAYING JOB IS A FACT OF LIFE

Even if you do keep working through your 60s, it is dangerous to assume you will be working in the same high-powered job that paid you a top salary in your 50s. Downsizing is a fact of life we all must be prepared for. And if you have been with one firm for a long time, there's a good chance that a new job in your 50s or 60s will not pay as well. And let's be sure to stand in another important truth: Working 40, 50, 60 hours a week in your 60s may not be something you want to do. Sure, you want to work, but at a less hectic pace. You may make less in your 60s because you choose to shift to a less demanding job. A 2008 study by the Center for Retirement Research (CRR) at Boston College found that the percentage of men between the ages of 58 and 62 who were still with the same employer they worked for at age 50 had dropped from 68% in 1983 to 46% in 2006. And that was even before the economic downturn in 2008 left so many across all age brackets unemployed. Moreover, the CRR also found that those who changed jobs after age 50—whether the switch was voluntary or not—made on average about 25% less in their new job.

Add up all those factors and the lesson here is that you cannot assume you will be able to maintain the same pay and same vigorous work schedule that you kept in your prime. You must aggressively save for retirement in your 50s so that you can afford to earn less in your 60s, and if necessary, stop working altogether at an earlier-than-expected age.

Yet here's what I hear so often these days from so many of you: Your plan, you say, is to never retire. I have to tell you, that is simply not a realistic plan. Please do not make the mistake of not saving for retirement (or not saving as much as you can) on the assumption you will be able to work forever—even if that's what you want.

YOUR WORK-LONGER GAME PLAN

• **Plan on making less in your 60s than you did in your 50s.** Maybe this won't come to pass, but now is the time to do as much saving as you can so in the event you can't work as long as you expect, or you take a lower-paying job, your retirement plans won't be thrown off course. That's another reason why I recommend paying off your mortgage sooner rather than later; if you are still saddled with a hefty mortgage payment in your early 70s or 80s you are walking quite a financial high wire.

• **Aim to delay your retirement until age 66 or 67.** When it comes to Social Security, your goal should be to wait until you reach at least your full retirement age (FRA) so you can claim your full retirement benefit. While your grandparents' FRA was 65, the system was tweaked in the early 1980s to gradually raise the FRA. Anyone born between 1954 and 1959 has an FRA between age 66 and 67; it depends on the exact year you were born. For example, someone born in 1957 has an FRA of 66 years and 6 months, while someone born in 1959 has an FRA of 66 years and 10 months. Everyone born in 1960 and later has an FRA of 67.

A Note About Potential Social Security Reform

Throughout 2011 as our government debated possible fiscal reforms to address the national debt and deficit, raising the FRA for Social Security was one of the options thrown into the conversation. Please understand that none of the proposals—and they are just that, proposals—would change the age requirements for people already in their 50s. One proposal to raise the FRA to 69 would impact today's toddlers, not you.

I'd love for you to keep working until you reach your FRA, if possible, so you don't feel tempted to draw your Social Security benefit beginning at age 62. As I will explain in the next lesson, delaying your Social Security start date is a great strategy to give you more income in retirement. And trust me, most of you will need it.

Delaying your retirement just 3 to 4 years—or more if you're willing and able—can have a tremendous impact on your retirement security. It reduces the number of years you will be living off your retirement income and allows your investments to continue to grow. So often the "How Am I Doing?" segment on my CNBC show involves a couple who want to retire in their early 60s and seek my opinion. In the vast majority of these calls my advice is to keep working. Here's what they and you need to understand: According to research by T. Rowe Price, if you retire at age 67 rather than 62 you could have nearly 40% more retirement income, and that assumes that from age 62 to age 67 you don't save a penny more for retirement. Delay retirement all the way to age 70—again assuming you stop saving at age 62—and your retirement income can be more than 60% higher than what you would have if you retired at age 62. The big increase is a function of your savings continuing to grow a bit longer, the fact that you will be living off your retirement savings for fewer years, as well as the benefit of waiting to take your Social Security payout at a later age. (We will cover this important step in the next lesson.)

- **Spend your 50s planning for your 60s.** Waking up at age 62 laid off or sick of your job is not the ideal time to think about what you might do to bridge the gap to age 66 or 67. You want to be planning for that day at least a decade before. If your dream is to transform a hobby into a part-time job that will bring in some income during those transition years, you need to start testing the waters and picking up any necessary new skills you may need. Or if you want to do something entirely different that requires formal training, get that schooling now, before you need it. In fact, if your employer offers education benefits, have your company help you pay for your next-stage career. If you anticipate you will want to segue into a consulting role in your area of expertise, well, now is the time to start doing a little bit of that on the side (assuming your employer has no objections), or focusing on building industry relationships that will make it easier to bring on clients when you do start your consulting work.

I also recommend you make an effort to develop relationships with the 20- and 30-somethings in your office and at industry networking events. Those are the folks who 10 to 15 years from now will be running the show when you are looking for a late-career job in your 60s.

LESSON 3. DELAY YOUR SOCIAL SECURITY BENEFIT

Nearly two-thirds of Americans rely on Social Security retirement benefits as their primary source of retirement income. Yet most Americans settle for a Social Security benefit that can be 30% to nearly 80% less than what they are entitled to because they choose to start receiving their benefit at an early age.

For our parents and grandparents, Social Security was a no-brainer—the benefit started to kick in and subsidized their retirement. But for baby boomers who are suddenly staring down retirement, it is a whole new ball game and it is so very important to learn the ins and outs of how Social Security works. And learning about this in your 50s is very important. If you decide that waiting until age 66 or 67 to begin your Social Security payments makes the most financial sense, that may impact other decisions, such as whether you will want to keep working—even if just part-time—until the time is right for you to start drawing your Social Security benefits.

I want to call attention to the fact that this is a whole new strategy I am presenting here, different from what I've written about in my previous books.

Changes in the economy and our retirement system necessitate this shift. For example, most of you will not have a steady pension to rely on in retirement; that ratchets up the need to be as strategic as possible in how you take your Social Security benefits. More-over, taking early benefits used to mean a maximum 3 years of early benefits, as past generations had an FRA of age 65. Today the FRA for people currently in their 40s and 50s is somewhere be-tween the ages of 66 and 67. That stretches the period—and the penalty—for early benefits from 3 years to as much as 5, and thus it changes the calculus of this important decision. Social Security to our parents and grandparents was a cornerstone of the Ameri-can Dream. For my generation and the generations that follow, So-cial Security is still a part of the American Dream of retirement, but because you may not have that steady pension, or because you may not have been able to save up enough on your own through your 401(k) and IRA, squeezing the absolute maximum amount from Social Security becomes one of your most important retire-ment planning strategies.

The time to learn how best to take your Social Security benefits is right now, when you are still young enough to be able to adapt.

SOCIAL SECURITY BASICS

We are all eligible to begin receiving our Social Security retirement benefit at age 62. But what you may not fully appreciate is that the Social Security program will give you a higher benefit for every month you wait to start, between the age of 62 and age 70.

The payment scale pivots around your full retirement age. As I explained above, the FRA for today's worker is somewhere between age 66 and 67; everyone born after 1959 has an FRA of 67.

If your FRA is 67, that is the age at which starting to draw your benefit will entitle you to 100% of what you have earned. If, however, you decide to start drawing an early benefit at age 62, it would be just 70% of your full benefit. In other words, when you start your benefit at age 62 you are locking in a 30% reduction compared to what you could earn if you waited a few years. Another way to look at this is that between the age of 62 and 67 Social Security will pay you 6% a year if you delay starting your benefit payments.

Even if you were to take the money early with the intention of saving it for your later retirement years, I think you'd be making a mistake. That 6% bonus each year is guaranteed. There is no way you could be absolutely assured your investments would generate that return. Maybe yes, maybe no. But either way you would have to invest in far riskier investments than what you can get guaranteed by delaying when you start to draw your Social Security benefit.

But that's not all. Let's say you reach age 67 and you are still happy to be working, or you have enough retirement savings you can rely on, so you don't need to begin receiving your Social Security payout. The Social Security Administration will pay you an 8% bonus for every year between the ages of 67 and 70 that you continue to defer your start date. That is, if you wait until age 70 to begin receiving your Social Security benefit it will be 24% more than the benefit you would be eligible to receive if you started at age 67 and about 80% more than the benefit you would be entitled to at age 62.

There is indeed talk of "reforming" Social Security to help address our fiscal shortfalls, but there is no proposal being discussed that would alter the benefit formula for Americans who are already in their 50s; any changes would be slowly phased in over many years; they may impact your kids and their kids, but not you. And as I explained in the previous retirement class, Social

Security is not going belly-up. The reality is that beginning in 2036, Social Security will not have enough money to pay 100% of the current benefits; it would be able to pay out at about 75% of its current promised benefit level. I am not suggesting that a 25% reduction is "nothing," but it is also far different than no payment at all. And in fact, if and when Washington chooses to look seriously at fixes, there are some reasonable ways to tweak the system that would keep the program on solid footing well past 2036.

How Your Start Date Affects Your Social Security Payout

- **Benefit at age 62:** 70%
- **Benefit at FRA*:** 100%
- **Benefit at age 70:** 124%

*Assumes FRA of 67

It is also important to understand that Social Security benefits are indexed to inflation; every year there is inflation, your benefit will be adjusted higher.

So how come the Social Security Administration is so generous if you delay? Well, it's nothing more than some actuarial math at work; the older you start, the less time, on average, you will collect that benefit. So the program can afford to pay you more.

That raises an important question I imagine you're pondering right now: If you die before you reach age 67 or age 70, won't you have "wasted" all that money you didn't ever get because you waited? Or what if you don't start to draw your benefit until age 70 and then you die at age 73? Won't you have left a lot of money on the table?

Given the changes in the economy, that's the wrong way to think about Social Security. If you have an illness or disability that makes it difficult or impossible to work past age 62, then of course it makes sense to draw your Social Security benefit at an earlier age if your other sources of income aren't sufficient. If you *need* to draw a reduced benefit starting before your FRA, that is always the right move. But for those of you who can in fact delay when you start receiving your benefit, it is hands down one of the best ways to improve your retirement finances.

That's especially true given our longer life spans. Remember, half of today's 65-year-olds will still be alive in their 80s. If your health and your family history suggest you might be in that pool of people who enjoy a long life, then it makes tremendous sense to consider delaying your start date; you are essentially buying yourself a higher payout during those later years.

MY SOCIAL SECURITY STRATEGY

• *Between Age 62 and Your FRA*

Make it a priority to hold off on starting your Social Security benefit. Of course, if you are unable to work, and you have no other assets to support you, then drawing a reduced early benefit is what you must do. But if you can afford to wait, you should.

I know that many of you simply do not want to keep working full-time once you hit age 62. If that is your truth, that is what you must follow. But I am still going to tell you that you should not start your Social Security payout. My recommendation is to work part-time at a job that will pay you the equivalent of what you would be entitled to receive from Social Security. Let's consider someone who is age 62 in 2012 and is eligible for a $1,500 a month benefit. Rather than collect that benefit, how about a part-time job for a few more years that brings in $1,500 a month? Not a 50-hour-a-week high-powered job, but something that provides the income you would otherwise be receiving from Social Security.

Note: If you decide you need to take your benefit before you reach your FRA, and you will still be working, you need to understand how your Social Security benefit may be impacted. In 2012, if you have not yet hit your FRA, you can earn $14,640 without any impact on your Social Security benefit. Your benefits will be reduced $1 for every $2 you earn above this amount. If you reach your FRA in 2012, you could earn up to $38,880 without any reduction in your benefit. Above $38,880 your benefits would be reduced

$1 for every $3 above that limit. Luckily, once you reach your FRA the amount of any reduction you had because of your earnings while you were drawing early benefits is added back to your benefit. However, I still think it's best to put off taking your benefit—so you can qualify for a bigger payout at a later age—particularly if you have other income coming in.

• *At Your FRA*

Once you reach age 66–67 I am fine with you beginning to take your Social Security benefit. Your patience will give you a payout that is up to 30% more, and that's a great achievement. But I also want you to consider if you can possibly delay further, all the way until age 70. If you can and want to keep working, then delaying your benefit makes tremendous sense. But even if you are ready to stop working, that doesn't automatically mean you must start your Social Security payout. I'd rather you live off other assets; remember that between age 67 and 70, for every year you delay starting your Social Security payout, you earn a guaranteed 8% increase in your eventual benefit. And that benefit is also adjusted for inflation. That's a risk-free return you can't earn anywhere else given where interest rates are as I write this in late 2011.

• *Special Strategy for Married Couples*

If you and your spouse are both eligible for a Social Security benefit you can create a best-of-both-worlds strategy that gives you some Social Security income before age 70 while also allowing you to earn the maximum age-70 benefit as well.

The way Social Security works, when both spouses are eligible for a Social Security benefit they have the option of claiming a benefit based on their individual earnings, or they are entitled to a benefit that is 50% of their spouse's benefit. When one spouse dies and the surviving spouse has reached her FRA, she can choose between her benefit or receiving 100% of her spouse's benefit, whichever is more.

Let's use an example where a husband is the primary earner. I would recommend he delay drawing his benefit at least until his FRA, but ideally wait until he reaches age 70. Given that women on average outlive men, that will leave his wife with the highest possible payout if she is widowed.

But if the couple wants to start receiving some Social Security income prior to the husband turning age 70, the wife can begin to claim a benefit. If she has paid into Social Security and is eligible for a benefit based on her own record she can collect a benefit as early as age 62. Or, once her husband reaches his FRA, she can claim a benefit that is 50% of his. (The husband does not need to collect his benefit; he can opt to "file and suspend," which entitles his wife to claim a benefit based on his earnings record while his own benefit continues to grow until he decides to start receiving a payment, ideally at age 70.)

Now let's say that the wife starts claiming a benefit based on her own earnings record, and her husband is indeed waiting until age 70 to collect on his own earnings record. Once the husband reaches his FRA, say at age 67, he can start to pocket some Social Security income by claiming a 50% spousal benefit based on his wife's earnings record. So from age 67 to 70 he and his wife are collecting 150% of her benefit.

Then when the husband turns 70 he can suspend his spousal benefit and start claiming on his own maximum age-70 benefit. Depending on the wife's own benefit at that juncture, it can also make sense for the wife to stop claiming her own benefit and start to receive 50% of her husband's benefit. If the wife survives the husband she would then be eligible to receive 100% of his benefit. Because he waited to start claiming his benefit until age 70 he has ensured his wife will receive the highest possible payout.

I realize that is a lot to absorb. The most important point to focus on is that married couples should aim to have the higher-earning spouse delay drawing a benefit on his or her earnings for as long as possible, preferably until age 70. You can learn more about spousal claiming strategies at www.ssa.gov.

LESSON 4. ESTIMATE YOUR RETIREMENT INCOME: HOW ARE YOU DOING?

Early in your career you would need a powerful zoom lens to look far into the future and see what your retirement savings and income might be. But now that picture can be viewed in a more refined close-up. With just a decade or so to go until retirement we can get a clear sense of what your savings and other retirement income sources might be worth in retirement. Perhaps you have a plan to pay off your mortgage early; perhaps you have found a way to save more and reduce your expenses; and you now know when you can expect to draw a Social Security benefit. So let's see how it all falls into place.

In this lesson I want you to actually calculate what you might realistically expect your income sources to be in retirement. For those of you familiar with my CNBC show, this exercise is your personal "How Am I Doing?" segment.

In retirement most of you will have two primary sources of income:

- Your Social Security benefit
- Your personal savings, be it in 401(k)s, IRAs, or regular taxable savings

Some of you will also have:

- Income from a traditional pension

If you work for the government or in the public sector this is probably your situation. And while private-sector firms rarely offer pensions to new employees these days, older workers may have been grandfathered into an old plan.

Let's walk through how to get a rough estimate of what your various sources of retirement income may be worth when you retire:

1. Estimate your Social Security benefit. If you have been paying into the Social Security system, you can get an estimate of your

benefit at the Social Security Administration website: www.ssa
.gov/estimator.

Your estimated monthly Social Security benefit at your FRA:
   $_____

**2. Estimate the value of all of your retirement accounts at your
FRA.** Next, we want to know what all your current retirement savings
might be worth when you reach your FRA, and from there we
can estimate how much monthly income you might be able to generate
from those savings.

One of the hardest challenges you face that your parents and
grandparents didn't have to stress over is how to spend your
401(k) and IRA money at a pace that won't put you at risk of running
out of money later in life. All your parents and grandparents
had to do was mosey on down to the mailbox and collect their
pension and Social Security checks. You need to calculate a sustainable
withdrawal rate from your personal retirement accounts
that won't put you at risk of outliving your money. Talk about a
changed retirement dream!

I am going to suggest that if you plan to start making withdrawals
in your late 60s, you aim to withdraw no more than 4% in
the first year. So, for example, if you have $250,000 in your 401(k),
your withdrawal in the first year would be $10,000. Then you can
adjust the amount you withdraw each year in line with inflation. If
you wait until you are 70 to start your withdrawals, you might consider
starting your withdrawals at a 5% initial annual rate.

Okay, did that news just give you a minor heart attack? Why
am I telling you to start with only a 4% or 5% annual withdrawal
rate? Well, it's that same old good news/bad news problem: your
life expectancy. Because we are living longer than past generations
we need to set a conservative withdrawal pace that would give us
a high probability that we would not run out of money in 25 or 30
years. Of course, this is just a rule of thumb. If you have other
assets you can tap—maybe you expect an inheritance—or your

family history suggests you may not live into your late 80s and 90s, then you might consider a slightly higher withdrawal rate. But please stand in the truth that your biggest retirement risk is also a blessing: the fact that you could live a very, very long time. A conservative withdrawal rate is your best strategy for making sure that long life will not come with financial stress.

My recommendation is to use a free online retirement calculator to help you estimate what the monthly income from your 401(k) and IRA investments may be. There are many variables that go into the calculation, including how much you will continue to save between now and retirement and the return you may earn. T. Rowe Price and Vanguard have calculators that use solid assumptions, including an initial 4% withdrawal rate.

> **Go to The Classroom at www.suzeorman.com:**
> There you will find links to the T. Rowe Price and Vanguard retirement income calculators.

Calculator tips:

- Exclude Social Security from your calculation, as we have already figured that out.
- Exclude your pension information as well; we will gather this in the next step.

Your estimated monthly income from your 401(k) and IRAs:
$_____$

3. Your pension. If you are eligible for a traditional pension your plan will be able to provide you an estimate of your expected monthly benefit. But here too you must make some choices as to how you want to receive your benefit. Many pension plans allow you to choose between taking a lump sum payout when you retire or opting for an ongoing payment—typically monthly—once you retire. The ongoing payment is called an annuity.

I highly recommend working with a trusted financial advisor to decide whether a lump sum or monthly annuity makes sense for you; there are many variables to consider. An advisor can offer expert guidance, but this decision will have a significant impact on your retirement security. That is why you must take responsibility and ownership of the decision.

Factors to consider if you opt for a lump sum payout:

• If you take a lump sum payment, I strongly recommend you do an IRA rollover that will transfer the money from your pension into your own retirement IRA at a discount brokerage. If you take the lump sum in a check, all that money will be considered income paid to you for the year and you will owe tax on all of it. That could be a huge bill. It is far better to do the rollover; you owe no tax until you start to make withdrawals from the IRA.

• If you do not need to live off your pension and you want to leave this money to your heirs, you would be better off taking the lump sum and doing a rollover rather than opting for the annuity payment. But please understand that you will be in charge of deciding how to invest that money once it is in the rollover IRA. And I want you to be extra careful here. The sad truth is that some unscrupulous advisors recommend inappropriate investments for the lump sum that generate big commissions for the advisor. If you want professional advice on how to invest your money, please work with a fee-only financial advisor. That means you pay a flat fee. This is a much better setup than working with a commission-based advisor, who will be paid based on what products he sells to you. Recommendations from friends and colleagues are always a smart way to find a trusted advisor; you can also locate fee-only advisors at the napfa.org website. (I also offer investing advice for retirees in the next chapter.)

Factors to consider if you take an annuity:

• If you want an ongoing monthly payment from the pension your employer will ask you to choose from a variety of payment options. The two most common types of pension options are:

1. **Single life only.** This will provide the payout to the retired worker. When that retiree dies, no beneficiary will receive a payout.

2. **Joint and survivor.** The monthly annuity will be paid to the retired worker, and a surviving spouse as well. You can typically choose a joint-and-survivor benefit that pays the surviving spouse 50%, 75%, or 100% of the employee's benefit. The lower the survivor benefit, the larger your monthly check. So if you opt for a 50% survivor benefit, your current monthly check will be larger than if you opt for the 100% survivor benefit.

• If you are married and you decide to opt for the annuity payout, I strongly recommend you choose the 100% joint-and-survivor benefit. This always elicits howls from couples who want the higher payout that comes from a 50% or 75% survivor benefit. But carefully think this through with me: If the pension will be a large part of your retirement income, could the surviving spouse live comfortably if the pension payment were cut by 25% or 50%? Remember, your spouse will also likely have less Social Security income at that time; if both of you were drawing Social Security checks, when one spouse died the survivor would be entitled to the higher of the two checks, but not both. If at that time they also lost 50% of the pension that you were getting that would make it very very rough unless you had serious sums of money. Choosing the 100% joint and survivor is a smart way to ensure the surviving spouse will have as much income as possible.

• If you decide you want to receive a monthly income check, please take the annuity directly from your pension. Do not let a financial advisor convince you to take the lump sum in a rollover that he can then invest in an annuity for you. The annuity from your employer will be a fixed guaranteed payment. An advisor can sell you an annuity that does the same thing if you take a lump sum, but in my experience many of the annuities sold by advisors have high fees, and sometimes you are steered into an annuity where your payment will vary based on the performance of investments. I think it makes more sense to go with the known rather than the unknown: Stick with the guaranteed fixed annuity from your employer.

• I also want you to have your antennae up for any advisor who tells you to take the higher single-life-only benefit and then use the extra amount of the payout to purchase life insurance that the survivor would receive. I don't like that advice at all. It's an opportunity for the advisor to sell you an expensive life insurance policy that no doubt earns him a large commission.

A note on pop-up provisions: Some pensions offer a provision that goes like this: If the spouse dies before the employee, the employee may be able to switch (pop up) to a higher pension payout. This is another issue to discuss with a fee-only financial advisor.

COMPARING THE LUMP SUM TO THE ANNUITY

To help you create an apples-to-apples comparison, let's see how much monthly income you might be able to withdraw from your lump sum and compare that to the monthly annuity option:

1. Take the amount of your lump sum that you could roll over into an IRA and multiply it by 4%. This is what you could afford to initially withdraw annually from your rollover without having to worry about running out of money if you were to live a long life.

    Enter that figure here: $_____

2. Enter the annual amount of the annuity you could receive. Choose a 100% joint-and-survivor option if you are married, or the life-only if you are single.

    $_____

I think you will be surprised to see that you will be getting considerably more by taking the annuity. That said, one important consideration is that most annuity payouts do not include an inflation adjustment: The payout you receive in year 1 will be the same as year 5, year 10, and so on. If you took the lump sum and invested it wisely you would have the opportunity for gains that would effectively allow you to keep pace with inflation. That is another factor a financial advisor can help you weigh.

**Your estimated monthly pension annuity
or annual income from your rollover IRA: $_____**

Is Your Pension Safe?

It is no secret that some pensions—both private and public—are facing financial challenges. But I want you to understand two important points: It is highly unlikely that any public or government pension will change the benefit formula for anyone near retirement. The rules, if they change, would affect new employees; there will likely be a grandfather clause for current employees, especially those near retirement age.

If you have a private-sector pension, you may wonder what happens if your company goes bankrupt or it can't fulfill its pension obligations. Please understand that the money your firm has in its pension accounts is kept separate from its other operations. And the plan is required to report each year whether it has enough money to pay its future obligations. This is called its "funded status." You have a right to receive an annual statement showing your plan's funded status. Request a summary plan description (SPD) to find this information.

So let's say your plan is in fact underfunded. Time to panic? No. Check the SPD to confirm if the pension plan is covered by the Pension Benefit Guaranty Corporation (PBGC). Most plans are. This is a federal agency that guarantees the payments for member firms. Its job is a lot like the FDIC for banks or the NCUA for credit unions: They step in and cover payments when member firms fall into trouble and can't make their pension payment.

Just as with FDIC or NCUA insurance, there are limits to what you can receive from the PBGC. If you are already receiving a benefit from your pension, the PBGC limit is set by your age at the time it took over your plan. In 2011 the maximum monthly benefit for someone age 65 was $4,500; for a joint-and-survivor benefit the maximum payout was $4,050. (At the website listed below you can check the benefit maximums for 2012 and beyond.) If you are under age 65 the PBGC benefit will be lower than those amounts; if you are older the maximum will be higher. At the PBGC website (www.pbgc.gov) there is a table of maximums based on age. If your plan is taken over by the PBGC before you retire, your maximum benefit will be tied to the age at which you begin to receive your benefit.

The bottom line is that even if you are concerned about your employer's future, as long as it is part of the PBGC and your expected payout is below the agency's limits, you should rest easy.

Now let's add up your various sources of retirement income.

Your Total Estimated Monthly Retirement Income:

Social Security $_____
+
Your investments $_____
+
Your pension $_____
+
Other sources of income
(rental properties, etc.) $_____
=
**Your total estimated
monthly retirement
income before tax** $_____

Please remember that any money you withdraw from a traditional IRA or 401(k), as well as pension payouts and Social Security (to a limited extent based on your overall income), is taxed as

ordinary income in the year it is paid. Through 2012, federal income tax rates vary from 10% to 35% depending on your total income, and some states tax retirement income as well. Just keep in
mind that the figure above is going to be lower once you settle your
tax bill.

ONCE AGAIN, IT IS TIME TO STAND IN YOUR TRUTH

Now compare this figure to your current expenses—the figure you
arrived at in Class 2, when you used the expense tracker tool on
my website. Of course we need to adjust your current expenses for
inflation. You can use the compound interest calculator in The
Classroom at my website to get a rough estimate. In the Initial Investment box input your current annual expenses. Leave the
Monthly Addition box empty and then for the interest rate plug in
4%. That is actually slightly higher than the long-term inflation
rate over the past few decades, but I think given what is going on
in our economy and with our fiscal deficit we could in fact see
above-average inflation in the coming years. Finally, input 10 years
past the date you expect to retire. Why so long? Well, if we just
plan to the date you retire we won't know what your expenses
might be down the road in retirement.

Note: if you plan to pay off your mortgage before you retire, remember to deduct that current expense from your calculation.

Okay, now you have a rough idea what your expenses might be in
retirement. I hope you're smiling because your expected retirement
income is plenty to cover your anticipated expenses. But if that's
not the case, and you see a shortfall, please do not panic. You have
time to figure this out. That's why we are doing this exercise now,
in your 40s and 50s. You have 15 or more years to make up
ground. It can also help you focus on some priorities, such as
working longer and delaying when you begin to draw Social Security. And perhaps you might recognize that my advice to focus on
your retirement rather than saving for your child's college costs
makes a ton of sense.

Or let's take a different approach: Maybe your next few vacations are to different parts of the country—or the globe—where the cost of living is lower than where you live today. Start scoping out possible places you might consider retiring to. There's no pressure; just make this an enjoyable adventure where you explore your options. Now is the time to do that exploring and planning. I am confident you can indeed reach your new retirement dream, but we are committed to standing in the truth that there may be some adjustments necessary between then and now to get you there.

Next I want to discuss one more important way you can increase your retirement security: Save more, and save smart.

LESSON 5. SAVING MORE, AND INVESTING STRATEGIES IN YOUR 50S

Obviously, one of the surest ways to improve your retirement picture is to save more over the next 10 to 15 years. In fact, the annual contribution limits for your 401(k) and IRA savings are higher once you turn 50.

In 2012 the limits are:

- **401(k)s:** If you are at least 50 years old, you can contribute $22,500. The maximum for younger employees is $17,000.
- **IRAs:** If you are at least 50 years old, you can contribute $6,000. The maximum is $5,000 for younger savers.

I think it is a smart time to consider saving more in those accounts. Don't expect HR or your 401(k) plan sponsor to send you a note on your 50th birthday informing you of this great opportunity. It's up to you to take the initiative here. My one caveat, as you have already learned, is that if you currently live in a home that you intend to retire in, and you can honestly afford to stay in that home, then it can make sense to divert some of your retirement savings to accelerate paying off your mortgage.

HOW TO INVEST SMART

It is so interesting to me that people in their 50s tend to take extreme positions when it comes to investing their retirement money.

At one end of the investing spectrum are the people who realize they are way behind in their savings. Therefore they decide they should put all their money in stocks; they think that is the only way to have a shot at the big gains they need to make in order to amass what they want by their targeted retirement date.

At the other extreme is the conservative bunch. They think that because they are retiring in 10 or so years they can't afford to own any stocks. After watching what happened in the bear market that began in 2008, they feel it would be a huge mistake to risk having any of their retirement savings lose value.

The truth is that neither camp is correct.

It was very frustrating to me in the wake of the 2008 financial crisis to see people in their 50s shell-shocked that their portfolio was down 40% to 50% or more. The only way that could have happened was if their portfolios had been 100% invested in stocks. If they had owned a more appropriate mix of stocks and bonds, the losses, while still steep, would have been far less devastating. While the S&P 500 stock index lost 37% in 2008, the leading index tracking the bond market gained 5% for the year. Someone who simply had an even split between stocks and bonds might have come out of 2008 with a cumulative loss of 16%, or less than half of what so many of you told me you experienced.

Now I realize that the 16% loss may not sound so good either. Because you are in your 50s you feel as if you don't have time on your side, so you can't afford to have any losses in your portfolio. I agree—as you near retirement you should definitely become more cautious with your investments, favoring bonds over stocks. But that does not mean you can afford to completely shun stocks. Remember, a 65-year-old today will on average still be alive into his or her 80s. That means anyone in their 50s today must consider that some of their retirement savings will not be used for another 25 to 30 years, and possibly longer. It is a mistake to look at your retirement date as your investing stop point. You must consider how long you will need your money to support you. In your 50s you should invest with the awareness that some of that money will not be touched for another 25 years at least. And that raises a potential problem if you were to prematurely move all your money into bonds or cash. The long-term trend tells us that those investments, while earning a steady return, won't typically earn enough to keep pace with inflation.

What's inflation got to do with this? Well, if you do live into your 70s and 80s the price of things you need and want to buy—from groceries to medications—will be higher. If your investments haven't grown at a pace that keeps up with inflation you will have to use more of your savings just to maintain your standard of living, and that raises the risk of running out of money too fast. The solution is to keep a portion of your money invested in stocks, which over the long term have the best potential for producing gains that beat the rate of inflation.

Have the Right Mix of Stocks and Bonds

So what's the right mix in your 50s? Well, I will be the last person to tell you there is any single right formula. You must decide for yourself. If you have so much money saved up that you are confident that you could keep 100% of your money in CDs and bonds and still be able to pay for everything in your 80s and beyond, then that is a wonderful truth! But the reality is that for most of you, you must think about the rising cost of things 20, 30, or 40 years from now. And that makes it wise to keep some of your money in stocks. A rule of thumb that is actually very sound is to subtract your age from 100. So at age 55 you might have 45% invested in stocks. At age 65 you might have 35% invested in stocks. (Every few years you should be rebalancing your retirement portfolios so you have less in stocks and more in bonds.) This rule of thumb is a guideline you can tweak to fit your emotional truth. If you want a little more or a little less in stocks, that is for you to decide. I just ask you to avoid any extreme allocation: 100% in stocks is way too risky. And unless you know for sure that you have ample savings so you don't have to worry about inflation, 100% in bonds and cash is too risky as well.

MAKING THE MOST OF WHAT YOU HAVE

A critical step in building your new retirement dream is to focus on how to maximize the money you have in all your retirement accounts. And if you have changed jobs through the years and have left behind old 401(k)s at former jobs, you are likely dropping the ball here. What you need to focus on is that once you leave a job, whether voluntarily or not, you no longer have to keep the money invested in your former employer's 401(k). You have the option to move your money out of the 401(k) and into what is called a rollover IRA, where your money will continue to grow tax-deferred. I believe that is often the smartest move you can make. I discussed IRA rollovers in the previous chapter about planning for retirement, so if the concept is new to you, I would encourage you to go back and reread that section. There you will learn where to open an IRA rollover account and whether to choose a traditional IRA or a Roth IRA.

One of the reasons I recommend rolling over old 401(k)s into one account at a single brokerage, and consolidating your IRAs as well, is so you have an easier time looking at the entire retirement pie you have. It will be infinitely easier for you to make sure your overall allocation of stocks and bonds/cash makes sense if you have everything under one roof; most discount brokerages and no-load mutual funds have free online tools that will produce easy-to-grasp pie charts that can show you what you've got. And if you are indeed rolling over old 401(k)s you will also benefit from the wider array of investment choices you have with an IRA at a discount brokerage, including investments in individual bonds and all sorts of specialty ETFs, such as precious metal and other commodity-based sectors.

And the reality is that by the time you are in your late 40s or have segued into your 50s, you—and your spouse or partner—no doubt have a mix of different accounts. I bet there are a few traditional IRA accounts, maybe a Roth IRA or two, a handful of "old" 401(k)s from past jobs, along with the retirement plan from your current employer.

Note: If you have old 401(k)s that include company stock, I recommend you work with a fee-only financial advisor before you roll over any of your 401(k)s into an IRA. There is a special way to handle your company stock that is in a retirement account—referred to as net unrealized appreciation (NUA)—that can help you boost your after-tax return on that stock. At my website I have more information about the NUA rules for handling company stock in an old 401(k).

A trusted financial advisor can also help you sort through whether it makes sense for you to convert some of your retirement savings into a Roth IRA rollover. Beginning in 2010, anyone, regardless of income, can do a Roth conversion on all or part of their IRA accounts, including money being rolled over from old 401(k) accounts. You will owe income tax at the time you convert the money, and the tax bill is based on a convoluted formula that includes more than simply the amount of money that is being converted.

That's why you want to work with a financial advisor or tax advisor who has experience with all of this. An added complication is that the amount you convert in any given year is added to your taxable income for that year, and that could bump you into a higher tax bracket. So one consideration is spreading out your conversion over a few years to make sure that no single-year conversion pushes you into a higher tax bracket. Again, that's why you want to have a pro run the numbers and walk through your options with you.

The advantage of doing the conversion today is that once your money is in a Roth you will be able to use it in retirement without owing any tax whatsoever. Moreover, you will not have to take a required minimum distribution from a Roth account (explained in greater depth in the next chapter); so if you don't need to tap that money for living expenses it can stay growing for your heirs.

After you consolidate your accounts (other than your current 401(k)s) under one roof, you can more easily consider a few strategic moves:

Focus on the Entire Pie

Your goal is to make sure that the sum of all your retirement assets is invested in a way that matches your long-term allocation strategy. So, for example, if your goal is to have 60% in stocks and 40% in bonds/cash, then your focus should be for all the various accounts in the aggregate to give you that 60/40 split. But that does not mean every single account must have the same split between stocks and bonds. You don't need your Roth IRA to be 60/40 and your 401(k) that you have at your current job to be 60/40. All that matters is that the total sum of all your money divided between stocks and bonds/cash lands at 60/40 (or whatever you have decided is the right truthful mix for you).

And one smart move to consider is how you are investing the money in your current employer 401(k). Of course you are limited to the investment choices offered in the plan, but because you are taking a holistic approach to your overall retirement pie, a smart move can be to pile your 401(k) savings into the least expensive option. I explain this in the next step.

Focus on the Cheapest Investment Offered in Your Current 401(k)

I want you to find the lowest cost mutual fund in your 401(k). As I explained in the previous chapter, every mutual fund has what is called an expense ratio. This is the annual percentage of your assets that is deducted from your investment each year to pay the mutual fund. That said, you don't really see the expense ratio as a line-item expense in your annual statement. It's levied in a somewhat invisible way, as it is deducted from each fund's gross return before the net return is credited to your account. For example, let's say a stock mutual fund has a 1% annual expense ratio and its gross return is 6%. That means your account will be credited 5% after the 1% expense ratio is siphoned off to pay the fund's fees.

I know this is a bit dry to think about, but it is very profitable. The expense ratio you pay can have a huge impact on your retirement security. As I noted in the previous chapter, I think it is prudent to set our expectations for future returns in the vicinity of an annualized 6%. As some of you may remember, that's one-third the rate of return for stocks during the 1990s, when in fact the S&P 500 grew at an annualized 18% rate for the decade. Let's imagine you owned shares in a mutual fund in the 1990s that had an annualized gross return of 18%, and the fund charged a 1% expense ratio, so your net return was 17%. Now let's assume you own the same mutual fund today and it still charges that 1% annualized rate of return. Today's truth suggests that future returns might be more like 6%. So that would mean your net return would drop from 6% to 5%. That 1% now eats up a bigger portion of your return; it is about 16% of the 6% return, whereas a 1% fee represents just 5% or so of an 18% return. Fees are always important, but you can see how they become even more important when your expectations for future returns are lower. You can't afford to waste any money paying a higher expense ratio than necessary. And mutual funds offered within 401(k)s can have wildly different expense ratios; some stock mutual funds may charge 1.5%, while others might charge just 0.20%, or even less. One of the best ways you can make money in the coming years is to reduce the amount you are paying in that fee.

That is why I want you to locate the fund in your current 401(k) plan with the lowest annual expense ratio. If that fund owns securities that you want to own, I would consider pouring the bulk of your money into that one fund. Remember, you don't need this specific 401(k) to have a mix of investments; all that matters is that your overall portfolio—of all your various retirement accounts—makes one cohesive pie.

Here's an example: Let's say you have a total of $250,000 in all your retirement accounts, and the 401(k) at your current employer accounts for $100,000 of that total. Now let's assume that you want to keep 50% of your money in stocks and 50% in bonds/cash. So that's $125,000 you have earmarked for stocks. If your 401(k) has a great low-cost stock mutual fund, you could put all of your account in that one fund. Then with the remaining $150,000 in your consolidated accounts (you will likely have more than one, since traditional and Roth accounts must be kept separate) you will want to put another $25,000 in a stock mutual fund or ETF. That brings your total stock investment to your target of $125,000. The rest can be invested in cash and bonds. Your total pie adds up to 50% stocks and 50% bonds, but you are strategically taking advantage of the lowest-cost fund within your 401(k).

I really like this approach because it is a great way to avoid ever having to invest in bond funds in your 401(k). I do not like bond funds at all—see page 180 to get my reasoning—and prefer that you invest directly in individual bonds, such as Treasuries. This strategy makes it easy to steer clear of bond funds in your current 401(k).

I want to be very clear here: If the majority of your retirement savings is in this 401(k) account, you obviously should not shift all of it into one fund. If your 401(k) is in fact your whole pie, then this must be a diversified pie. For your stock portion I recommend you keep 85% in U.S. stock funds. If your plan offers a fund with the name Total Stock Fund, that can be a great option, as it invests in a mix of large established firms, mid-size firms, and small firms. So-called large cap stocks tend to offer steadier returns—and often dividends—while stocks of smaller companies typically offer more growth potential. If your plan offers an index fund with "500" in its name, that means it focuses on the large company stocks in the Standard & Poor's 500 stock index. That's a fine choice as well, and you can also invest in a mid-cap and small cap fund offered in your plan. As a guide for how to split that money among the different funds, you might follow how a Total Stock index fund allocates money: about 70 percent is in large caps, 20 percent in mid-caps, and 10 percent in small caps.

The remaining 15% of your stock portfolio should be earmarked for international stocks. There are two broad ways to invest in international markets: developed countries, such as Japan and most of Europe, and emerging markets, such as China and India. My recommendation is to have most of your international stock money invested in developed markets and reserve just 5% of this 15% slug for emerging markets. Fast-growing emerging markets are more volatile. So you don't want to overload your portfolio with exposure to them. And keep in mind that those those big multinational blue-chip U.S. stocks that make up 85% of your 401(k) stock allocation do a lot of business selling their goods and services into the emerging markets. So your 401(k) will be tied to the fortunes of emerging markets through those U.S. firms.

Locate the international fund offerings within your 401(k). If your plan has one fund, well, you're good to go. But if you see two (or more) international funds, that means one of them focuses on developed markets; it will often have *EAFE* in its name. That's a tip-off that it is a fund focusing on developed markets in Europe, Australasia, and the Far East. The other offering probably focuses on emerging international markets.

Before you put 10% of your stock portion in the developed fund and 5% in the emerging markets fund, I recommend you take a look at the portfolio of the developed fund. While the bulk of its assets will be in developed markets, you may find that a fund has 10% or 20% invested in emerging markets. If that's the case, then you can just invest in that fund and forget about adding the emerging markets fund as well.

Your 401(k) plan should provide you easy access—online or over the phone—to the latest available portfolio mix of each fund. If not, go to morningstar.com. Type the ticker symbol for your fund into the search box (it is a five-letter string of letters ending in X that will be listed alongside a fund's name in your 401(k) material). Then click on the portfolio tab, scroll down, and you will see a breakdown of how much of that fund is invested in developed markets and how much is in emerging markets. Please investigate *The Money Navigator* newsletter offer on page 156. The newsletter includes portfolio recommendations for popular funds used by many 401(k)s.

BEST INVESTMENTS OUTSIDE YOUR CURRENT 401(K)

Let's talk about the right investments for your rollover accounts as well as any regular taxable accounts. The advice here is exactly the same advice I gave to younger investors in the previous class. For retirement assets outside your 401(k), you have the freedom to choose among the thousands of investments offered by the discount brokerage you use. That includes mutual funds, individual stocks, and individual bonds, as well as exchange-traded funds (ETFs). Please go to pages 185–87 for my investment advice.

BOND INVESTMENTS

For the bond portion of your IRAs and any taxable accounts, I recommend you invest in individual Treasury bonds. Because the U.S. government backs these you do not have to worry about default risk. If you were to invest in corporate bonds you would need to build a diversified portfolio of 10 or more issues, and unless you have $100,000 or more to devote to bonds, the commission you would end up paying would be too expensive.

The discount brokerage where you keep your IRA should offer the ability to buy Treasury securities. Just remember to stick with shorter-term issues—maturities of five years or less.

• *No Target Funds Allowed*

At this stage of your life I am going to put my foot down and insist that you do not rely on target retirement funds. It's for the very reason I mentioned earlier: I do not like bond funds in any way, shape, or form. And a target retirement fund when you are in your late 40s and 50s will in fact have plenty invested in bond funds. It varies by each different fund company but it might be 30% to 60% or more of the target fund's assets. In the previous class I told younger adults that if they didn't think they had the discipline to create their own portfolio of mutual funds among the offerings in their 401(k), I would allow them to opt for a target retirement fund because at a young age a target fund wouldn't have much invested in bond funds. But as you age, a target fund's glide path—that's the term used to describe how its mix of different types of investments changes over time from higher risk to lower risk—will naturally shift into more bond funds.

You do not have my permission to stay in a target-date retirement fund once you are in your 50s. Nor do I want you using a target retirement fund for your rollover and taxable accounts. Time to stand in your truth. You are here in this class because you have a dream to retire. And to retire knowing you will be financially secure. That is your children's dream as well. The more you can build true financial security for your later years, the less likely you will need your children to step in with financial support.

No matter how unfocused you may have been on making the smartest retirement investing choices in the past, you have reached a crossroads moment. You are standing at an important intersection: You can continue down the same road of not paying much attention; if you choose that path, there is no way to say whether you will in fact realize your retirement dreams. Or you can choose to become actively engaged in managing your retirement accounts and take control of steering your retirement to success. The choice is yours; which way will you go?

I understand that some of you may feel too overwhelmed to handle all the decisions on your own. There is nothing wrong with wanting to hire help. But I ask you to think of a financial advisor as a coach who is there to offer expert advice and help devise a strategic game plan. But you must be an active participant in the process as well. Hiring a financial advisor is not the end of your work. There is no end here. This is your retirement we are talking about, this is your money, not anyone else's money. As I have said so many times: What happens to your money in the coming years affects you and you alone. So no matter how talented and smart an advisor is, if you blindly hand over your money and the decision making to someone else, that is a failure to stand in your truth. Hire a financial advisor to *help you* make the right choices for your future.

In previous books I have offered detailed advice on how to identify a solid financial advisor. At my website you can read the steps I recommend you take when interviewing possible fee-only advisors. But I do want to be very clear here: Fee-only advisors are in fact the only financial advisors you are to ever work with. Fee-only advisors charge a flat hourly fee, or if they oversee your investments, they will charge a small percentage of your total assets. But they do not make any money through sales commissions on the investments you buy, sell, and own.

An advisor who is reliant on commissions has an inherent conflict of interest. To get paid, an advisor who relies on commissions or trade-based fees needs you to buy certain investments to get paid. So that raises a question: Are you being advised to make an investment or trade because it is the right and smart move for your future, or because it generates a commission for the advisor? You should never put yourself in a situation where you have to ask yourself that. Working with a fee-based advisor is the way to go.

I hope what I am about to say will be ridiculously obvious to all of you, but history tells me this is an age-old problem: A referral from a friend or family member is not all you need to find a financial advisor. Bernie Madoff had great word of mouth for decades. Gather leads from people you admire and trust, and then do your own legwork to verify that the advisor is not only legit, but is someone you feel understands you and your financial situation. In the second class of this book I discussed my belief in trusting your gut—if something does not feel right to you, you must honor that. You are never to take a leap of faith, particularly when it comes to choosing someone who will be instrumental in the handling of your finances, simply on the basis of what someone else says. You have to get in there face-to-face and assess the situation for yourself.

LESSON 6. PLAN FOR LONG-TERM CARE COSTS

One of the most important decisions to make by your 50s, one that can have a huge effect on your retirement years, is whether to purchase a long-term care (LTC) insurance policy. Long-term care insurance helps pay for your care if you can no longer take care of yourself without assistance. LTC insurance can pay for someone to help within your home and it can also be used to help with nursing home costs. I think buying an LTC policy now is a seriously smart move to make because the policy will be much more affordable. However, you will once again have to factor the cost into your annual expenses for years to come—possibly all the way to age 84. Why 84? That is the age when people typically need this type of care. It will do you no good to purchase a policy now, pay for it for ten years, and then have to give it up in retirement because you can't afford it. No one wins in that situation except the insurance company. But if you can afford it, I would urge you to buy it. I remember suggesting to my mother that she buy a long-term care policy about twenty years ago. I even told her I would pay for the premiums, but she refused. She said she would never need such a thing. She even refused to sit for an exam. In April 2012 my mother, God bless her, turns 97. Her expenses in an assisted living facility are approximately $20,000 a month. If my mom did not have my help in covering these costs, I cannot imagine the life she would be living right now. So know that this is a subject I take very seriously—and so should you.

WHEN TO BUY

In the past I have recommended you wait until age 59 to purchase an LTC policy. Given recent changes to these policies, I now say that is the latest you should consider making a purchase. Your age at time of purchase and your health status determine your premium cost. If you purchase a policy before age 59 you will likely pay a premium of less than $2,500 a year. Furthermore, what you want to avoid is being turned down outright because of a health issue; the older you are when you apply, the more likely you are to have a preexisting condition that could impact whether you are able to buy a policy, or the cost of that policy. It's just a fact of life that medical issues increase as we age. That is why I recommend you make your LTC decision no later than 59.

Go to The Classroom at www.suzeorman.com: I have more information on how health issues can impact your ability to qualify for LTC insurance.

THE FINANCIAL CASE FOR BUYING LONG-TERM CARE INSURANCE

The fact that on average we are all living longer creates a bit of a good news/bad news situation for your retirement planning. A longer life span increases the likelihood that at some point you may no longer be able to take care of yourself.

Some of us may need nursing home care. The median daily rate for a private room in a skilled nursing home in 2011 was $213, according to Genworth Financial's comprehensive survey of long-term care costs. A semiprivate room at a private nursing home carried a median daily rate of $193. And that's just today's cost. Like most of our healthcare system, long-term care costs have been rising more than the general inflation rate, about 5% a year. At that pace, the cost in 20 years could easily be $512 a day for a private room, or more than $185,000 a year.

What's really eye-opening, though, is the cost of at-home care, something that many more of us will likely require. At some point we may well need to hire people to come into our homes to help us manage the daily rhythms of life after a serious accident or as we age. And that can end up being even more expensive than nursing home care. The median hourly salary in 2011 for a home healthcare aide, according to Genworth, was $19; that adds up to more than $450 a day for round-the-clock care. Moreover, assisted living facilities carry a median monthly rate of about $3,260. Even adult day care is around $60 a day. It's all expensive and something you must plan for if you are going to live a long life without outliving your money.

HEALTH INSURANCE, MEDICARE, AND MEDICAID

Please know that your current health insurance policies and Medicare do not cover your long-term care needs. Medicare offers limited financial assistance for short-term recovery periods of less than three months. If you have been hospitalized (for at least three days) and then move to a Medicare-approved skilled nursing home facility, Medicare will only pick up the full tab for 20 days. For days 21–100 you must contribute to the cost of your care—called a copay. Beyond 100 days there is no coverage. Medicare coverage for at-home care is also limited. The bottom line is that Medicare will provide limited help in covering your long-term care needs. At Medicare.gov you can download a free booklet that explains Medicare coverage.

A Promising Development: A Partnership Between LTC Insurance and Medicaid

In the past, Medicaid (MediCal in California) has paid for long-term care only after people have spent down most of their own money. As I have said many times, if you think choices where you can receive care when you are on Medicaid are as good as when you are a private-pay patient, I am here to tell you that you are wrong.

But a promising program called the Partnership for Long-Term Care makes it possible to hold on to more of your assets if you were to ever need to apply for long-term care coverage that is provided within the Medicaid program. Under partnership plans, states allow consumers who purchase a state-approved LTC policy to be able to keep assets equal to the benefits paid out by your policy. The idea is that you buy as much private insurance as you can afford from an insurance company that participates in the Partnership program and if it isn't enough, you can then use Medicaid as a safety net to help pay for your care for the rest of your life without spending most of your hard-earned money first.

You can learn more about these programs—including whether your state has a program in place—by typing "State Partnership Programs" into the search box of the government's long-term care website (www.longtermcare.gov) or in The Classroom at my website.

Clearly, planning for how you will be able to cover later-life care expenses is a big piece of your retirement puzzle. It is also of extreme importance for your children as well. In the Family Class

I discuss how to stand in the truth while raising your kids—instilling good money values and helping them establish a firm financial foothold in their young adult years. Well, Mom and Dad, one of the most incredible gifts you can bestow on your grown children is to do your very best to plan ahead so you can cover your care costs later in life. That will help your kids reach their retirement dreams by reducing the likelihood—or the cost—of helping you out down the line. That is not just a financial gift; it carries tremendous emotional power as well. Releasing your adult children from the worry of how they might have to simultaneously care for you and their own family gives them more breathing space to live their lives to their fullest. That's part of your legacy as well.

And that is why I think everyone who can truly afford a solid LTC insurance policy should have one. Please read that carefully; the point I am going to stress here again is affordability. I am not just talking about the cost of a policy you buy today. The biggest challenge is to make sure that you will be able to afford paying an LTC premium year after year. You should anticipate an increase of 50% in that premium cost, too, over time. The LTC insurance industry is still in its early growth stages and insurers have yet to figure out how to properly price the policies to cover their claims. What has been happening is that many LTC insurers have raised their rates on existing policies by double digits. And some insurers have recently decided to stop selling new policies, period (don't worry; they are still honoring existing policies). I do not think that is a reason to avoid LTC insurance. But it does make it very important to shop wisely and make sure the policy you buy today is a policy you will still be able to afford if it incurs a price hike.

You can learn more about LTC policies at the website www .longtermcare.gov. The consumer section of the American Association for Long-Term Care Insurance (www.aaltci.org) is also a good resource for learning about LTC insurance as is the Life and Health Insurance Foundation for Education (www.lifehappens .org). Below I walk through the ins and outs of LTC; after you read what I have to say I encourage you to explore these websites and learn more.

LONG-TERM CARE BASICS

Long-term care insurance is a lot like car or home insurance. You choose the parameters of your coverage and pay an annual premium to keep the policy in force year after year. Eventually, if your physical or mental capacities decline and a doctor deems you need care, you then file a claim on your LTC policy that will give you money you can use to pay for your care. During any period when you are receiving an LTC insurance benefit you are not required to pay the premium. The challenge is that you must carefully think through exactly what coverage you want; unlike car or auto insurance, there are no mandated guidelines. You are in charge of building your own custom policy that fits your family's needs and, most important, your budget.

I highly recommend you work with a qualified insurance broker who specializes in long-term care insurance. An LTC specialist can help you build the right policy for your situation and will get you quotes from multiple LTC insurance companies. Ask friends for leads, or refer to the websites I mentioned above for more information on how to locate qualified LTC insurance agents.

Here are the key points you want to discuss with an LTC insurance agent:

- **The daily or monthly benefit amount.** This is one of the most important decisions you will have to make. How much will your policy pay you per day, or monthly, to cover you if you need care at home or in an assisted living facility or a nursing home?

- **Find out what care costs in your area.** The cost of care—be it home care, assisted living, or nursing home care—varies widely depending on where you live. Genworth Financial publishes a comprehensive annual cost survey that breaks down costs by state and metro region. You can get a free copy of the report at www.genworth.com.

- **Buy only what you can afford.** One of the biggest mistakes people make when evaluating LTC insurance policies is to think that they must buy a policy that covers 100% of the cost in their area for a certain number of years. A 100% policy is a nice goal, but it may not be realistic for many of you. Please do not be discouraged. And please do not stretch your finances to buy a policy that is not really affordable. That makes no sense.

I want you to focus on what is possible and realistic. Focus on what you can do, not what you can't. Every penny in LTC benefits you can realistically afford today is a penny that you—and your children—will not need to pull out of your own savings if you indeed require care at some point.

- **How your benefits will be paid.** There are four basic ways you can receive payment.
  1. **Reimbursement.** You are paid back for daily or monthly costs you incur.
  2. **Indemnity.** You receive a set daily or monthly benefit regardless of your expenses for that period.
  3. **Cash.** You receive a check each month and can use the money as needed. This means you can use it to pay informal caregivers like family, friends, neighbors, or sitters, as well as companions provided by a caregiving agency. Be aware, though, that if you choose this method you will likely be responsible for the Social Security, Medicare, and unemployment tax of people you pay for care.
  4. **Hybrid.** This is a new offering that allows you to take up to 70% of your home healthcare benefit in cash to use in any way you choose. A qualified LTC insurance agent will help you sort through the best choice for your circumstances.

- **The type of care that is covered.** You can choose a policy that will only pay a benefit if you are in an assisted living facility or a nursing home, or you can opt for a plan that offers coverage for at-home care in addition to coverage for care in an assisted living facility or nursing home. I highly recommend you consider as broad a policy as possible that covers not just nursing home care, but all types of care. Nearly 70% of current LTC claims are made for at-home or assisted living care. Flexibility here is so important.

- **The elimination period.** Sounds awful, doesn't it? This is simply the number of days you must pay out of your own pocket before your policy begins to make payments. It is the LTC version of an insurance deductible. You can typically choose a 30-day, 60-day, or 90-day elimination period. The longer the period, the lower your premium will be. But please be very careful here and make sure that if you choose a longer elimination period you can afford to cover those costs on your own. Ask your agent to calculate the expected daily cost at age 75 and age 85 and then multiply those costs by 30, 60, and 90 days. That is what you must have in savings to pay for your own care during the elimination period.

- **An inflation rider.** We all know that healthcare expenses in our country keep going up and up, far more than the general inflation rate. And long-term care is no exception. That is why I absolutely insist that you purchase only an LTC policy that includes an annual inflation adjustment that increases the value of your benefit each year. I recommend you lock in a 5% annual inflation adjustment and make sure that the inflation is calculated using "compounding" rather than simple interest. Compounding will give you the largest benefit increase over the years if you start in your 50s.

Note: State-approved partnership policies require some type of inflation benefit if you are under age 76 when you buy, and compound if you are under age 61.

> **Go to The Classroom at www.suzeorman.com:**
> You will find more information there about the various inflation choices you have when purchasing an LTC policy.

- **Spousal/partner policies.** Couples have some LTC options that can reduce their total costs, including having access to each other's benefit pool if one needs more care or to inherit unused benefits when one dies. Another option is to buy one policy that either person can use. Make sure your agent explains how a combined policy could work for you and your spouse. Also, if you are in a same-sex relationship many policies will also give you a discount if you and your partner both apply. In most cases you just need to be living together and be able to prove that you are in fact a true partnership.

- **How long you want benefits to be paid.** The average claim period for an LTC policy is about three years. Common choices are 2, 3, 4, 5, or 6 years, and unlimited. A policy that pays benefits no matter how long you need care can be very expensive; a policy that will pay for three years of care will be far less expensive. Ask your agent to explain the difference in premium costs if you were to purchase a policy with a three-year, five-year, or unlimited benefit pool.

Note that this is where the Long-Term Care Partnership plans I mentioned earlier can be especially helpful. With a partnership plan you buy the amount of time you can afford and if you wind up needing care longer, the state will let you apply for Medicaid's help while keeping assets equal to what your policy has paid out in benefits. But please also think about more than money here. If your family has a history of dementia or Alzheimer's or other long-term debilitating illnesses, you will want to weigh the possibility of needing care for more years, not fewer.

As you can see, there are many variables that will impact the cost of your premium. You want to work with an LTC agent who will get you quotes for a variety of scenarios, and then you can sit down together and carefully assess what makes the most sense. If you do not have access to a local LTC insurance specialist, or cannot find good references, contact LTC insurance consumer advocate and educator Phyllis Shelton at GotLTCi.com for advice. Phyllis is a tremendous resource; she helped me purchase my own LTC insurance policy. And just to anticipate a question: I have no business arrangement with Phyllis and do not receive a penny from any policy you might purchase.

Employer-Sponsored LTC Insurance Policies Can Be a Great Deal

Be sure to check and see if your employer offers access to a long-term care insurance policy. This can be a great way to get coverage, as there is typically a more lenient process for assessing your health status for new hires or when an employer first offers this benefit.

If your employer does sponsor an LTC insurance benefit you can purchase, other family members—parents, grandparents, siblings, and adult children—may be eligible to apply and will have access to the same premiums as you. The same idea works in reverse as well: Ask your adult kids if their employer offers an LTC insurance benefit that is extended to family members.

As you narrow your choices, please make sure you follow these two steps:

1. Add 50% to the quoted premium. When you buy an LTC insurance policy in your 50s, you could pay the premium for decades before you ever make a claim. And the reality is that over those years there is a very real possibility your premium will rise. Insurance companies are not allowed to raise premiums on an individual-by-individual basis; they must apply to the state insurance commission for an across-the-board hike that is applied to all policyholders in that state, or within a group policy. But I need to be up front here: We are seeing some insurers win very large premium increases of 25% to 40% as the insurers are learning that their claims are running much higher than anticipated.

So that's why I want you to compute what a premium quote you receive today would cost you if it were to rise as much as 50%. Let's hope you aren't hit with such a big premium increase. But I need you to decide if you could in fact afford the premium if it were to rise that much. Please face up to this possibility, because it is so important. It makes no sense to buy a policy today if you cannot handle an increase. I am so saddened by the many people who have been hit with a large increase and then abandon their policy after having paid thousands of dollars in premiums. That is such a tragic waste of money.

So what do you do if you already own an LTC policy and your premium has increased to a point where you can't afford it? The worst possible outcome is that you walk away from the policy entirely. Talk to your LTC insurance agent about how you may be able to keep the cost affordable, possibly by reducing your benefits. I also encourage all parents to talk to their adult children about what is happening. If you drop the coverage entirely it raises the likelihood that you and your children may one day need to pay all the costs for care. I would recommend you ask your children if they could help you pay for the increase in the premium. I know how hard that is to contemplate, but please think through what a gift this may be for them. By contributing $1,000 or $2,000 or so a year now to help you pay your premium, they are buying insurance for themselves as well: the insurance that they will not need to pay what could be tens of thousands of dollars a year if down the line you need care and you do not have the LTC policy.

Now, if after adding 50% to the current cost you decide the policy is unaffordable, that doesn't mean you shouldn't buy LTC insurance. What you want to do is rethink the level of coverage so you can reduce the premium enough today that it will still be affordable if in the future you face a premium increase.

2. Consider policies from financially strong insurers that have been in the LTC business at least 10 years. When you purchase an LTC policy it is with the expectation that the insurance company will still be alive and well 10, 20, 30 years from now when you might make a claim. I want you to focus on insurers who have strong financial strength ratings from one of the major rating agencies—Standard & Poor's, Moody's, or A.M. Best. Each firm uses a slightly different rating scale. Here's a guideline for what constitutes a very strong rating for each insurer:

- Standard & Poor's: AA or better
- Moody's: AA or better
- A.M. Best: A or better

I also recommend you only work with an insurer that has a good track record in the LTC market, and that has not run into complaints with your state insurance commissions for unjustly denying LTC benefits claims. To find a list of companies selling LTC insurance in your state go to www.naic.org/state_web_map .htm. You can research complaints at https://eapps.naic.org/cis.

Some good companies currently writing new LTC policies as of late 2011 are Country Life, Genworth, Mass Mutual, Mutual of Omaha, New York Life, Northwestern Mutual, Prudential, State Farm, Transamerica, and UNUM.

Being able to qualify for long-term care insurance is a precious gift. If you can get it, I encourage you to do so and not allow anyone to talk you out of it. LTC coverage, in my opinion, offers more than financial protection for you. If your children don't have the money to pay for your care, they may wind up making really difficult lifestyle choices in order to care for you themselves. They may have to give up a promising career that could affect their ability to pay for your grandchild's college education. Or they may have trouble maintaining a committed relationship because your care becomes their first priority. This is why I want to leave you with the thought that long-term care insurance is really about taking care of your family and preserving your dignity.

LESSON RECAP

We should have a special graduation exercise for making it to the end of this class. It feels more like you've earned a degree, given all the topics we have covered, than having taken a class.

I want you to know that I understand just how easy it can be to read through this class and be overcome with anxiety. It's a huge amount of information to process—and it's not just facts and figures; every fact carries an emotional component. There is no way that the subject of retirement finances can be discussed in a lab, devoid of the human cost of every calculation. Add to that the anxious economic news of the past several years and it creates a cauldron of worry. I get it. But I also know that misinformation and ignorance are what anxiety thrives on, and the only way to combat it is through knowledge and action. That is why the information imparted in this class is so dense and so comprehensive. Now that we've reached the end, I hope I've at least been able to alleviate your concerns about not knowing what to expect. The emotional impact of the information I cannot dismiss so easily, but I can tell you what you need to know and what you need to do to face down that vast unknown territory just over the hilltop of your working life. I've been down that road with many of you before. It's where I started when I wrote my first book.

When I wrote *You've Earned It, Don't Lose It* in 1994, I thought the retirement planning process was complicated enough. But in retrospect, retirement in those days could still well be called the golden years. The majority of my private clients had old-fashioned pensions to look forward to; our work was to figure out what the best payout method for them was. Today the issues are so much more complex; you must set aside your own money in retirement accounts, you must figure out how to invest that money, and then in retirement it's up to you to figure out how to withdraw that money without risking that the well runs dry before you die. And fifteen years ago far fewer people within a decade or so of retiring were still staring at huge mortgages and massive bills for their children's college education. Nowadays, you may have earned it, but the ways in which you can lose it are much more varied and in many ways more treacherous.

I've been asked numerous times over the years to update my first book or to write a new book about retirement. I resisted, until now. As you can see from this chapter, the subject is a complex one in so many ways: from the changes in legislation to the seismic economic jolts to the way we see ourselves aging in society . . . this is one tough subject to tackle. Maybe the toughest. But there was no way to write a book about the New American Dream without a top-to-bottom reconsideration of retirement. The image our grandchildren will have of us in our golden years will no doubt be radically different than the way we viewed our grandparents in their dotage. And so our Act III will shape their notion of the American Dream. It's just one more reason—not that you needed another!—why it is so important to make the most of these decades that precede retirement. Reimagining the American Dream is the legacy you will hand down to future generations. I urge you to face this challenge with all the courage you can muster and a generous amount of hope. Here's to a better tomorrow, and the best possible retirement in a decade or two.

Once more, let's run down the major points of this class:

- Consider paying off your mortgage before you retire.
- Start planning for how you will be able to keep working well into your 60s.
- Save more today so you will be okay if you can't afford to save in your 60s.
- Make it a goal to delay when you start drawing Social Security, so you can earn a benefit that could be 80% bigger than if you start early.
- Make sure all your retirement accounts are invested to complement one another.
- Decide no later than age 59 if long-term care insurance should be part of your retirement plan.

CLASS

8

LIVING IN RETIREMENT

THE TRUTH OF THE MATTER

The impact of the recent financial crisis has made life anything but easy for today's retirees. Believe me, I know: Those of you who are living off your savings and Social Security have been among the hardest hit these past few years.

Ever since the downturn took hold in 2008, the Federal Reserve has aggressively reduced the federal funds interest rate in an effort to encourage businesses to borrow and lend more. That may have helped our economy avoid an all-out depression, but as every retiree knows only too well, the Federal Reserve policy means that all short-term interest rates are now at near record lows. In late 2011, a six-month certificate of deposit (CD) has a yield of less than 1%. In 2008, before the crisis, that same CD was yielding 5%. Let's say you had $250,000 that you kept safe and sound in CDs. Three years ago that portfolio might have generated $12,500 annually in interest. In 2011 the same account would have earned just $2,000. And with the Federal Reserve's announcement that it will keep short-term interest rates low into mid-2013, what you can safely earn on your cash is not going to improve anytime soon. How are you supposed to make ends meet on a fixed income, when your income just fell by nearly 85%?

And then there is the frustration with Social Security. There was no cost of living increase added to your benefit in 2010 or 2011, even though many of your daily expenses cost more than they did in 2009. For 2012, the cost of living increase is 3.6%. And even if you had the energy and determination to go back to work part-time to bring in some extra cash, it's not exactly an easy time for anyone, especially retirees, to find work.

It is indeed a very tough time for retirees. Tough, but not insurmountable. Even if you are living on a fixed income, there are steps you can take today that can help. The core of this class is instruction on how to maximize your savings so they earn as much as possible for you. That entails a lesson in knowing what to do—invest in dividend-paying stocks—as well as what not to do: Avoid long-term bonds and bond funds.

I look back to 1994, when I published my first book, *You've Earned It, Don't Lose It,* and the temptation is to see it as a much simpler time. True, we tend to view times past with that kind of nostalgia, but in this case, the description fits. My advice back then was focused on how soon-to-be-retirees and retirees should handle their retirement income. Most of my clients back then came to me with a fairly simple task: how best to take their pension from their employer. Those ample pensions along with Social Security were a solid foundation for being able to live comfortably.

But for so many of you today, you may not have a pension, or your benefit was frozen years ago. Another interesting trend is that many of you may have opted to take a lump sum from your pension, and now you are struggling with how to make that lump sum last, and generate income for you.

In 1994 investing for income was relatively easy. Back then we could earn more than 4% in a 12-month Treasury bill. As I write this in fall 2011 the current rate is 0.1%. And back then, if we chose to lock in higher yields in longer-term bonds, the risk was far less than what you face today. In the mid-1990s we were still in the early stages of a cyclical decline in interest rates from a high that had peaked in the early 1980s. As you may know, when interest rates fall, the price of bonds rises, so even though the yield we could earn on bonds was falling, the value of those bonds was climbing. Today we face the exact opposite scenario. We are now at the end of that long cyclical decline, and in the coming years we will see interest rates climb. When that transpires bond prices will drop. That makes it an especially dangerous time for retirees today; if you are venturing into long-term bonds and bond funds because of their higher yields, you may well find your portfolio stung by falling bond prices going forward when rates rise.

And we have to be honest: Some of your income may still be going toward paying down debt. Unlike the majority of my clients from 15 and 20 years ago, today's retirees tend to have more debt than retirees of generations past. The prevalence of retirees still with mortgages or home equity lines of credit is higher today than it was 15 and 20 years ago. Nor have retirees been able to steer clear of credit card debt. At the same time, medical costs above and beyond what is covered by Medicare keep growing at a rate that exceeds the general rate of inflation.

There is no question that living in retirement today is more challenging for more of us than it has been at any point in the past 75 years—probably since the Great Depression. That may sound like cold comfort, but some hard-to-find perspective could be your greatest asset right now. I have heard from so many of you how devastated you are that your sizable retirement portfolio lost $100,000 or more during the recent bear market. You are right to be upset; a loss of any magnitude is hard to swallow. But let's think through how that loss impacts your month-to-month living. As I explain later in this class, you probably don't want to withdraw more than 4% of your retirement fund each year. So let's say your $500,000 portfolio fell to $400,000. At a 4% annual withdrawal rate that means you might need to reduce your withdrawal from $20,000 a year to $16,000. That's $333 a month. I realize that is not an inconsequential sum. But in practical terms that is easier to manage than a onetime $100,000 hit. Convert it into its tangible impact on your life today—$333 a month—and it becomes a little easier to cope with. The challenge then becomes how you might rein in your spending until your portfolio recovers.

Because everyone could use help in navigating this passage, I have organized this Retirement Class into six lessons:

- Home Finances: Stand in the Truth of What Is Affordable for You
- Coping with the High Cost of Healthcare in Retirement
- Stick to a Sustainable Withdrawal Rate
- Avoid Long-Term Bonds and Bond Funds
- Earn Higher Yields by Investing in Dividend-Paying ETFs and Stocks
- Double-Check Your Beneficiaries and Must-Have Documents

LESSON 1. HOME FINANCES: STAND IN THE TRUTH OF WHAT IS AFFORDABLE FOR YOU

If you are already retired and you're feeling the pinch of a mortgage that is yet to be paid off, I must ask you to consider if you can truly afford to stay in that home. I recognize the weight of that consideration and how upsetting an idea it can be when you first confront it; after all, having to leave your home was probably not a part of a retirement forecast made years before. But I am making a few assumptions here: First, if you are reading this chapter you are likely in your late 60s or your early 70s. Your income-earning days are probably behind you, yet there is a very good chance you have at least another 15–20 full and rich years ahead of you. If a mortgage payment is already weighing you down each month and causing anxiety, then that stress will not get better with time, as you grapple with other rising costs, such as healthcare not covered by Medicare; it will only get worse.

If you recognize yourself in the paragraph above, then I encourage you to read the advice I give in the prior class about paying off your mortgage on an accelerated schedule. Beginning on page 199 you will find a detailed strategy for how to tap retirement savings to pay off the mortgage.

The first crucial question you must address, of course, is whether you can indeed afford to pay off your mortgage. That is, if you were to use a portion of your savings today to pay off the mortgage, would you still have enough in your retirement accounts to support you for years to come?

This is your stand-in-the-truth moment. I need you to summon a lifetime's worth of courage and honesty. For if the truth is that paying off your mortgage would deplete your retirement savings to a level that could impact your ability to live comfortably, then we need to face the fact that perhaps it is time to consider moving to a less expensive home, perhaps in a less expensive neighborhood or region of the country.

What about a reverse mortgage? Yes, this is indeed an option. But as I explain in the Home Class, if you feel the need to do a reverse mortgage in your 60s and early 70s, that is a signal to me that your finances are already too stretched. The costs and trade-offs of a reverse mortgage are indeed steep. Please read that section of the Home Class and then ask yourself if it makes sense to stay in your home or if it is the unspoken root of your anxiety.

I have to tell you that as hard as the decision may be for you today, it will be a gift for you and your family if you can summon the strength to make that decision sooner rather than later. What I see so often is retirees refusing to contemplate the affordability issue, and then in their 80s it falls to their kids to make that most difficult of calls. And if you need to move at that juncture, the upheaval will be so much more taxing emotionally and physically.

I encourage you to make this a family discussion. Let's all be realistic here: In the coming years your adult children may need to step in with some financial assistance—just as you may have done for your parents. That is part of the rhythm of life across the generations. My suggestion here is that you ask your grown children for their input. It may be that your children have the ability to help you get the mortgage paid off today; and if you and they believe that staying in your home is the best course for all parties concerned, then that could be a wonderful option. But perhaps in having this conversation you get your children to open up about their financial situation as well. And the fact is, many of them may already be stressed over how to make their own household's finances work. The prospect of needing to help you as well—now or later—could be something that is already of concern to them. It's not that they don't want to help; it's that they don't know how they will be able to help, given their own retirement concerns, lower home equity, and financial commitments to their own children.

So I ask you to please start talking, so you can decide together and examine how these financial decisions will impact other generations. And if you haven't yet read the Family Class, please make it your next stop. As I suggest in that class, in some families it might be worth considering combining households, be it with your children, siblings, or cousins. I know, I know—that will strike many of you as a horrendous idea that compromises your fundamental independence. But I take issue with the stigma that seems to be attached to this idea. Not only can it be a great financial move, it can also provide companionship for all. Countless studies have shown the health and psychological benefits of elderly people staying engaged with family and community; and we know in our hearts that grandparents can enrich the lives of their grandchildren in so many meaningful ways. In my opinion, it's certainly something worth considering.

LESSON 2. COPING WITH THE HIGH COST OF HEALTHCARE IN RETIREMENT

If you are already enrolled in Medicare you no doubt have come to realize something important: It doesn't cover everything. Now, one bright spot for many of today's retirees is that your former employer may be subsidizing your healthcare expenses that aren't covered by Medicare. But that benefit too could be heading toward extinction for those not in public-sector jobs. The percentage of large firms (500+ employees) that offer retiree health coverage has fallen from 40% in 1993 to 21% today. The percentage is far lower for employees of smaller firms. In most instances the retiree is wholly responsible for paying his or her premium cost.

A reality we must all accept is that the price of medical care is rising at a pace that far outpaces the general inflation rate. And to date, Washington has yet to address ways to bring costs down to a more manageable growth rate. So the likelihood is that your out-of-pocket medical costs will keep eating up a greater percentage of your annual income. I mention that not to scare you, but to focus you on reality. Any extra saving you can do today means more money you will have to cover those costs.

If you don't yet have long-term care insurance and you are still in relatively good health, I also want you to carefully read through the LTC lesson in the previous class. As I explain, the ideal time to purchase LTC insurance is before age 59, but that does not mean you cannot or should not purchase a policy if you are older. Yes, the premium will be more expensive. And that may mean you will need to consider a policy with less coverage than you might have been able to afford if you had purchased a policy in your 50s. But there is still so much security to be gained from purchasing a policy today, if in fact you can afford to do so.

And I would urge you to include any grown children in this decision. I think a family strategy for LTC insurance is something that can have a huge benefit for both generations. Let's say you get a quote for an LTC insurance policy that is for $4,000 a year. You crunch the numbers and know that all you can truthfully afford is $2,500 a year. Before you walk away from the idea, or ask for a new premium quote with lower benefits, please talk to your children. If you have two grown children who can each pitch in $750 a year (less than $63 a month), they can help you afford the $4,000 premium. And I have news for you: They are not doing you a favor; you are doing them the favor. I can't overstate this fact: While your kids will do anything and everything to take care of you in your later years, many of them are in a slow panic over how they will be able to afford helping you while also supporting their own family. By asking them to help you purchase an LTC insurance policy, you have just given them an incredibly affordable means to protect themselves from much of those future costs. Please do not get trapped in misplaced pride. Asking your children to share in this insurance cost is ultimately an act of caring.

What to Do If Your Current LTC Policy Has a Huge Premium Increase

In recent years, many people who already own an LTC insurance policy have been hit with budget-busting premium increases of as much as 40%. I can imagine how unsettling that is for households that were so careful and responsible to buy LTC insurance, only to struggle with whether they can afford to keep the policy. And as I explain in the LTC lesson in the previous class, the trend toward higher premiums could be here to stay for many years.

If you ever are hit with a steep premium increase, please promise me that you will do everything possible to keep some level of insurance. For starters, please reread the advice I just gave: Your kids may be very eager to step in and help with the added cost. If that is not practical, then talk to your agent about how you can adjust the level of coverage—maybe shorten the lifetime benefit or increase the elimination period—to bring down the cost of the new premium.

LESSON 3. STICK TO A SUSTAINABLE WITHDRAWAL RATE

I have stated this elsewhere in the book, but I want to make sure retirees have heard this: If you have made it to retirement age, there is a very good chance that you will live two or three decades in retirement.

A 65-year-old man today has an average life expectancy of age 82 and a 65-year-old woman has an average life expectancy of age 85. Understanding what *average* means is important: If you are 65 years old with a life expectancy of age 85 you have a 50-50 chance that you will still be alive at 85. Life expectancy is not a statistical estimate of when you will die; it is a measure of the age at which 50% of an age group will still be alive. And if you in fact make it to those life expectancy milestones, your life expectancy resets again—about five years or so. My mom, God bless her, is still alive at the age of 96.

So that is why I want those of you retiring today to follow the 4% withdrawal rule in the first year of retirement if you are going to begin making those withdrawals in your 60s. That is, you should aim to withdraw no more than 4% or so of your savings in the first year of retirement. You can then adjust that amount upward each year for inflation, but try to keep your early withdrawal rate at 4%. If you have an age-appropriate mix of stocks and bonds, at a 4% withdrawal rate you minimize the chances your money will run out too quickly. An analysis by T. Rowe Price estimates that a retiree with a portfolio that is invested 40% in stocks and 60% in bonds would have a 90% probability of his money lasting 30 years if he chose a 4% initial withdrawal rate that was then increased each year to keep pace with inflation.

Now pay attention here: If that retiree instead chose a 6% withdrawal rate the probability he would still have any money left after 30 years falls to 24%. This person went from a 90% chance of having his retirement money last 30 years to a 24% chance because of a 2% increase in withdrawals. Wow—take a minute to process that. Let's say you have a $500,000 retirement portfolio that you are going to start making withdrawals from this year. A 6% annual withdrawal this year comes to $30,000, or $2,500 a month. (Remember, though: Withdrawals from traditional 401(k)s and IRAs will be taxed as ordinary income, and you may owe a capital gains tax on withdrawals from regular taxable accounts as well.) But that $2,500 a month comes with a big risk that you might run out of money. To have a 90% probability your money will outlast you requires that you make do with a 4% initial withdrawal rate. That's $20,000 a year, or $1,667 a month—nearly $1,000 less each month, in this example. It's a significant difference, but then again, is there anything more important than the certainty that your money will last you throughout your retirement? In that two-percentage-point variance lies a world of difference.

Now, if you are many years into retirement, you may well be able to pull out more each year. If you manage to wait until your 70s to begin to make withdrawals, you can consider starting with a 5% withdrawal rate. And of course, if you have other reliable income sources such as a bountiful pension, you may indeed be fine with a higher withdrawal rate. But again I would caution you to be careful. I appreciate that with interest rates so low, the yield you can earn on your bond and cash investments has made it hard, if not impossible, to generate enough income to pay your bills. But the answer is not to withdraw big sums from your account. If you eat into that principal too much and you are fortunate enough to enjoy a long life, I am sorry to tell you that you very well may run out of money.

In the next two lessons I explain how to invest in today's environment so that you can earn 4% to 5% interest on your retirement money. Can it be done? You bet, but it is not as easy as just walking into a bank or credit union and asking for a CD or leaving your money in a money market fund. To create your New American Dream you are going to have to be involved with your money, to know what to do and what not to do. And believe it or not, we are going back to the future. We just may have to do it the way our grandparents did, years ago.

HOW TO MAKE TAX-SMART WITHDRAWALS

When you make withdrawals from your retirement accounts, the tax you owe will be based on the type of account. In these times when you want to maximize every penny of your retirement income, you need to devise a withdrawal strategy that allows you to keep your tax bill as low as possible.

• **Traditional 401(k)s and traditional IRAs** are subject to a required minimum distribution (RMD) by April 1 of the year after you turn 70½. The firm that holds your retirement accounts can tell you what your RMD must be, or you can use the online calculator at apps.finra.org/Calcs/1/RMD. (If your spouse is the beneficiary of your accounts and is 10 years younger than you, your RMD will be lower than the amount shown in the calculator. I recommend you consult with your tax advisor.)

The tax you owe on RMDs is based on your individual income tax rate.

It is very important to follow the RMD rules; there is a 50%

penalty (of the amount that should have been withdrawn) if you fail to make your annual withdrawal. That 50% is in addition to the income tax you owe on all withdrawals.

RMD Tip: If you have multiple tax-deferred accounts, you do not have to take an RMD from each one. You can calculate the total amount due across all the accounts, but then make your withdrawal from just one account. That can cut down on administrative headaches. It also gives you more control over which assets you want to sell.

While you must take your annual RMD from your traditional 401(k) and IRA, I recommend you do not take out more than the RMD if you have other money you can access first. It is always smart to leave money that is sheltered from tax growing for as long as possible. If you have other savings you can tap, that is preferable, especially when those other accounts will bring a less painful tax bill.

• **Roth IRAs:** Withdrawals of money you contributed to a Roth IRA are always tax-free. To withdraw earnings from your account tax-free you must be at least 59½ or have had the account for at least five years.

• **Regular taxable accounts:** Money you withdraw from regular accounts will be taxed only if you have a gain, that is, if you are selling the asset for more than you paid. If you have owned that asset for less than one year, you pay the tax at your ordinary income tax rate. But if you have owned the asset for at least one year it is eligible for the long-term capital gains tax rate. The long-term capital gains rate is either 10% or 15%, depending on your income. Those rates are in effect through 2012. A maximum long-term capital gains tax rate of 15% is a lot better than what you might pay on ordinary income; the top income tax rate is 35%.

Another important consideration is that any loss you have in a taxable investment can be used to reduce your tax bill. (You cannot claim losses from 401(k) and IRA investments.) You can use any loss to offset any capital gains for a given tax year. If you don't have any tax gains, you can claim up to $3,000 of your losses as a deduction. If your loss is more than $3,000 you can keep claiming more losses in subsequent years—either to offset gains in those years, or as a deduction.

Here is how I want you to think strategically about which accounts you withdraw money from to support yourself in retirement:

1. **If you are at least 70½:** Fulfill your RMD on traditional IRA and 401(k)s but do not withdraw more than the RMD.
2. **If you are under 70½ or you need more income than is generated by your RMDs:** Withdraw money tax-free from a Roth IRA.
3. **If you don't have a Roth IRA:** Withdraw money from taxable accounts.
4. **If you don't have a taxable account:** Make additional withdrawals from your traditional 401(k) and IRA accounts.

LESSON 4. AVOID LONG-TERM BONDS AND BOND FUNDS

One of the biggest mistakes I see retirees making today is investing in long-term bonds (and bond funds) because they offer the highest current yields. That is an especially risky move to be making right now. Going forward it is likely we will see interest rates begin to rise and when that happens, the value of long-term bonds will fall. This hasn't really been an issue for nearly 25 years, as we have been living in an extended period where interest rates have been falling. That cycle is coming to an end, and I fear that an entire generation of retirees is about to get a very costly lesson in how rising interest rates can hurt them.

Please read the next section carefully. If your retirement dream relies on income from long-term bonds that you are purchasing today, you may in fact be putting your dream at great risk.

WHAT YOU MUST UNDERSTAND ABOUT BONDS

The longer the maturity of a bond, the more its price will fall when rates rise. Since 1983 we have been in a long cycle of falling interest rates, and that has been great for long-term bonds. But now we are at the end of that falling-rate cycle. So going forward, it is the long-term bonds with the highest yields that will suffer the biggest price declines. Sure, if you buy a 20-year Treasury bond at 4% and you hold it until maturity you are indeed guaranteed to get 100% of your principal back. But during that 20 years your 4% yield will not budge, and it will be less than what you could earn if you invested in new debt. While you are stuck with your 4% yield, new debt in a rising rate environment could yield 5%, 6%, etc. Now when that happens, you could decide to sell your 4% bond so you could reinvest at the higher rates. But remember, the price you will get when you sell a bond before it matures, and with a below-market yield, will be less than what you paid for it. And here is what is also so very important. When interest rates rise so does inflation. Therefore, as your cost of living goes up, your retirement income should also increase. If you are stuck with 20-year bonds paying only 4% when you could be getting 5% or 6% or more you will not be very happy as you struggle to pay your bills or are frustrated your money isn't earning more.

Because we will eventually be seeing interest rates rise, my recommendation is that you invest in bonds with maturities of less than 3 to 5 years. If you own shorter-term issues, when they mature you will have the ability to reinvest at what I expect will be higher rates.

HOW TO BUILD A BOND LADDER

A smart way to deal with the prospect of higher interest rates in the future is to construct your bond portfolio so you have some bonds maturing every year or so. This will allow you to reinvest that money in a higher-yielding bond. It's what is known as bond laddering. I'll give you an example. Let's say you have $50,000 to invest. Rather than taking all $50,000 and investing it in a 5-year bond you could divide up the money among different maturities. For example:

- $10,000 in a 1-year bond
- $10,000 in a 2-year bond
- $10,000 in a 3-year bond

- $10,000 in a 4-year bond
- $10,000 in a 5-year bond

That way every year you have $10,000 that will mature and you can reinvest it in a higher-yielding bond, assuming rates do rise. Even if rates don't rise, your laddering strategy gives you more income than if you stuck with super-short maturities, and also protects you from the very real risk of rising rates. Given where we are with historically low rates, the important fact to stay focused on is that at some point rates will indeed rise. Bond laddering is a strategy I want you to keep handy for the future; once we see rates rise, you should think about staggering your maturities in order to have money available every year to reinvest at those potentially higher rates.

But I have to tell you that bond laddering is not the best move for right now. As I write this in late 2011, we have a very abnormal situation given how Federal Reserve policy is keeping all short-term Treasury issues very low. The yield of a 1-year Treasury bill (the technical term for Treasury bonds with shorter maturities) is 0.1% and the yield on a 5-year Treasury is 1%. As I noted earlier, based on Federal Reserve statements, those low rates will persist into 2013. At the same time you may be able to earn 1% in a 1-year bank or credit union certificate of deposit.

It does not make sense to invest in a longer-term security with a lower yield. My recommendation: Rather than ladder your portfolio as long as Treasury yields are so low, stick with a safe and simple bank or credit union CD. (Remember, up to $250,000—and potentially more depending on your mix of different accounts—is 100% safe if it is deposited at a federally insured bank or credit union.) You should be able to earn 1% or more. You can shop for the best deals at Bankrate.com.

Beware of Long-Term Bond Funds

I always prefer direct investments in individual bonds rather than investing through a bond mutual fund. There is no set single maturity date with a bond fund because the fund owns dozens or hundreds of different bonds that are being bought and sold. I think that's a huge disadvantage when interest rates rise—as I expect them to in the future. At least with a high-quality individual bond you know that if you hold it until it reaches maturity you will be repaid your principal. There is no such guarantee with a bond fund.

That is one reason why I always recommend that once you leave a job (or turn 59½) that you move money out of a 401(k) and into a rollover IRA. Most 401(k)s only offer bond funds, whereas with an IRA at a discount brokerage you have the flexibility to invest directly in individual bonds.

And the big lesson here is that bond funds that own long-term issues will be the most vulnerable if interest rates rise. Remember, when rates rise the price of bonds declines. The longer the maturity, the bigger the decline. If you want to have your money in short-term bond funds (maturities of 3 years or less), that's okay; given the very short maturity, your potential loss will be much less in a rising rate environment. But I have to point out that in late 2011 the yield on a supersafe 1-year bank or credit union CD looks a lot smarter to me. Any money you don't expect to need for a year or more just might be better off in a bank account.

BEYOND TREASURY BONDS: OTHER BOND INVESTMENTS

Investing in Treasury bonds offers important safety: The bond is backed by the full faith and credit of the United States Treasury. No matter what you may think of our current state of affairs, that promise is rock-solid. The decision by Standard & Poor's in August 2011 to downgrade the U.S.'s credit rating from AAA to AA+ was not based on the ability of the Treasury to make its debt payments. Rather, S&P stated their concern over how Congress was choosing to address our debt and deficit debate. That is a very important distinction.

As solid as Treasuries are, there is an obvious trade-off: Typically the interest you can earn on Treasuries is lower than other types of bonds. Here is what you need to know if you want to venture beyond Treasury issues:

Municipal Bonds

I have made no secret of the fact that since 2007 I have been in love with municipal bonds. But investing in municipal bonds is indeed tricky today. Not only have bond values already risen sharply, but we now must consider the troubling finances of states and municipalities that could impact their ability to pay their bond interest. I want to stress that to date, muni bond defaults have been extremely rare. But the fiscal straits of many states and cities are very real. That just increases the need to be extra careful and smart in how you invest in municipal bonds.

Municipal bonds are issued by state and local governments and public agencies to help finance public projects. There is no federal income tax on the interest you earn on a municipal bond. If you live in a state that levies a state income tax, interest from a bond issued by an entity within your state can also be free of state tax. If your retirement income is still high enough that you are in the 35% federal tax bracket, the tax-free yield can be a good advantage. There is of course the risk that if the state or municipality that has issued a bond falls into dire financial shape it could have trouble making all its interest payments. To date this has been extremely rare. Still, I would only recommend you invest in municipal bonds if you have a trusted advisor who specializes in building a well-diversified portfolio of high-quality municipal issues.

Trusting most of the rating agencies and buying bonds with safe ratings is not good enough today. Nor is buying general obligation bonds in certain states. I myself have switched from buying general obligation bonds to general revenue bonds that are tied to an essential public service, such as water service. I think general revenue bonds for essential services can be a smarter investment in this environment. People tend to keep paying their bills for essential services, so bonds whose own payments are made from that revenue flow are likely to have a steady source of money to keep paying their bond interest. As I write this, the states that currently are in the biggest financial trouble are California, Illinois, New York, New Jersey, and Florida. That is not to say all the other states are healthy, mind you; you have to do your homework here.

You have to know what backs the bonds, the condition of the state, and the risk you can afford to take. So if you are going to invest in municipal bonds at this point in time, you really have to know what you are doing. Again, I would encourage you to seek out the help of an expert in municipal bonds and make sure you are thoroughly diversified among various states—and be aware that you might end up owing state taxes on some of those.

Corporate Bonds

Please be very careful if you are buying corporate bonds. I recommend sticking with high-quality bonds rated above BBB. And the same maturity rule applies; I don't think you want to own corporate bonds that mature in more than 5 years. Now, I know many of you may be investing in high-yield corporate bonds, which are also called junk bonds. They definitely pay much higher yields; in fall 2011 the average yield for an index of junk bonds was near 8.5%. I want you to understand, however, that junk bonds are nothing at all like regular bonds. They pay that higher yield because there is a higher risk that the company that issued the debt could run into financial trouble and not be able to honor its payments. Even if that doesn't come to pass, when the markets are volatile, junk bonds will resemble stocks more than bonds. Consider that in October 2008, as the financial crisis was deepening, an index of junk bonds fell 20%! My recommendation is that if you want to invest in junk bonds, you think of them as part of your stock portfolio, not your bond portfolio, because of the risk factor.

Okay, I bet you're getting a little frustrated with me as I tell you not to chase higher yields in the bond market. Stick with me. I actually have a plan that will allow you to earn yields of 3% to 5% or higher without investing in long-term bonds.

LESSON 5. EARN HIGHER YIELDS BY INVESTING IN DIVIDEND-PAYING ETFS AND STOCKS

Yes, as I write this in fall 2011, I am recommending ETFs and stocks over bonds for generating income to help you meet your living expenses.

Stocks belong in most every retiree's portfolio. From a pure planning perspective, if your retirement spans 20 or 30 years, having a small portion of your assets invested in the stock market, with its history of providing inflation-beating gains, makes a lot of sense. And for those of you who intend to leave assets to your heirs, your time horizon is even longer. You need to consider the life span of your beneficiaries—your children and grandchildren.

There is also a timely reason to consider investing in stocks. As I explained in the prior lesson, it is likely that we will see interest rates rise in the coming years and that will present challenges for bond investors. As tempting as it is to think that bonds are the best place to be right now, that is only using the rearview mirror as your guide. And you must look at the road ahead. In an economy where interest rates are rising, bond returns will not be as great as they have been over the past 20 years.

Let's be clear: I am not telling you to sell all your bonds and invest everything in the market. What I am recommending is that you take time to consider seriously what the proper mix of stocks and bonds would be for you to meet your goals. As a retiree, most of your money absolutely belongs in bonds and cash. Most, but not all. Let's go back to that very good rule of thumb: Subtract your age from 100. That is how much you might consider investing in stocks. So if you are 75 I am recommending you consider keeping 25% of your investments in stocks. That is just a guideline; if you have lots of other retirement income—pensions, etc.— and you don't think you need stocks, that's fine. Or if you want to focus on a longer-term strategy for your heirs and keep 30% in stocks, that's also fine. You must stand in the truth of what is best for your life, right now and in the years ahead.

THE CASE FOR DIVIDEND-PAYING ETFS AND STOCKS

Not all companies pay a dividend, but many do. Dividends are a retiree's best friend. Actually, they are great for investors of all ages, but they are especially smart for retirees in search of income.

To start this lesson I want to review a point I made earlier:
As I write this in fall 2011, a six-month certificate of deposit

(CD) has a yield of less than 1%. In 2008, before the financial crisis, that same CD was yielding 5%. Let's say you had $250,000 that you kept safe and sound in CDs. Three years ago that portfolio might have generated $12,500 in interest. In late 2010 the same account would be earning just $2,000.

I mentioned all of that at the start of this class, but I think that is shocking enough that it deserved to be written twice.

And I know it is creating a dangerous problem for many of you. Because your bank deposits and CDs aren't producing enough income, you are withdrawing more of your principal to make up the difference. Using the same example, if you needed to make up the $10,000 shortfall, you would withdraw the money from your $250,000 balance, leaving you $240,000. That leaves you less money to be earning interest. And you and I both know that if you have to withdraw even more—and keep it up for years—you are putting yourself in danger of running out of money. I cannot imagine a more harrowing way to spend your golden years than watching your funds dwindle.

So what I am about to suggest is a strategy that our grandparents and their fellow retirees used to pay their bills years ago. If you focus your investments on dividend stocks with a long history of paying out, you will have yourself a steady income stream. As I write this in early 2011 there are many high-quality stocks that have dividend yields of 3% to as much as 6%. Compare that to the 1% you can currently earn on a short-term CD and you can see why I think dividend stocks can be a great solution to your income shortfall.

Now, that said, it is absolutely true that any stock investment is going to be more volatile than investing in a CD or a short-term bond fund. I do not recommend that you invest any money you think you will need within 10 years or so in stocks. But remember how we talked earlier about the need to own stocks as well as bonds and cash? The fact is, the stock portion of your portfolio can do double duty for you right now. It can provide the opportunity for long-term growth that we know is important given the odds you will live a long time. But while you are investing for that long-term growth you will also receive an income payout—the dividend—that is in fact higher than what you can get in bonds these days. And unlike bond interest rates that are fixed, a dividend can increase over time. That's an important way to keep your money growing along with inflation.

I want to repeat this important point: As long as you know you will not need to sell a stock in the next 10 years or so to cover your living expenses, dividend-paying stocks are a great way to generate income.

I think the smartest way for most of you to invest in dividend stocks is by investing an exchange-traded fund (ETF) that specializes in dividend-paying stocks. An ETF will typically own at least a few dozen individual stocks, so with one investment you will own a diversified portfolio of stocks. For those of you with at least $100,000 or so to invest in stocks, direct investment in individual issues can indeed make plenty of sense. That is how I invest in dividend stocks. Later on in this class I share some guidelines for how to build a portfolio of individual dividend-paying stocks. But I want to stress that I think using ETFs that focus on dividend-paying stocks is a great way to own a diversified portfolio of dividend stocks.

Why do I want you to be protected by diversification and not just buy individual dividend-paying stocks? Let me answer that one by giving you an extreme example. For years BP, British Petroleum, paid shareholders 6% dividends, month in, month out. Then in April 2010, disaster struck in the Gulf of Mexico when a BP oil rig exploded, killing eleven people and touching off an environmental disaster. The stock price crashed, falling more than 50% by July, when the spill was brought under control, and the firm stopped paying its dividend for 2010. And as some of you may have experienced, in the wake of the 2008 financial crisis many banks abolished or sharply reduced their dividend and have yet to restore those payments. Diversification affords protection from the volatility of any given individual stock.

I also want to stress another point about ETFs that invest in dividend-paying stocks: While I think they deserve to be a permanent part of your retirement portfolio given their ability to help you manage inflation, at the same time I recognize that there is indeed much greater peace of mind for many of you by sticking with bonds. As I have explained, the current interest rate environment makes it likely that we will see bond rates rise in the coming years. Until that happens, I hope you will consider adding dividend-paying ETFs or stocks to your portfolio to produce more income. But then, once you see rates rise to a level that you are comfortably certain will provide you plenty of income, you can consider redirecting more of your money into bonds, if that is the truth that will make you feel more secure.

STOCK DIVIDEND BASICS

Some publicly traded companies choose to give a portion of their profits back to their shareholders over the course of a year. That payment is called a dividend. For every share of stock you own, you are entitled to the per-share dividend. For example, let's say you own 10 shares of the XYZ Corp. And the XYZ Corp. pays a quarterly dividend of 25 cents. That means that four times a year you get 25 cents for each share you own. So over a year you would collect $1 for each share you own; in this case, your 10 shares would entitle you to a dividend payout of $10 a year. You are paid that dividend simply because you are a shareholder.

Dividend yield is the per-share dividend divided by the share price of the stock. So let's say you buy a share of the XYZ Corp. for $35 and the company pays a per-share annual dividend of $1. The $1 dividend divided by the $35 share price means your dividend yield is 2.86%. In fact, some solid companies have dividend yields of 3% to 5% or higher. Utility and telecommunication firms such as ConEd and Verizon were yielding 4% or more in late 2011. By way of comparison, a 10-year Treasury bond in late 2011 had a yield of about 2%. And remember, a 10-year bond maturity is way too long, in my opinion, given that when general rates rise, longer-term bonds will suffer the biggest price declines, and so if you hold on to that 10-year bond for the entire 10 years you have no chance of earning a higher yield. In other words, there is indeed "risk" in owning a 10-year Treasury. So what if you were to keep your money in a 1- or 2-year Treasury bill instead? Well, your yield in early 2011 was less than 1%.

See why I think dividend stocks yielding 3% to 5% or more can be a smart part of your retirement portfolio?

The Protection of a Stop-Loss Order

For those of you who are interested in owning dividend-paying stocks but are also worried about downside volatility, I recommend you learn how to place a stop-loss order on an investment. With a stop-loss order, you instruct your discount brokerage to sell any stock once it hits your designated price. So, for example, if you bought an ETF at $35 a share but can't bear the thought of your principal investment losing more than 15%, you could place a stop-loss order on your account that directs the brokerage to sell your shares if the ETF price falls to $29.75. But please know that in a volatile market there is no guarantee you will be cashed out at exactly $29.75. With a stop-loss order you are basically telling your brokerage to get you the best market price once it hits your target.

HOW MUCH TO INVEST IN DIVIDEND-PAYING ETFS

Here are my recommendations:

• **Determine how much of your portfolio you can comfortably devote to the stock market.** I know I am repeating what I said above, but this is so important I want to make sure you hear me loud and clear: No stock investment, even an ETF portfolio of dividend payers, is to be mistaken for a cash investment, or a bond investment. You are to only invest money in dividend-paying ETFs that you will not need to tap for at least 10 years.

• **Diversify.** There are two ways to invest in dividend-paying stocks. You can do it via ETFs that focus on dividend payers, or you can build your own portfolio of individual stocks that pay dividends. If you want to own individual stocks your portfolio should have a minimum of 10 to 12 stocks. It is never smart to have a larger portion of your retirement funds invested in one stock. No matter how stable that stock looks, we can never be sure of its future. If the money you want to devote to stocks is not enough to buy that many individual shares, then I recommend you focus on dividend-paying ETFs.

HOW TO CHOOSE A DIVIDEND-FOCUSED EXCHANGE-TRADED FUND

If you choose to invest in a diversified portfolio of stocks through an ETF, there are in fact many good options to choose from. ETFs tend to have lower expenses than many no-load mutual funds. And many brokerage firms are allowing you to buy and sell certain ETFs for free. As of late 2011, firms that were waiving their commission on certain ETFs included Fidelity, Schwab, TD Ameritrade, and Vanguard.

ETF Fees: All ETFs, like mutual funds, have an expense ratio (the annual charge for administrative and management costs). It is expressed as a percentage. The average expense ratio for a stock mutual fund is about 1%, but some funds charge 1.5% or higher. Every penny that goes to pay the expense ratio is money you lose. And expenses are the one factor that is entirely within your control. You are the one who decides if you will pay high expenses or low expenses. In today's world, where you want to earn as much as possible on your investments, focusing on minimizing the expenses you pay becomes crucial.

Below are some ETFs you might consider for your portfolio. They all focus on dividend-paying stocks and have low expense ratios.

EXCHANGE-TRADED FUNDS THAT FOCUS ON DIVIDEND STOCKS			
ETF (TICKER SYMBOL)	FOCUS	YIELD AS OF NOVEMBER 2011	ANNUAL EXPENSE RATIO
SPDR S&P Dividend (SDY)	Companies that have managed to increase their dividend payout for at least 25 consecutive years	3.3%	0.35%

ETF (TICKER SYMBOL)	FOCUS	YIELD AS OF NOVEMBER 2011	ANNUAL EXPENSE RATIO
Vanguard Dividend Appreciation (VIG)	Screens for the highest-quality corporations that have increased dividend for at least 10 years	2.1%	0.18%
iShares S&P Global Communi-cations (IXP)	Telecom firms, including Verizon and AT&T, that historically offer above-average yields	4.7%	0.48%

TIPS FOR OWNING INDIVIDUAL DIVIDEND-PAYING STOCKS

If you are interested in building a portfolio of individual dividend stocks rather than purchasing an ETF that holds a basket of dividend payers, make sure you follow a few key steps in putting together a strong portfolio:

• **Avoid the highest yielding stocks.** As I write this in late 2011, the yield of the S&P 500 stock index, considered a solid benchmark of "the market," is 2.2%. That average yield includes some firms that have lower yields and others with higher yields. For example, the utility and telecommunications sectors have mature companies that tend to offer higher dividend yields; the average payout right now for those two sectors is 4.5% for utilities and 5.7% for telecom stocks.

Those are good benchmarks to keep in mind when investing in dividend stocks. When you see a dividend yield of 8%, 10%, or higher, that should be a big warning signal. When a stock yield is that high it is a sign that the company may be in trouble and unable to continue to make its dividend payout. It's important to remember how a dividend yield is calculated: dividend/price. A $1 dividend on a $30 stock is a 3.3% yield. But let's say that company runs into a big problem and its stock price falls to $10. Its yield is now 10% ($1/$10). Not because the dividend grew but because the stock price has taken a huge plunge. (Note: You will be averaging only 3.3% if you bought it at $30, but new investors will be getting 10%.)

My recommendation is to avoid the highest-yielding stocks. Stick to solid blue-chip firms that have a long history of making dividend payments. They will typically yield anywhere from 2% to 6% or so, depending on their industry.

Stock Tip: Standard & Poor's maintains a Dividend Aristocrats index of firms that have managed to increase their dividend payouts for at least 25 years. It's a good resource for anyone looking for investments to research. As of late 2011 the Aristocrats included:

3M	Cincinnati Financial
Abbott Laboratories	Cintas
Aflac	Clorox
Air Products & Chemicals, Inc.	Coca-Cola
Archer Daniels Midland	Consolidated Edison
Automatic Data Processing	Dover
Bard, C. R.	Ecolab
Becton, Dickinson & Co.	Emerson Electric
Bemis	Exxon Mobil
Brown-Forman	Family Dollar Stores
CenturyLink	Grainger, W. W.
Chubb	Hormel Foods

Johnson & Johnson	PPG
Kimberly-Clark	Procter & Gamble
Leggett & Platt	Sherwin-Williams
Lowe's	Sigma-Aldrich
McCormick & Co.	Stanley Black & Decker
McDonald's	Target
McGraw-Hill	VF
PepsiCo	Walgreen
PitneyBowes	Wal-Mart Stores

- **Diversify among different types of businesses.** You want to build a portfolio that owns a mix of stocks that operate in different fields. For example, make sure you don't own all energy stocks, or all consumer stocks.

- **Buy at the right time.** There is one tricky aspect of investing in dividend stocks. Every company that pays a dividend chooses a date at which all shareholders as of that date will be entitled to the next dividend payout. For example, let's say XYZ declares a dividend on September 15, with an ex-dividend date of October 15 and a payment date of October 31.

The most important date to pay attention to is the ex-dividend date. This is the cutoff date for receiving the dividend; if you buy the stock on October 16 you will not be entitled to the dividend. The actual dividend payment will be made on October 31.

You want to purchase your shares before an ex-dividend date to be eligible for the upcoming dividend. When you are considering selling shares of a dividend stock, if you wait until the ex-dividend date you can sell at any time between that date and the payment date and you will still receive the dividend. Just know that when it comes to buying and selling a dividend paying company, they reduce the price of the stock by the amount of the dividend so in the end it all comes out about the same.

One of the sources that I use to pick good quality dividend stocks for my own portfolio is the newsletter published by Dividend.com. Founder Paul Rubillo writes a newsletter that is full of great information and is easy to understand. Not only does Paul offer tips on what to buy, but he also shares his insights on when a stock should be sold as well.

WHERE TO FIND MORE INCOME

Retirees in need of more income may want to consider a reverse mortgage. A detailed lesson on reverse mortgages is in the Home Class, but I ask that you carefully consider the often high costs and risks involved.

No Free Lunch

During your retirement years you may be invited to many luncheons where a financial advisor will present you with what he believes is the answer to your retirement needs. Please be careful. All too often, what is pitched to you as a great solution to your income shortage is in fact an inappropriate and expensive investment you should never make.

My quick list of investments to avoid:

- A whole-life insurance policy
- A variable life insurance policy
- A variable annuity
- A universal life insurance policy
- A mutual fund that charges a load (sales commission)
- An immediate annuity (only as long as interest rates are low)

LESSON 6. DOUBLE-CHECK YOUR BENEFICIARIES AND MUST-HAVE DOCUMENTS

It may be years, if not decades, since you first opened your retirement accounts or purchased a life insurance policy. That is a long time for any number of life-changing events to have occurred. Marriage. Divorce. The death of a spouse. A remarriage. Children from a remarriage. Stepchildren. Grandchildren. Stepgrandchildren. A part of your legacy is to make sure you have updated your beneficiary statements to reflect your most current wishes. Please don't leave this to memory. If you are not sure, go back and check.

I also want you to pull out your must-have life documents and make sure they are also up to date. If you have any doubt as to whether you have all the documents you must have in my opinion, then please consult the Family Class, where I run them down in detail.

The good news is that any estate planning—such as trusts—you have reviewed with your estate-planning attorney sometime in the past few years is likely in good shape. In late 2010 Congress voted in increases in the estate tax exemption. The current law, good through 2012, exempts the first $5.12 million ($10.24 million for married couples) from estate tax, and the tax rate on sums above that amount is 35%.

LESSON RECAP

Now that you have made it through this retirement class I hope you are feeling more confident about how you can best navigate what you and I both know are very challenging times for retirees. But as we discussed in "Stand in Your Truth," sometimes the most powerful action we can take is to be willing to change our perspective. Instead of becoming stuck in frustration and fear over what you have lost, or how much harder it has become, please stand in this truth: With the right perspective, I am confident you can make the necessary changes to keep your retirement dream alive and well.

- Recognize that even once you retire, you still have 20+ years that you need your money to last.
- Make sure that at the rate you are withdrawing money, your savings will last your lifetime; a 4% annual rate is a good rule of thumb.
- Protect yourself from a future in which interest rates will likely rise: Do not invest in long-term bonds or bond funds.
- Consider dividend-paying ETFs or stocks for a portion of your portfolio; many currently pay double the income yield of bonds.

CLASS

9

THE ULTIMATE LESSON

I have a confession to make. *The Money Class* has been the most difficult book for me to write. For months I struggled to come to terms with just why I was having such a hard time with it, and that in itself was quite a jolt. After all, this is my tenth book; I wasn't exactly suffering from a case of first-time jitters. Eventually what I realized is that I myself was having some trouble coming to terms with the very strong, sobering message of the book. I came to understand that I needed to dig deep before I could start to tell you how to dig deep.

I want to share with you the process I went through in overcoming my personal roadblocks in writing this book. I offer this last lesson to you in the spirit of shared experience. I know that your journey has yet to begin; you end this book at a starting point. It's now time for you to find the strength and resolve to put the lessons of *The Money Class* into action. It is my hope that in sharing the process I went through to bring this book to life I can provide added motivation for you.

I never wavered in my enthusiasm for this project. When I approached my publisher to discuss the idea for the book I was eager to get rolling. When I wrote *Suze Orman's 2009 Action Plan* during the height of the financial crisis in the fall of 2008, I saw myself as an emergency room doctor; I needed to act fast to get you out of harm's way. The message for that time was about survival, in the short term. How to get through. But I knew even then that I would soon want to follow up that crisis management book with a more expansive discussion of how to move forward once the worst of the crisis was past. To use the hospital analogy just one more time: Once you make it out of the ER and ICU, the next phase is often long-term rehabilitation, which takes a more holistic approach to how to live the best—most healthy—life going forward.

The Money Class is that long-term rehabilitation plan. The focus and intent of this book have not changed conceptually from those early planning days. But I soon became bogged down in the enormousness of what I was going to ask you. The financial advice wasn't the problem. I knew exactly what I needed to teach you. But I began to realize that the overriding message of the book was anything but easy to digest. The death of the American Dream as we know it is not exactly the sort of uplifting, inspirational message that has always been the powerful undercurrent propelling my financial advice.

I was always clear that the New American Dream was the right message. I knew that if you agreed with the premise—that the new realities of life in these times require a reimagining of the dream—and followed my advice you would begin to shed your anxieties and fears and build a life defined by calm and confidence. But what slowed me down was that I was well aware of how incredibly difficult it was going to be for many of you to get from here (old, broken dream) to there (new, realistic dream). The attitude reform and the specific measures I was going to ask you to take were more drastic than anything I had ever suggested before. We are long past the days when trimming the cable bill and stretching out the time between haircuts was enough. As you now know, *The Money Class* asks you to contemplate far more life-altering changes.

Granted, I am not exactly shy when it comes to telling the truth. As my friends who worked on *The Oprah Winfrey Show* liked to say, I am not afraid to deliver a Suze Smackdown when necessary. But it's all in the service of what I see as my mission: To help you be the best you can be. To help you to live the life you not only want to live, but deserve to live. Am I direct and honest? Guilty. Do I react passionately? I sure do. But I think you appreciate that it is done with the best intentions: to help you fix what isn't working, quit habits that aren't empowering, and gain the confidence to know how to move forward toward a better life. In *The Courage to Be Rich* I wrote of how to create a life of material and spiritual abundance. More recently, *Women & Money* was about creating the power to own your destiny. Abundance. Destiny. Such powerful words. And if you've read those books you know the power I place on the words we choose: Your thoughts, your words, your actions—all must be in harmony.

Yet here I was, sitting at my computer, writing a book that pronounced the American Dream dead. Not exactly a fabulous truth to share. I worried that the power of those words would be crippling to the traits I prize so very much and rely on to power us through: optimism, courage, hopefulness, clarity. I worried that the message I had to deliver would affect your very ability to dream.

My breakthrough came when I finally reminded myself to take the advice I dispense early in this book. I had to change my perspective. Yes, I was telling you that an outmoded version of the American Dream was over and that its demise—no matter how good for us in the long term—would create a period of difficult transition. But the real message I had for you was not about that death, but about the rebirth each and every one of you can experience once you let go of the dreams that are broken.

I came to see that the New American Dream I am asking you to embrace and build for yourself and your family is in fact my most inspirational message ever. The steps I have laid out for you in this book, the truths that I have presented, and the truth I am asking each of you to locate within yourself will propel you into a future that is so much more hopeful and enjoyable than what I know many of you feel right now.

Will the transition be difficult, will it test your strength and commitment? Yes. I am not going to sit here and pretend that walking away from a home is easy, or that accepting a job that pays 15% less than your previous job is a snap. The road ahead no doubt has its bumps, potholes, and pitfalls. But navigate it you will. I have to ask you: What is the alternative? Do nothing, change nothing, and you will get nowhere. Commit to making change and you have the power to get it right once and for all.

I hope you are spared the months of angst I went through and can, right here, right now—as you read these words—train your perspective on what you are moving *toward*. Take your eyes off the rearview mirror. I ask you to let go—surrender what is no longer relevant to your well-being, so that you can step into that better future.

With time I also came to see that the central message of this book is not in fact hard or beyond your grasp. And that, too, released me from my writer's block. "Stand in your truth" is my clarion call that you have faith in yourself. To have faith that what you choose to do with your life—the conscious choices you decide to make—is what brings abundance and allows you to control your destiny. And I know that each and every one of us has that ability to turn inward and trust ourselves to take care of ourselves far better than anyone else.

What we collectively experienced over the past two decades has ultimately been a hard lesson learned. And in an odd way, that is why I am so hopeful that you are ready to act on the lessons I have shared in *The Money Class*. We now understand that change is necessary. We are motivated to rethink our ways, because, well, we're feeling anything but abundant and in control of our destiny.

The authentic, sterling values of old are ready to make their comeback. Our grandparents and great-grandparents had a pretty good handle on standing in their truth, and that is what propelled us individually and as a nation for so many generations. It is time to turn back to them for help in making our way forward. The payoff is not merely a better life today and next year, but a life of lasting integrity and honesty whose effects are far-reaching—for us, our children, our community, and beyond. Most important, we will all be back on track, creating an enduring legacy for future generations. And that, my friends, is the greatest dream of all.

ABOUT THE AUTHOR

SUZE ORMAN is a two-time Emmy Award–winning television host, #1 *New York Times* bestselling author, magazine and online columnist, writer/producer, and one of the top motivational speakers in the world today.

Orman has written nine consecutive *New York Times* bestsellers and has written, co-produced, and hosted seven PBS specials based on her books. She is the seven-time Gracie Award–winning host of *The Suze Orman Show,* which airs on CNBC, and host of *America's Money Class* on OWN: The Oprah Winfrey Network. She is also a contributing editor to O: *The Oprah Magazine.*

Twice named one of the "*Time* 100," *Time* magazine's list of the world's most influential people, and named by *Forbes* as one of the 100 most powerful women, Orman was the recipient of the National Equality Award from the Human Rights Campaign. In 2009 she received an honorary doctor of humane letters degree from the University of Illinois at Urbana-Champaign and in 2010 she received an honorary doctor of commercial science from Bentley University.

Orman, a Certified Financial Planner™ professional, directed the Suze Orman Financial Group from 1987 to

1997, served as Vice President—Investments for Prudential Bache Securities from 1983 to 1987, and was an account executive at Merrill Lynch from 1980 to 1983. Prior to that, she worked as a waitress at the Buttercup Bakery in Berkeley, California, from 1973 to 1980.

NOTES

NOTES